D1810430

# THE
# CHRISTMAS
## DECEPTION

# THE CHRISTMAS DECEPTION
## THIRD EDITION

Tommy Hale

XULON PRESS

Xulon Press
2301 Lucien Way #415
Maitland, FL 32751
407.339.4217
www.xulonpress.com

© 2021 by Tommy Hale

All rights reserved solely by Tommy Hale. Tommy Hale guarantees all contents are original and do not infringe upon the legal rights of any other person or work. No part of this book may be reproduced in any form without the permission of Tommy Hale. The views expressed in this book are not necessarily those of the publisher.

Unless otherwise indicated, Scripture quotations taken from the King James Version (KJV)–*public domain.*

All non-scripture content of this book is protected under the copyright laws and shall not be used for profit, reproduction, sale or resale without written Permission from Tommy Hale. Any non-profit use of this material used for preaching or evangelism purposes is permitted without written permission. My contact address is:

800 Prairie, Highlands, Texas 77562.

Printed in the United States of America.

Paperback ISBN-13: 978-1-6628-3258-1
eBook ISBN-13: 978-1-6628-3259-8

# SOUNDS OF

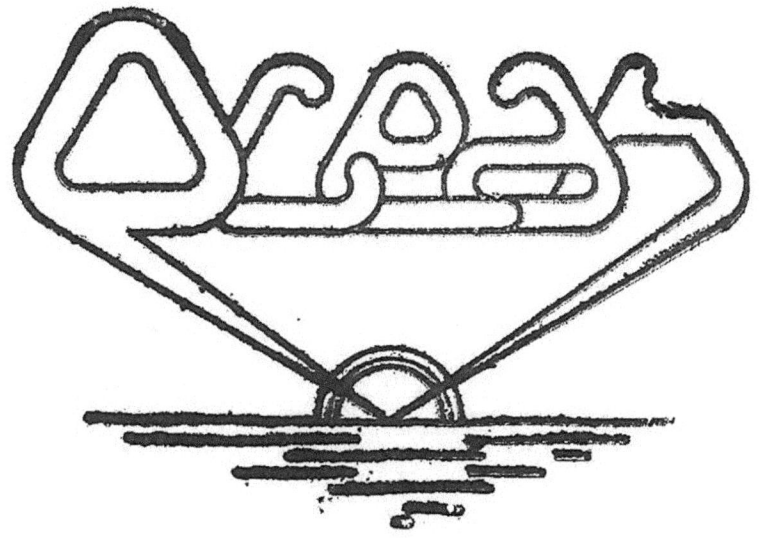

# PUBLISHING

## Copyright © 2021 Thomas Hale

# CONTENTS:

# THE CHRISTMAS DECEPTION
## THIRD EDITION

Tommy Hale
A Sounds of Ocean Production

# TRADITION WITHOUT IDOLS

You notice there is no "About the Author" in this book. There is a little bit of information about me related to the subject of Christmas included in various places in this book; but I didn't want to waste a lot of time on me in this book. If you are really interested in my story, I suggest you pick up a copy of my book, "Salvation the simple truth". Available at Amazon.com and Barns and Noble.com. There is a chapter called "A lot about the Author". You will find an abundance of information there. Also, my grammar is horrible. I was criticized a lot on the first edition of this book because of my bad grammar and misspelled words. People didn't pay attention to the content of the book because they were too busy pointing out my mistakes in grammar and spelling. With this third edition, I have gotten a lot better at it than I was. But still, words and spellings may have slipped by the grammar check and spell check of my computer. If so, please, just ignore my ignorance and try to make out what I am trying to say. The message of this book is far more important than my lack of intelligence.

Before I get started on this, I would like to say that there is a mindset in this country that prevails in most of the population. Some people call it "the good ole boy syndrome." Treat everyone good, live a moral life for the most part. Go to church occasionally and then meet at the bar for some beers. This type of person is usually a live and let live type of person and doesn't try to push his religion or politics off on anybody. This type of person probably walked the isle at church and got baptized but doesn't spend a lot of time searching the scriptures to find the deeper things of God. He is satisfied with getting his information from a Sunday sermon more than seeking it out in God's Word for himself. This type of person has always known Christmas as a good moral expression of Christianity and celebrates it yearly without questioning any of its content. He thinks it is the most spiritual time of year and anyone that would speak anything against it must be some kind of reprobate unbeliever. But because he never goes deeper into the things of God, he spends his life on the edge of Christianity never wading more than ankle deep into God's Word. This is the type of Christian that this book is written for. I want every Christian to know the truth about this pagan ritual that masquerades as Christian. The way some of these vain traditions get started is by advertisers that structure their advertising in a way to make you feel guilty if you don't participate. When I stopped celebrating Christmas, I also quit exchanging Christmas gifts with friends and family. I told them ahead of time not to buy me any gift because I no longer wish to participate in that tradition. The typical reaction from some of my friends was accusations that I was cheap and selfish and that I probably quit celebrating Christmas so I wouldn't have to buy everyone presents. I have endured more persecution from that one act than anything else. The world does the same thing with all the occasions they have created to make you buy something for someone for a day that they created to do so. Then they make you feel guilty if you don't. Look at the commercials for these occasions; "have you bought your wife or girlfriend or your mother a valentine's gift yet"? Making you believe that if you haven't, then you are some kind of selfish person that doesn't appreciate them. I wouldn't be surprised if they someday came up with a second cousins' day or a people with blue eyes day or school bus driver day, just to get you to buy presents on these occasions. But Christmas is by far the biggest of these occasions and gift buying at Christmas time far surpasses all others. So, you may ask, what is wrong with that? We will answer that question in detail later on in this book, but the main problem is that Christmas is not what it appears to be. It is a tradition of idol worship. Some traditions are good. Family get togethers are good. But you can still have family get togethers. There is nothing wrong with a get together with family to have a family meal even on that day. Just don't call it a Christmas dinner. It's just a good time to have a family get together because everybody is off work and everything is closed, so everyone is available. I am not legalistic about these things. You can allow some limited participation in some of the fun aspects of the season for the kids without letting the actual pagan tradition into your house. You can buy presents for your kids at that time so they wouldn't feel left out. Just don't put them under a tree. And don't tell your kids that they are Christmas presents from Santa Claus. Simply leave out the tree and tell them that they are a gift from you. Don't impose the idea that it is an exchanging of presents time. You can tell them ahead of time not to buy you a present. Instill the idea in your kids that you don't need a gift in return for giving them a gift. The exchanging of gifts type of thing is a pagan practice, not Christian. There are alternatives to other worldly and pagan celebrations also. Some churches have what they call a Halleluiah Festival as an alternative to Halloween. Kids dress up like Bible characters and play games for candy. If you take away the false deities involved and take the lies out of it, and take the dark costumes away, and don't honor the day by calling it what the world calls it; it then just becomes having fun with Bible characters. Sometimes we must decide what is crossing the line in cases like this. For instance; you can hide colored eggs at Easter if you leave the mythical bunny out of the picture and don't give credibility to the Easter celebration for what it stands for, which is a celebration of the goddess of spring. Simply tell your kids that you are merely coloring eggs and hiding them for them to find. Don't tell them that the Easter bunny left a basket full of candy for them to find and then hid eggs for them. Don't tell them that it is the time when Jesus was crucified on the cross, then raised from the dead three days later. That happened at Passover, not Easter. I'm not here to take fun away from people. I'm all for creating an alternative for the fun associated with traditions like this so when your kids see all the other kids having fun, they can have fun also, but without the idolatry and lies associated with the day. So, yes, do what you can so that your kids wouldn't feel left out of the fun. Just be careful not to bring any of the actual idolatrous tradition into it. Family get togethers and giving presents are not things that The Bible would forbid. But the difference is, there should never be a tree set up in your house for the occasion. There shouldn't be the traditional Christmas decorations around the house and especially no celebrating the false day of the birth of Jesus or the false day of His death and resurrection at Easter, or celebrating ghost, goblins, jack o' lanterns and trick or treat at Halloween. Your kids should never be told they should tell Santa Claus what gift they want to receive and that he can go around the world and leave those gifts to every child that was good that year. I never tell anyone merry Christmas, happy Easter, or happy Halloween. For one thing, merry, in The Bible means to get drunk.

> **1 Samuel 25:36**
> **36 And Abigail came to Nabal; and, behold, he held a feast**
> **in his house, like the feast of a king; and Nabal's heart was**
> **merry within him, for he was very drunken: wherefore**
> **she told him nothing, less or more, until the morning light.**

I suspect that is where the term "merry Christmas" came from. The Bible is not against having fun; as long as that fun doesn't involve getting drunk, lies, dark underworld characters or false gods by any name. With a Halleluiah Festival instead of Halloween, you are not participating in Halloween. You are doing away with Halloween and having a Halleluiah festival. With just hiding colored eggs, you are not celebrating Easter. You are only coloring eggs and hiding them for your kids to find. If you keep the bunny out of the picture and you are not celebrating the pagan spring festival called Easter, then it is just a day of having fun. If you give your kids presents at Christmas time and have a dinner; and don't call it Christmas presents or a Christmas dinner or say that it is the birthday of Jesus; and don't tell them that a mythical character called Santa Claus magically left them presents. In other words, you are not calling Tammuz Christ, and you are not lying to your kids and you are not setting up a Christmas tree. It is then only a casual get together to have a good time. I'm telling you this to possibly give you some alternatives to powerful traditions filled with lies and idol worship. If you take the lies and idol worship out of it, we are free to do what we want. But common sense tells you that verse 22 below is not talking about allowing sin or idol worship in your life, and Christmas is idol worship. This is more like what is talked about in 1 Corinthians chapter 8 about eating meat sacrificed to idols. Some can do it without feeling condemned because they don't worship those idols and they know that those idols are not real and they can't affect the meet. Others feel condemned simply because the meet had been sacrificed to an idol and they feel like that act condemned the meet itself. Today it would be like deciding to drink a glass of wine with your meal. Some would consider that a sin and would feel condemned doing it, verse 21 below. Others allow themselves to have it with no condemnation of themselves, verse 22 below.

> **Romans 14:21-23**
> **21 It is good neither to eat flesh, nor to drink wine, nor any thing whereby thy brother stumbleth, or is offended, or is made weak.**
> **22 Hast thou faith? have it to thyself before God. Happy is he that condemneth not himself in that thing which he alloweth.**
> **23 And he that doubteth is damned if he eat, because he eateth not of faith: for whatsoever is not of faith is sin.**

Participating in idol worship would not be included in that option to allow in our lives with no condemnation. That would be like saying: I want to allow adultery in my life because I feel no condemnation doing it. Adultery is a sin whether you allow it or not. So is idol worship. With Christmas, you are calling a false deity by The Name of The true Deity and claiming that the birthday of the false deity is the birthday of The true Deity. You are keeping the idol worship and just changing its name. That would be like getting saved and not changing your old ways to new Christian ways, but instead, keeping your old sins and just changing their names. Using the example of adultery again, if you are an adulterer and you get saved, you must quit committing adultery. So, you reason within yourself that you will just change the name of adultery to "friends with benefits" and keep on doing it because you think that because it's not called adultery any more, that makes it okay. That is the same reasoning for continuing the idol worship practice of Saturnalia. You just call it Christmas and continue to do it. You don't stop doing something by just doing the same thing under a different name. There are many things that when we first get saved, we simply don't know is against what The Bible says, so we must make adjustments as God reveals those things to us. Christmas was one of those things for me. When I surrendered my life completely to The Lord, I was excited when the first Christmas after that came along. The Church group that I was meeting with was a strict: (what does The Bible say about it) kind of group. We met in each other's homes because we couldn't afford a building. As it came closer and closer to Christmas, I notice that no one had a Christmas tree up in their house. One day I ask them when they were going to put a tree up. I told them I was looking forward to Christmas this year because I had just completely surrendered my life to The Lord that year. I believed in The Lord when I was 13 years old and received Him as Savior at that time. I truly was sincere but I was weak back then. My life didn't change a lot. I had come to the realization that hell was real and I wanted fire insurance to escape that prospect, so I accepted Jesus as my Savior but my desire to serve Him wasn't as strong as my desire to just escape hell. I kind of lived as a backslidden Christian for years after that until I met Dennis Evans at college. He was preaching right there in the middle of the hallway between classes at that college when me and some friends of mine were going to our next class and we stopped to listen to what he was saying. He made me feel ashamed that I had been a Christian for so long and hadn't done anything. His boldness made me even doubt that I had been saved before. So, to make sure, He helped me to pray to Jesus to rededicate my life and if I wasn't really saved, to surrender my life totally to Jesus right there on that college campus. It is my opinion that I was really saved, because I wanted to serve God, but my spiritual walk was not what it should have been. For one thing, I wasn't studying His Word and at the same time I let sin take me in a wrong direction. I didn't realize and appreciate what I had. But The Lord did not abandon me, which is why I think He led me to cross paths with Dennis. So, this time I surrendered my whole life over to Jesus and began attending that home church group I mentioned led by Dennis. He discipled me for years after that and he taught a strict Bible doctrine that you believe nothing unless it can be backed up in The Bible. Anyway, when I ask them about the tree; the answer I got changed my life. Dennis said: "We don't celebrate Christmas." He showed me only one scripture in The Bible to explain why. That scripture was Jeremiah 10:1-5. We will discuss this scripture later but in general, it describes a Christmas tree, and it says that the people of God are not to set one up in our homes. This provoked me to investigate this further because I had always loved Christmas time. It was very disturbing to me that anything could be wrong with celebrating it. I thought perhaps they had made a misinterpretation of that scripture. I had never heard anything bad about Christmas before. I thought to myself at the time: "What have I stumbled into? Is this some kind of cult or something?" If it wasn't right there in The Bible, I would have thought they were crazy, but I couldn't dismiss that scripture. As a newly committed Christian, I was very zealous about The Word of God and I was like a sponge wanting to soak up as much of God's Word as possible. This was probably a good thing because a lot of people that have been a committed Christian for a while lose the excitement of their conversion and wouldn't take the time to investigate something like this. It didn't take me long to find out that he was telling me the truth. But to make sure, I did an extensive study on it. It took me ten years to investigate this thing called Christmas. I could not have even imagined what I would run in to with this subject. What I found was beyond my wildest expectations. I found far more than just that one scripture about the tree that I was first shown. In fact, the whole Christmas celebration is only a small part of the extensive zodiac system of idol worship that I found. I searched for information on the subject so long that even some of the Church group I was with; yes, the ones that enlightened me about this in the first place, accused me of taking the subject too far. But my zeal only grew as I found out more and more about it. I found that it was a pagan festival deeply rooted in widespread pagan worship that goes all the way back to after the flood with Noah's great grandson who established the kingdom of Babel. And that pagan system of worship is still alive and well today. It is woven throughout all the world and deeply entrenched in society even infiltrating the church. I found that Christmas was nothing more than a deception designed to lull Christians into idol worship without them even knowing it. I was so surprised about my findings and that it was so easy to find, that I wondered why I had never heard anyone talk about it. I couldn't accept the notion that ministers didn't know about this. To my surprise, I found many things that the church teaches as Bible that are simply tradition and not Bible at all. I don't have time to cover all the things that I found, so I decided to focus on the one that, in my opinion, is the most widespread and by far the most dangerous. And that is **The Christmas deception.** Now, don't get me wrong. I am not a pastor or a person of any authority. I am just like you. A common everyday person seeking the truth. In importance, I am a nobody. But in Jesus; I am somebody because I have The Holy Spirit living inside of me making me somebody. Because of the sheer volume of what I found; I felt led to write this book. Not that there is any new revelation or even any new information revealed in this book.

There has been no more new revelation from God given after all the books of New Testament were completed sometime near the end of the 1st century AD probably around 90 AD. The information found in this book is already out there to find. I have just found it and written it down for you to clearly see. All I am doing is exposing this false teaching that is not inspired by God. And I have used the already completed inspired Word of God and good historical references that have been documented for hundreds and sometimes thousands of years. I'm just bringing to light this already known information. I didn't want to quote all the references I found information in due to legal reasons. I didn't want to get bogged down in the legal quagmire of getting permission to quote some other author on something that is common knowledge on things that happened long ago and is well documented in history. So, I didn't quote any of those writings, but only used commonly known historical information that is not copyrighted, and I used my own words to say it. I figured that if you want more specific information with names and dates and the more detailed information that these copyrighted authors have given; then you can look up their easily found writings for that more specific information. The only source I quote directly is The King James Version Bible which has no copyrights. Most people will not take the time to research history, therefore, this information gets forgotten. I'm here to bring out general information on those things that people have conveniently forgotten.

# IS IT GOD OR IS IT BABYLON?

To start with, Christmas started as a Babylonian winter solstice celebration. It is interesting to compare the Babylonian Kingdom with God's Kingdom. A man named Nimrod was the builder and leader of Babel and some other cities. In giving you this comparison, just realize that you cannot compare anything or anyone to God. He is far above anything or anyone in this earth. There cannot be a comparison that would come close to equaling God. This is strictly for comparing a worldly system that thinks it can become like God which it can never do; to the one and only true God. So, this is comparing the kingdom of God to the Babylonian kingdom which represents this present world's system trying to build a tower to worship their false zodiac gods and to come against the true God. They will fail.

God...God is the creator of the heavens and the earth and all things in them.
Babylon...Nimrod is the builder of Babel.

God...God created man in His own image.
Babylon...Babylon created a false god in the image of the sun.

God...God created Adam starting out in Innocence.
Babylon...Babylon stared out as sin and rebellion against God.

God...God created the 1$^{st}$ family and community of man to worship Him

Babylon…Babylon established the 1st community of man to worship false gods.

God…Man was driven from the Garden of Eden by God.
Babylon…Man was driven from the tower of Babel by God confusing their
language.

God…God gave us knowledge. and stability and the knowledge of good and
evil.
Babylon…Babylon gave us confusion. Babel means confusion.

God…God represents supernatural power.
Babylon…Babylon represents natural power.

God…God is The true God worthy to be worshiped.
Babylon…Babylon represents world religion and the worship of false gods not
worthy of worship.

God…God created the true system of worship for all mankind.
Babylon…Babylon established the worldwide false system of worship.
God…God became a man (Jesus Christ)
Babylon…A man became a false god. (the sun god)

God…Jesus was crucified on the cross, but The Spirit of God raised Him
bodily from the dead after three days and three nights.
Babylon…A king was claimed to have died and risen from the dead over night without his body into the sun and became the sun god.

God…God's Kingdom is established because of the death, burial and resurrection of Jesus Christ

Babylon…The Mystery, Babylon the great, was established by the self-proclaimed

queen of heaven after her husband died and was buried, then was claimed by her to be resurrection into the sun, becoming the sun god.

God…The bride of Christ (the Church) is to reign with Him in His Kingdom

as The Lambs wife.

Babylon…The bride of Babylon reigned in the Babylonian kingdom. She married

her son, Tammuz, that she proclaimed to be her reincarnated husband and the son of the sun god; the false Christ. Thus, proclaiming herself the wife of the sun god and the queen of heaven.

God…Jesus is The true Christ.

Babylon…Tammuz is the false Christ.

God…God's Kingdom is to be established in the earth and is forever, and will

survive even the end of the world.

Babylon…The Babylonian kingdom, will be destroyed once and for all and

forever. It being a worldly kingdom cannot survive the end of the world. But it will be destroyed a thousand years before this world is.

God…Salvation is by faith in Jesus Christ and by His grace alone.

Babylon…A false salvation is by following the works of the zodiac and obeying its

commands.

The devil always tries to imitate and corrupt what God does. All he can do is copy. He has no power to create something new, and he has no power to force you to do his will unless you give him that power. All he can do is try to use us to do his work through his lies and deceitfulness, but only if we let him. Resist him and he will flee from you.

**1 Timothy 3:7**

**7 Moreover he must have a good report of them which are without; lest he fall into reproach and the snare of the devil.**

**2 Timothy 2:25-26**

**25 In meekness instructing those that oppose themselves; if God peradventure will give them repentance to the acknowledging of the truth;**

**26 And that they may recover themselves out of the snare of the devil, who are taken captive by him at his will.**

**Matthew 4:1-11**

**1 Then was Jesus led up of the Spirit into the wilderness to be tempted of the devil.**

**2 And when he had fasted forty days and forty nights, he was afterward an hungred.**

**3 And when the tempter came to him, he said, If thou be the Son of God, command that these stones be made bread.**

**4 But he answered and said, It is written, Man shall not live by bread alone, but by every word that proceedeth out of the mouth of God.**

**5 Then the devil taketh him up into the holy city, and setteth him on a pinnacle of the temple,**

**6 And saith unto him, If thou be the Son of God, cast thyself down: for it is written, He shall give his angels charge concerning thee: and in their hands they shall bear thee up, lest at any time thou dash thy foot against a stone.**

**7 Jesus said unto him, It is written again, Thou shalt not tempt the Lord thy God.**

**8 Again, the devil taketh him up into an exceeding high mountain, and sheweth him all the kingdoms of the world, and the glory of them;**

**9 And saith unto him, All these things will I give thee, if thou wilt fall down and worship me.**
**10 Then saith Jesus unto him, Get thee hence, Satan: for it is written, Thou shalt worship the Lord thy God, and him only shalt thou serve.**
**11 Then the devil leaveth him, and, behold, angels came and ministered unto him.**

**James 4:7**
**7 Submit yourselves therefore to God. Resist the devil, and he will flee from you.**

As you can see, Jesus didn't let Himself be used by the devil. He didn't fall for the devil's cleverly disguised deception. There are two systems operating in this world today. God's system, and the world's copycat system. What you have to decide is if you're going to be sucked into a false religious system through the deception of the most popular day of the year that looks like it is of God but falls short of lining up with His Word? Or are you smart enough to see through the popular view and think for yourself? We have something that the devil and his demons don't have. The devil cannot create anything new because he doesn't have that part of God in him. We have the part of God in us that gives us an advantage over all other created beings. We have the creative power of God in us that separates us from all other created beings. Have you ever heard of an angel building himself a house or creating something of his own idea? When I say creative power, I mean power to invent and do something new. I am not talking about creating something from nothing. Only God can do that. But God breathed the breath of life into man giving us a living soul and giving us a spirit when Adam was created. God gave us the ability to love or not love. Love is only attainable through God because God is Love. There is no love but of God. Even atheist and unbelievers could not possibly love any one unless they have that part of God in them. It is God that gives them that ability whether they believe in God or not.

**Genesis 2:7**
**7 And the Lord God formed man of the dust of the ground,
and breathed into his nostrils the breath of life; and man
became a living soul.**

**Zechariah 12:1**
**1 The burden of the word of the Lord for Israel, saith the
Lord, which stretcheth forth the heavens, and layeth the
foundation of the earth, and formeth the spirit of man
within him.**

**Ecclesiastes 12:7**
**7 Then shall the dust return to the earth as it was: and the
spirit shall return unto God who gave it.**

**1 John 4:8**
**8 He that loveth not knoweth not God; for God is love.**

**1 John 4:16**
**16 And we have known and believed the love that God hath
to us. God is love; and he that dwelleth in love dwelleth in
God, and God in him.**

Everyone has this soul and spirit from God whether you are saved
or not, which gives everyone that part of God that only humans
have and makes us a triune being possessing a spirit, body and soul
which gives us creative power. But today, if you are saved, you
also have The Holy Spirit of God living in you to communicate
with your spirit giving you the mind of Christ allowing you to
receive spiritual instruction directly from God that an unsaved
person cannot receive. We will go over this later in chapter 4, but
this reasoning power of The Holy Spirit allows us to figure out
spiritual thing like the hidden manna of hidden idol worship that
the devil uses to deceive us. The only way you can be deceived
when you possess The Holy Spirit is if you will not listen to what

He is telling you and you choose to be deceived. The Holy Spirit reveals the truth only to those that are willing to receive the truth.

**1 Corinthians 2:14-16**
**14 But the natural man receiveth not the things of the Spirit of God: for they are foolishness unto him: neither can he know them, because they are spiritually discerned.**
**15 But he that is spiritual judgeth all things, yet he himself is judged of no man.**
**16 For who hath known the mind of the Lord, that he may instruct him? But we have the mind of Christ.**

**Ephesians 3:17-19**
**17 That Christ may dwell in your hearts by faith; that ye, being rooted and grounded in love,**
**18 May be able to comprehend with all saints what is the breadth, and length, and depth, and height;**
**19 And to know the love of Christ, which passeth knowledge, that ye might be filled with all the fulness of God.**

# OVERVIEW

Before I get into the meat of this book, I'll give you a short overview of the origin of Christmas. It started out with the worship of the sun, the moon and the stars as in the zodiac. This started at Babel where Nimrod ruled. A tower was built to battle with God and to reach their sun god. A lot of humanity at this time after the flood was gathered in the land of Shinar. There were several cities here that Nimrod had built. This is where all false religions of the world began. This is talked about in Zachariah about the mystery, Babylon the great that shall be established throughout the earth. Verse 3 and 6.

> **Zechariah 5:1-11**
> **1 Then I turned, and lifted up mine eyes, and looked, and behold a flying roll.**
> **2 And he said unto me, What seest thou? And I answered, I see a flying roll; the length thereof is twenty cubits, and the breadth thereof ten cubits.**
> **3 Then said he unto me, This is the curse that goeth forth over the face of the whole earth: for every one that stealeth shall be cut off as on this side according to it; and every one that sweareth shall be cut off as on that side according to it.**
> **4 I will bring it forth, saith the Lord of hosts, and it shall enter into the house of the thief, and into the house of him that sweareth falsely by my name: and it shall remain in the midst of his house, and shall consume it with the timber thereof and the stones thereof.**

**5 Then the angel that talked with me went forth, and said unto me, Lift up now thine eyes, and see what is this that goeth forth.**

**6 And I said, What is it? And he said, This is an ephah that goeth forth. He said moreover, This is their resemblance through all the earth.**

**7 And, behold, there was lifted up a talent of lead: and this is a woman that sitteth in the midst of the ephah.**

**8 And he said, This is wickedness. And he cast it into the midst of the ephah; and he cast the weight of lead upon the mouth thereof.**

**9 Then lifted I up mine eyes, and looked, and, behold, there came out two women, and the wind was in their wings; for they had wings like the wings of a stork: and they lifted up the ephah between the earth and the heaven.**

**10 Then said I to the angel that talked with me, Whither do these bear the ephah?**

**11 And he said unto me, To build it an house in the land of Shinar: and it shall be established, and set there upon her own base.**

This is saying that out of the land of Shinar, also known as the land of Nimrod, Micah 5:6, shall come a worldwide false religious system originating at Babel, verse 11, and dividing into many false religions but all originating at the tower of Babel. This false religious system is referred to as a woman. The base is the headquarters of this religious system. This base is Rome, but represents Babylon through this woman. The Romans are the ones that brought this woman into the church, one of the two women in verse 9. The woman is the mystery religion of Babylon. I believe this lead covering in verse 8 represents this woman kept in check in the ephah, or bushel, only ruling from her base. But later will set her rule in the whole world. When the church is raptured, this religious system will be let loose and join the antichrist.

**2 Thessalonians 2:1-8**

**1 Now we beseech you, brethren, by the coming of our
Lord Jesus Christ, and by our gathering together unto him,
2 That ye be not soon shaken in mind, or be troubled,
neither by spirit, nor by word, nor by letter as from us, as
that the day of Christ is at hand.
3 Let no man deceive you by any means: for that day shall
not come, except there come a falling away first, and that
man of sin be revealed, the son of perdition;
4 Who opposeth and exalteth himself above all that is called
God, or that is worshipped; so that he as God sitteth in the
temple of God, shewing himself that he is God.
5 Remember ye not, that, when I was yet with you, I told
you these things?
6 And now ye know what withholdeth that he might be
revealed in his time.
7 For the mystery of iniquity doth already work: only he
who now letteth will let, until he be taken out of the way.
8 And then shall that Wicked be revealed, whom the Lord
shall consume with the spirit of his mouth, and shall
destroy with the brightness of his coming:**

Like I said, in Zachariah 5:9, the two women probably represent
the unbelieving Jews and the part of the church that participated
in this false religious system. There are too many false gods and
false religions to debunk all of them and The Bible just doesn't
get into the details of all these false religions. But I can give you
a general consensus of these from years of study of these false
religions. They all originated in this land of Shinar, verse 11, at
Babel, where they came up with the idea of substituting false gods
for The one and only True God by worshiping the creation instead
of The Creator. They worshiped the sun, the moon, the stars, the
seasons, the earth, the things in the earth, the animals in the earth
and man. This worship is still here even today, and a lot of it is
called the zodiac. They also worshiped the changing of the seasons.

One of those seasonal celebrations was the winter solstice and it involved the pagan sun god. It was the birth of the new sun. It occurred at the winter solstice at the shortest day of the year. After which the days start getting longer again in the northern hemisphere. There were others, like the spring celebration at the vertical equinox. It is called Easter. There are many more, but this book will concentrate on the winter solstice festival that would later be called Saturnalia. The original celebration was celebrated more than 2000 years before Jesus was born and is still here even today. Then one day, in the 4th century AD, there came along an emperor of Rome named Constantine whose actions led to Rome being proclaimed a Christian Empire which led to the banning of all pagan celebrations. But their pagan celebrations were deeply entrenched and had been traditional for more than two thousand years. They had become quite elaborate and very popular. So, fearing a rebellion in the kingdom, the emperor told his people that they could celebrate their pagan festivals with one condition; they had to make them pertain to Jesus Christ instead of the sun god deities. So, they kept their celebrations with all their traditions and only had to change the names of the festivals and the false gods involved into Christian names. In Rome at this time, the winter solstice celebration was called Saturnalia. It already involved the birthday of a false Christ, so it was easy to keep everything the same and just change the names involved from pagan names to Christian names. They changed Saturnalia to Christmas, Tammuz became Jesus, the queen of heaven became Mother Mary, and so on. As time went on, a government church was formed under the name of Christ and that government church accepted these pagan celebrations along with these pagan gods with their names changed and mixed them in with the worship of Jesus. Most of the true Christians of that day would not accept this government church with these traditions because of their pagan origin. This angered the government church because they didn't want these Christians going around trying to stop their pagan festivals that they proclaimed to be Christian. Most of the people of this government church at that time were not really Christians. They were still pagans proclaimed to be Christians by the Roman Empire. This government church made it mandatory to be a Christian because the Empire was proclaimed by the emperor to be a Christian Empire. These pagans were okay with the Empire proclaiming them Christians and changing the names of their pagan gods to Christian names as long as they could keep celebrating these festivals even under Christian names. But the true Christians of that day seen through this false Christianity and wouldn't participate in these pagan festivals that were accepted by this government led church. But the government led church didn't like these true Christians trying to stop these celebrations because they were very popular and the government didn't want to stir up the pagan population by banning these celebrations transformed to Christianity. This anger led to a great persecution of the true church in which millions of Christians were tortured and killed for not accepting the government's religion. This persecution lasted for centuries, but later, a movement began that would lead to the great reformation of the 16th century. At that same time, England decided to break away from the Roman church and establish its own church in England. This was a major event in the breakup of the government church and the church officials of Rome wouldn't stand for this reformation and break up one bit. But even the newly formed English church wasn't freedom from these pagan holidays. So, the true Christians began to flee to the new land in the west to escape being forced to take part in this false religious system that came out of that Babylonian zodiac. That land later became the United States of America. As the government church seen themselves losing control with the reformation of the 16th century, and with the breakaway of the church at England from the Roman church, and this new land of America providing religious freedom; The Babylonian queen started influencing other nations through the Roman church to try to regain control to force England to again accept the church at Rome which led to World War 2. When that failed, because they lost that war; that great religious Empire finally fell from global dominance. As time went on and persecution ended as Rome became less of a factor in the powers of the world; spiritual forces behind this government church continued as people began to forget why their ancestors came to America, and people began to slowly accept these pagan zodiac festivals again not knowing the facts about them; which brings me to this book. I am here to remind you of why your ancestors came here to this country, and what they were escaping from. This is all the devil has. So, all he can do is try it again. He is a one trick pony. Look what happened to Israel and Judah in the Old Testament. Over and over again God would deliver them from the woes of their turning to idol worship, then later they would fall right back in it again as if they completely forgot what they did before. The devil is a liar and all he can do is try to manipulate you with lies. When that doesn't work, he will wait until you forget the truth and then try to spring the same lies on you once again hoping you didn't learn from history or remember that it was a lie. So, when people came to this country to escape the Babylonian religion, they eventually forgot about that and seen this great holiday that they could celebrate for Jesus not realizing that it was that very same celebration that their ancestors escaped from in the first place. The devil will be patient. All he has to do is wait for people to forget so he can use the same tactic all over again. Like I said, he has no new tricks. This is all he has, so he has to depend on it working over and over again. That is exactly why I am informing you of this truth that has been lost and obscured through the years. All I can do is tell you what I know and warn you about this celebration known as Christmas. I urge you to read all this book and give the truth a chance. Then you will be able to make an informed decision on the facts as they are; not on what you've been told. I will cover all the parts of this overview in detail as this book progresses. I just wanted you to have a general idea of what I will be talking about so there will be no confusion. I hope you are as thirsty for the truth as I was when I found out the truth about Christmas. If so; you will have no trouble at all seeing for yourself that Christmas, with all its tradition, is one holiday that we, as Christians, can do without.

# A LETTER FROM SANTA

This letter is a fictional story made up by me. It is only a depiction of what I have perceived from what I have seen concerning Santa Claus. But before you read this letter, I would just like to make this statement. If you are a Santa Claus at Christmas, it is not my intention to degrade what you are doing. please don't take offense at what I am about to say. I realize the selflessness it takes to bring joy to kids for what you believe to be a good work. I have some very good friends that play Santa Chaus at Christmas time and the last thing I want to do is offend them. People that do this are very generous and kind people. But the devil has used this image of a Santa Claus to imitate kind of a false deity that he has incorporated into this character very subtilty and hidden to escape our reasoning. All I am doing in this section is enlightening you to the possibility of Satan taking your innocent pretrial of the legend of this historical figure and twisted it into something else.

## The following is an image I perceive to be of Santa Claus as if he would honestly write a letter to your child about Christmas:

Dear innocent and unsuspecting child:

It is Christmas time again and I wanted to let you know that I'll be in your town to see you... Oh, and at the same time, I can be all over the world to see all the little children everywhere. I can do that you know, because I am able to be in more than one place at once. In fact, you can see me on just about every street corner and in most every mall and store. Seek me out and find me and come to my throne and be seated with me. Then you can ask what you will, and I will give it to you on Christmas morning.

**John 15:7**
**7 If ye abide in me, and my words abide in you, ye shall ask what ye will, and it shall be done unto you.**

You shall have the desires of your heart. But first you must wait because you know not the hour in which I will come. Watch therefore and be diligent to do good because your deeds shall be made manifest before my eyes. I am all-knowing and can know if you've been naughty or nice. Then on that day, Santa himself shall descend from the heavens with a shout, [HO-HO-HO], and with the voice of Christmas, "MERRY-CHRISTMAS"

**Psalms 37:4**
**4 Delight thyself also in the Lord; and he shall give thee the desires of thine heart.**

**Matthew 25:13**
**13 Watch therefore, for ye know neither the day nor the hour wherein the Son of man cometh.**

And behold, I come quickly, and your gift is with me to give to children that have been good. Fear not, because I am well able to visit every house in the world in one night before I return to my home at the north pole. Be sure to cut a tree out of the forest, the work of the hands of the workman with the axe. Then fasten it with nails and hammer that it stands upright and moves not. Then you can deck it with silver and gold.

**Revelation 22:12**
**12 And, behold, I come quickly; and my reward is with me, to give every man according as his work shall be.**

**Jeremiah 10:2-4**
**2 Thus saith the LORD, Learn not the way of the heathen, and be not dismayed at the signs of heaven; for the heathen are dismayed at them.**
**3 For the customs of the people are vain: for one cutteth a tree out of the forest, the work of the hands of the workman, with the axe.**
**4 They deck it with silver and with gold; they fasten it with nails and with hammers, that it move not.**

You can also put hangings on the tree.

**2 Kings 23:7**
**7 And he brake down the houses of the sodomites, that were by the house of the LORD, where the women wove hangings for the grove.**

And you can also put an angel of light on top, so he can oversee things

**2 Corinthians 11:13-14**
**13 For such are false apostles, deceitful workers, transforming themselves into the apostles of Christ.**
**14 And no marvel; for Satan himself is transformed into an angel of light.**

When I come, let me find you sleeping, because I always work alone in darkness when everyone is asleep. And I can know if you are asleep or awake.

**1 Thessalonians 5:5-7**

**5 Ye are all the children of light, and the children of the day: we are not of the night, nor of darkness.**
**6 Therefore let us not sleep, as do others; but let us watch and be sober.**
**7 For they that sleep sleep in the night; and they that be drunken are drunken in the night.**

Then when the sun comes up, you can rise up and run to the tree and bow down on your knees before it and receive your gift. Don't forget that the Sunday before Christmas, you must go to church. You can skip the rest of the year, except Easter. But at these two times, I have instructed most pastors to tell you that it's okay to celebrate these two times of the year, even though neither one has anything to do with Jesus, but it just carries His Name so as to deceive the world. I have also instructed most pastors and parents to tell you that it's the birth of Jesus that you are celebrating, even though it's all a big lie. Many people will throw a big party in honor of Jesus and get very drunk and have drugs and fornication available. Then afterwards, many will try to drive home; and because they are drunk or high on drugs, they will kill many people on the hi-ways. Others that don't get invited to these parties and are alone at Christmas time will simply be so depressed that they will kill themselves because they can't handle being alone at Christmas. Others will go and buy so many things for Christmas that they will max out their credit cards and pay it back all the rest of the next year. Don't worry though, they can just do without so they can pay back all those charges. Either that or they can file for debt settlement and cheat their creditors out of the money they agreed to pay back. Because of many people doing just that, other people that pay their bills will have to make up the loss to that creditor through higher interest rates to all the ones that pay their bills. If they don't have the money or credit, don't despair, they can buy your toys with a hot check. But really, try not to think of all that bad stuff. It's Christmas time! You can worry about your troubles later. You can actually make all this evil appear good if you just put your mind to it. Just kick back and watch all those Christmas specials with all their magic, witchcraft, and sorcery. Oh! and drive around and enjoy all the lights on the houses and trees. Don't even give a second thought to how those lights short out and catch dried out Christmas trees on fire and burns down houses and kills many people and leaves others homeless. Just enjoy all the good parts of Christmas, getting toys and gifts for yourself. Think of it, you can show all your friends how much more stuff you got than they did... Especially the poor, whom I hardly ever give anything to because they are poor. I'm sure you will have much more than them. I rarely visit poor kids because they don't have enough money for me to even bother with unless their parents can come up with some cash somehow or they might receive a present from a charity. Oh! by the way, don't read your Bible too much, because it speaks against all these things that I have told you... But if you must, only read the parts that can support Christmas. Of course, I know that The Bible does not support Christmas; but if you stretch a verse here and twist a verse there, you can make it appear to say anything you want.

**Santa**

You may think this letter is silly. But you know as well as I do that the things said in this letter do happen. I have seen things like this myself. It is real life, not the make-believe world of Christmas. In Genesis 3:5, the serpent tempted Eve with the thought of her and Adam being as gods.

> **Genesis 3:5**
> **5 For God doth know that in the day ye eat thereof, then your eyes shall be opened, and ye shall be as gods, knowing good and evil.**

The trick of the Devil is to make you think you can be your own god. Santa Claus is portrayed by the world as a direct parallel to God. Keep in mind that Jesus is God, The Son. Look at this comparison and see if you can see the parallel.

1. God is the only one that can know all things, yet Santa Claus claims to be able to know when every child is sleeping or awake and if they have been naughty or nice all year.

> **1 John 3:19-20**
> **19 And hereby we know that we are of the truth, and shall assure our hearts before him.**
> **20 For if our heart condemn us, God is greater than our heart, and knoweth all things.**

2. Jesus will descend from heaven with a shout, with the voice of the archangel when He comes for His church.

> **1 Thessalonians 4:16-17**
> **16 For the Lord himself shall descend from heaven with a shout, with the voice of the archangel, and with the trump of God: and the dead in Christ shall rise first:**
> **17 Then we which are alive and remain shall be caught up together with them in the clouds, to meet the Lord in the air: and so shall we ever be with the Lord.**

This is not the second coming, but The Lord coming for His church, and He doesn't come all the way to the earth, but comes to the clouds and calls us up to meet Him in the air to go to the Judgement Seat of Christ to receive our reward.

> **2 Corinthians 5:10**
> **10 For we must all appear before the judgment seat of Christ; that every one may receive the things done in his body, according to that he hath done, whether it be good or bad.**

Santa comes down from the clouds too, and doesn't come all the way to the ground, but he parks on the roof tops of the houses. He shouts with his Ho-Ho-Ho, and merry Christmas, then he leaves your gift.

3. Jesus has a host of angels at his command to work for him. Santa has a host of elves at his command to work for him.

**Matthew 26:53**
**53 Thinkest thou that I cannot now pray to my Father, and he shall presently give me more than twelve legions of angels?**

**Mark 1:13**
**13 And he was there in the wilderness forty days, tempted of Satan; and was with the wild beasts; and the angels ministered unto him.**

**John 1:51**
**51 And he saith unto him, Verily, verily, I say unto you, Hereafter ye shall see heaven open, and the angels of God ascending and descending upon the Son of man.**

4. White stands for Jesus and his righteousness and purity.

**Matthew 17:2**
**2 And was transfigured before them: and his face did shine as the sun, and his raiment was white as the light.**

**Matthew 17:1-2**
**1 And after six days Jesus taketh Peter, James, and John his brother, and bringeth them up into an high mountain apart, 2 And was transfigured before them: and his face did shine as the sun, and his raiment was white as the light.**

**Revelation 20:11**
**11 And I saw a great white throne, and him that sat on it, from whose face the earth and the heaven fled away; and there was found no place for them.**

Many times, in The Bible, red stands for sin. Santa's colors on his suit are red and white in which he always wears, mixing the white purity of Jesus with the crimson red of sin. His boots on his feet are black. This could represent a foundation of walking in darkness. His belt is also black in contrast with Ephesians 6:14.

> **Ephesians 6:14**
> **14 Stand therefore, having your loins girt about with truth, and having on the breastplate of righteousness;**

He girts his loins with the blackness of lies. Wearing these colors don't make you like that, but these colors are his standard colors that he always wears which could represent these things:

> **Isaiah 1:18**
> **18 Come now, and let us reason together, saith the Lord: though your sins be as scarlet, they shall be as white as snow; though they be red like crimson, they shall be as wool.**

> **John 12:35**
> **35 Then Jesus said unto them, Yet a little while is the light with you. Walk while ye have the light, lest darkness come upon you: for he that walketh in darkness knoweth not whither he goeth.**

> **1 John 1:6**
> **6 If we say that we have fellowship with him, and walk in darkness, we lie, and do not the truth:**

5. God has chariots of fire.
Santa has a flying sled.

> **2 Kings 6:17**
> **17 And Elisha prayed, and said, Lord, I pray thee, open his eyes, that he may see. And the Lord opened the eyes**

of the young man; and he saw: and, behold, the mountain
was full of horses and chariots of fire round about Elisha.

6. The city of our God is on the sides of the north.
Santa's home is at the north pole. We will go over this in detail later.

> Psalms 48:1-2
> 1 A Song and Psalm for the sons of Ko'-rah. Great is the
> LORD, and greatly to be praised in the city of our God, in
> the mountain of his holiness.
> 2 Beautiful for situation, the joy of the whole earth, is mount
> Zion, on the sides of the north, the city of the great King.

7. God is omnipresent and can be everywhere at one time.
Santa is omnipresent and can be on every street corner and in every
mall all at the same time.

8. Jesus can answer every prayer.
Santa can answer every child's wish list at Christmas in one night
for the whole world.

9. God is on His throne. And we can come boldly before the throne
of God with our prayers, and He says to ask what you will, and He
will give it to you according to His will.

> John 15:7
> 7 If ye abide in me, and my words abide in you, ye shall
> ask what ye will, and it shall be done unto you.

> Hebrews 4:16
> 16 Let us therefore come boldly unto the throne of grace,
> that we may obtain mercy, and find grace to help in
> time of need.

At Christmas, Santa is on his throne, and your kids can come boldly to the throne of Santa to ask of him what they want for Christmas. And he claims he will deliver it to them on Christmas morning.

**10. We are told not to let The Lord find us sleeping at His return.**

**Mark 13:35-36**
**35 Watch ye therefore: for ye know not when the master of the house cometh, at even, or at midnight, or at the cockcrowing, or in the morning:**
**36 Lest coming suddenly he find you sleeping.**

Kids wait in anticipation on Christmas night for Santa to come. They know not the hour in which he will come, but they must be sleeping, because if he finds them awake, then he won't come yet. Notice the difference here. The Bible says don't sleep. But Santa says that he must find you sleeping. That's because Jesus makes manifest the light. Santa works in darkness. Who else works in darkness?

11. Jesus lives forever and is never changing.
Santa always stays the same and never ages or changes.

Again, these comparisons may seem silly to you, but I think we can see a subtle pattern emerging here. Do your kids look to The Lord for what they want and need? Or is it Santa they look to for their desires, and then can't wait till Christmas morning so they can receive their gift from Santa. And kids are brought into this practice by Christians that celebrate this religious event without questioning its origin. And in doing so, enter into a lie that is, "The Christmas Deception".

# THE CHRISTMAS DECEPTION

## THIRD EDITION
### BY TOMMY HALE

# CHAPTER 1
# BELIEVE IT OR NOT

I didn't give references in this book because I only used general historic information that is pretty much available everywhere you look. So, every place I looked had the same information. I searched countless encyclopedias and historical books and the internet. If I listed them all, there would be pages of references. I didn't quote any one source of information that would infringe on anyone's copyrights. I only used general information that you can find in all the writings. The only source I quoted directly is The King James version Bible. The first and second editions of this book are out of print and not available. This is the third edition of this book. All of the information of the first and second editions is included in this edition with a lot more information added for this third addition. Each time I put out another edition, I try to include more information. I started writing this book in 1980. Information on the origins of Christmas at that time was plentiful, but there was no internet the first few years I was writing the first edition and when it did become available, at about the middle of writing it, I couldn't afford it back then. So, I had to go to libraries. The second edition became easier to find that kind of information when the internet became available to me. But I have noticed in researching for this third edition of this book, that information on the internet began to be suppressed. You could still find it, but it was harder. I know this because I have researched this subject now for over 40 years and I have noticed drastic changes in some historical references that have been the same for decades, but now, going back to them, many today have reworded their comments to exclude the connection to Christmas and just talk about the other historical aspects of it. They can't change the history connected to Christmas. They simply no longer include it in their comments. They have taken some names connected directly to The Bible and left out that important connection and just included the title of that person without saying his name. That makes it harder to connect that person that is actually mentioned in The Bible to the person in history. I'm sure that was done to submit to public opinion. I also noticed that new Bible translations that came out began to change some verses I have previously used in an earlier edition of this book. Thankfully though, I didn't use their translation. I always use the King James version and I didn't have to change those because the KJV doesn't change for public opinion. But in some of these other versions, the information was altered to be worded in a different way as to soften the case against Christmas. Most versions repeat close to what the KJV says, but some versions almost sound like a different subject in how it is changed. One unrelated example of this is; because of today's public opinion, one of the most popular translations of The Bible that most pastors use today came out with a gender-neutral version of their Bible that excludes gender identity even though we can clearly see in The Bible that gender identity is extremely important. The Bible is very clear on the differences between male and female. A lot of people these days are not comfortable with that concept. The popular position today is that there is no difference between male and female. The idea of: "wives, submit yourselves unto your own husbands, as unto The Lord" is repulsive to them.

> **Ephesians 5:22-23**
> **22 Wives, submit yourselves unto your own husbands, as unto the Lord.**
> **23 For the husband is the head of the wife, even as Christ is the head of the church: and he is the saviour of the body.**

I prefer to believe The Bible that also goes on to say: "husbands, love your wives, even as Christ also loved the church, and died for it".

**Ephesians 5:25**
**25 Husbands, love your wives, even as Christ also loved the church, and gave himself for it;**

I'm sorry if you're irritated that I'm not politically correct. I would rather be Biblically correct than politically correct. The Bible is clear on gender identity issues. I would love to show you; but that is not what this book is about. But it does affect this book because there are some historical theories that I put in the first and second editions of this book that have been challenged and some facts changed by some theologians giving into politically correct and sometimes religiously correct theories. The historical facts still hold to be a solid theory, but like I said, some of the names put to the figures in these theories have been challenged. Therefore, in this third edition, I have just left out those names in question and used the title of the person such as the queen of heaven, or a man or a king that became a false god. Because of this, you may find it harder to quickly verifying some of the things written in this book. Not impossible, just harder. If you are really wanting to know more specific information, I suggest you pick up one of those books that have that information. Just look for books with the name Babylon in the title of the book or go to a book store and ask them for a book on Mystery, Babylon. People don't like you messing with their favorite pagan holidays. And in the world, the pagan culture wins out in the facts being smoothed over in history. That is what people do to history that they don't like. This has been done to many historical facts that certain people don't like being a fact, so they alter it. But there is far too much evidence of this false religious system of worship talked about in history to ignore. It speaks for itself in history. It is accepted, mostly without question, all over the world that December 25th is the day that our Lord Jesus Christ was born. Most people participate in this occasion traditionally without question with an annual celebration known worldwide as "Christmas". Traditional holidays and celebrations are usually followed with little or no opposition as long as they seem moral and right. A few are New year's, Valentine's Day, Easter, 4th of July, Halloween, Thanksgiving, Christmas, Birthdays, etc. Some of these celebrations hold a good place in society and in our personal lives, such as 4th of July, celebrating the declaration of our independence. Although today, some left-wing groups say that this country was founded unjustly, and they don't like celebrating how this country was founded. But again, that is another story. There is thanksgiving; in giving thanks for God's many blessings and our freedom in this land. But others have deep seeded roots of pagan and Babylonian origins often hidden from the public eye. In this book, I am going to expose one of these traditions; and that is "CHRISTMAS". There are others, but this one is the most widely accepted and most well-known, and without a doubt, the most dangerous of any. It is not my goal to stop the world from celebrating Christmas. This is the world's day to celebrate. Nothing I say is going to change that. And why should it? This book is not for the world. It's for Christians. If you are not a Christian, you are not going to be interested in anything I have to say anyway. The world is going to be the world and is not going to care what The Bible says about what they are doing. And nothing that I say is going to stop the world from doing anything. What the world does doesn't interest me much either. My ultimate goal is to preach the gospel to a lost world so that some will possibly receive the calling from God and turn from the things of this world and believe in The real Jesus and get saved. And for those that do get saved, or are already saved; my goal is to inform them about this worldly celebration that has deceived the whole world and that a Christian has no business participating in. Now, before you tear this book in half and throw it in the garbage screaming blasphemy and sacrilege, which I have seen done to some books that dare to expose a lie; all I am doing is exposing what The Bible says about mixing idol worship with the worship of God. So, it's not me; it's what The Bible says. And before you think that I am an extremist or cult leader; let me say that I am a Christian. I believe in Jesus Christ and have received Him as my Savior. I have been born again into His glorious Kingdom, I have been baptized and I am a member of His Church. I am not of any denomination that doesn't believe that Jesus is Almighty God. I meet with a local Bible believing group of believers. I have a music ministry with that congregation where they graciously allow me to do my music in a Saturday evening service broadcast live over social media under the name of the pastor, Charlie Tutt, and is called The Power Service. Feel free to join in on Saturday evening for a one-hour concert. To find it, just look for the name Charlie Tutt on social media. There are several by that name, so you will need to find the right one. He is pictured with his wife. He has a beard and he looks a lot like Elvis Presley's drummer who is his cousin. He is pastor of East Houston Revival Center in Channelview Texas 77562. The time of the concert changes from time to time, but the concerts are posted so you can watch any of the past prerecorded concerts and find out when it is being held live at that time. But it is always on Saturday evening. It is only the time that changes now and then. Right now, it is at 5pm, but that could change, but it will always be around that time. I believe in one God manifested into three persons: The Father, The Son, and The Holy Spirit. I believe that the earth and all that is in it was created by God, The Son, Who Is The Word. Then, The Word became flesh in The Person of Jesus Christ, Son of God, and dwelt among us, His own creation. I believe in the virgin birth of Jesus Christ, and that He walked this earth as God in the flesh in The Person of Jesus Christ. I believe that while here, He was still fully God, but He set aside His full glory as God while He was here. He lowered Himself to live as a man to be able to die for our sin. He lived a perfect, sinless and righteous life as fully man but without sin. He then willingly submitted to the will of God, The Father, and He was obedient to suffer the cross for the purpose of redeeming us from our sin while He was on that cross. He then suffered death on that cross and was separated from God, The Father, for three days and three nights after which The Spirit of God raised Him from the dead and He now sits at the right hand of the throne of God, the Father with all of His former glory He had before. He willingly gave Himself as a sacrifice for our sin on that cross of Calvary; paying in full the penalty for us so we could have eternal life. I believe that the only path to salvation is to receive The Father's invitation to be saved by confessing with your mouth Jesus as Lord and believing in your heart that He suffered and died on the cross for all sin and He was raised from the dead after three days and three nights. Then accept Jesus as your Savior and be born again. I believe Jesus will then give you The Holy Spirit to teach you all things. Some verses for these beliefs are as follows:

**Romans 10:9-13**
**9 That if thou shalt confess with thy mouth the Lord Jesus, and shalt believe in thine heart that God hath raised him from the dead, thou shalt be saved.**
**10 For with the heart man believeth unto righteousness; and with the mouth confession is made unto salvation.**
**11 For the scripture saith, Whosoever believeth on him shall not be ashamed.**
**12 For there is no difference between the Jew and the Greek: for the same Lord over all is rich unto all that call upon him.**
**13 For whosoever shall call upon the name of the Lord shall be saved.**

**John 3:3**
**3 Jesus answered and said unto him, Verily, verily, I say unto thee, Except a man be born again, he cannot see the kingdom of God.**

**Genesis 1:1-2**
**1 In the beginning God created the Heaven and the earth.**

2 And the earth was without form, and void; and darkness was upon the face of the deep. And the Spirit of God moved upon the face of the waters.

John 1:1-3

1 In the beginning was the Word, and the Word was with God, and the Word was God.

2 The same was in the beginning with God.

3 All things were made by him; and without him was not any thing made that was made.

John 1:14

14 And the Word was made flesh, and dwelt among us, (and we beheld his glory, the glory as of the only begotten of the Father,) full of grace and truth.


Isaiah 9:6

6 For unto us a child is born, unto us a son is given: and the government shall be upon his shoulder: and his name shall be called Wonderful, Counsellor, The mighty God, The everlasting Father, The Prince of Peace.


John 3:14-16

14 And as Moses lifted up the serpent in the wilderness, even so must the Son of man be lifted up:

15 That whosoever believeth in him should not perish, but have eternal life.

16 For God so loved the world, that he gave his only begotten Son, that whosoever believeth in him should not perish, but have everlasting life.


Romans 3:20-24

20 Therefore by the deeds of the law there shall no flesh be justified in his sight: for by the law is the knowledge of sin.

21 But now the righteousness of God without the law is manifested, being witnessed by the law and the prophets;

**22** Even the righteousness of God which is by faith of Jesus Christ unto all and upon all them that believe: for there is no difference:

**23** For all have sinned, and come short of the glory of God;

**24** Being justified freely by his grace through the redemption that is in Christ Jesus:

**1 Corinthians 12:12-13**

**12** For as the body is one, and hath many members, and all the members of that one body, being many, are one body: so also is Christ.

**13** For by one Spirit are we all baptized into one body, whether we be Jews or Gentiles, whether we be bond or free; and have been all made to drink into one Spirit.

**Ephesians 4:4-6**

**4** There is one body, and one Spirit, even as ye are called in one hope of your calling;

**5** One Lord, one faith, one baptism,

**6** One God and Father of all, who is above all, and through all, and in you all.

**1 John 5:7-13**

**7** For there are three that bear record in heaven, the Father, the Word, and the Holy Ghost: and these three are one.

**8** And there are three that bear witness in earth, the spirit, and the water, and the blood: and these three agree in one.

**9** If we receive the witness of men, the witness of God is greater: for this is the witness of God which he hath testified of his Son.

**10** He that believeth on the Son of God hath the witness in himself: he that believeth not God hath made him a liar; because he believeth not the record that God gave of his Son.

11 And this is the record, that God hath given to us eternal life, and this life is in his Son.

12 He that hath the Son hath life; and he that hath not the Son of God hath not life.

13 These things have I written unto you that believe on the name of the Son of God; that ye may know that ye have eternal life, and that ye may believe on the name of the Son of God.

John 8:31-32

31 Then said Jesus to those Jews which believed on him, If ye continue in my word, then are ye my disciples indeed;

32 And ye shall know the truth, and the truth shall make you free.

Hebrews 12:2

2 Looking unto Jesus the author and finisher of our faith; who for the joy that was set before him endured the cross, despising the shame, and is set down at the right hand of the throne of God.

Matthew 1:23

23 Behold, a virgin shall be with child, and shall bring forth a son, and they shall call his name Emmanuel, which being interpreted is, God with us.

Luke 1:27-32

27 To a virgin espoused to a man whose name was Joseph, of the house of David; and the virgin's name was Mary.

28 And the angel came in unto her, and said, Hail, thou that art highly favoured, the Lord is with thee: blessed art thou among women.

29 And when she saw him, she was troubled at his saying, and cast in her mind what manner of salutation this should be.

**30 And the angel said unto her, Fear not, Mary: for thou hast found favour with God.**

**31 And, behold, thou shalt conceive in thy womb, and bring forth a son, and shalt call his name JESUS.**

**32 He shall be great, and shall be called the Son of the Highest: and the Lord God shall give unto him the throne of his father David:**

**Hebrews 4:15**

**15 For we have not an high priest which cannot be touched with the feeling of our infirmities; but was in all points tempted like as we are, yet without sin.**

I believe whole heartily that The Bible is The complete and inerrant Word of God, and that It is profitable for doctrine, for reproof, for correction, for instruction in righteousness, that the man of God may be perfect, throughly furnished unto all good works.

**2 Timothy 3:16-17**

**16 All scripture is given by inspiration of God, and is profitable for doctrine, for reproof, for correction, for instruction in righteousness:**

**17 That the man of God may be perfect, throughly furnished unto all good works.**

I believe that The Bible can only be correctly interpreted by a spiritual or saved person possessing The Holy Spirit and using scripture to interpret scripture.

**1 Corinthians 2:12-14**

**12 Now we have received, not the spirit of the world, but the spirit which is of God; that we might know the things that are freely given to us of God.**

**13 Which things also we speak, not in the words which man's wisdom teacheth, but which the Holy Ghost teacheth; comparing spiritual things with spiritual.**
**14 But the natural man receiveth not the things of the Spirit of God: for they are foolishness unto him: neither can he know them, because they are spiritually discerned.**

But the time will come when people will not endure sound doctrine but shall be turned to fables.

**2 Timothy 4:3-4**
**3 For the time will come when they will not endure sound doctrine; but after their own lusts shall they heap to themselves teachers, having itching ears;**
**4 And they shall turn away their ears from the truth, and shall be turned unto fables.**

Just for clarification, I use this next statement in all my books to qualify why I am using the King James Version of The Bible, hereafter referred to in this book as (KJV). Most people don't use the KJV much today because of the Elizabethan Shakespearian type wording with all its thees and thous. And I acknowledge that it takes some getting used to. But there are reasons I use only the KJV. There are versions of The Bible out there that have all those words corrected to fit the modern-day language of today. But I only use the KJV because all the other translations of the English Bible used unreliable manuscripts that the King James counsel rejected. The Alaxandrinus, Vaticanus and Sinaiticus manuscripts were rejected by the KJV translators because these manuscripts have all been found to be about five percent in error but were used anyway by the translators of all other English versions of The Bible including the New King James version because these translations are older than the original copies that were used in the KJV. My guess is that they figured that because they are older, they must be better. The KJV was taken from the more reliable

Ancient Copies, Tyndale, Matthews and Geneva manuscripts. And all of the translators of the KJV were under the penalty of death if they mistranslated any of the manuscripts they were using. That is a pretty powerful incentive to get it right. None of the other translators of any of the other English Bibles were under that kind of penalty if they got a translation wrong. Plus, today, some of those new translations design their version to better fit modern public opinion which changes with the times and is not always scriptural. Another reason I use the KJV is that it is the only popular version of the English Bible today that you can use in a book like this without permission from the owners of the copyrights for that version. The KJV has no copyrights that are owned by man. The KJV has withstood the test of time and is called The Authorized version of The Bible all over the world. Once you get used to the thees and thous and all the other words never used in our modern English; it is really quite easy to understand and even clarifies some words that were changed by those other versions that are not as effective as the original KJV rendition of that word. I have gotten good enough at reading it that I can usually change the out-of-date words to today's words on the fly as I am reading it. Now, let me clarify. I don't change any word that would change the original meaning of that word. Many words like this have already been changed in the current KJV from what the original 1611 KJV was. No, the KJV was not revised or rewritten or retranslated. Just certain words were changed to be able to understand what it is saying or else today it would be like reading a foreign language. But they didn't change any words that would change the meaning of the word. I can give you an example of this on a word that was never changed to modern day language. In The KJV Bible today, the word eventide is used. That word today is evening. So, if they updated the language of The KJV Bible today and changed eventide to evening, that would not be retranslating The Bible. It's the exact same word that was pronounced differently back then than it is now. So, these are the types of words that I just change on the fly without even thinking about it when I am quoting a verse to someone. However, in this book, I left the original KJV language as is so there would be no confusion. There is a lot of benefit to using the King James Version of The Bible that was translated at a time when they better understood the meaning of the writings they were translating. Be very careful when reading other translations. Most all of them diminish the deity of Jesus in places like 2 Timothy 3:16 that clearly states that Jesus is God, but most all other translations take that part out because it is in italics. Words in italics were added to clarify a thought that wasn't clear in the English language. So, words were added to complete the thought of the original text that there was no single word in English that could relay the meaning of that one word. But they were added with careful consideration of scripture interpreting scripture with plenty of other verses that confirm Jesus as God. So why take it out of a translation that got it right? Unless you don't like Jesus being God. I would be very careful claiming that there are mistakes in the KJV; a Bible that God has allowed to be the authorized English version of The Holy Bible for over 500 years now. Language changes through the years, but we don't need a whole other translation to be able to read The Bible. Some of those other translations have translated verses to make them suggest a works salvation. You have to understand that there are some denominations out there that have influence on some of these translations of The Bible, and sometimes these denominations very subtly change some verses to conform more to their doctrines. You have to be very careful what you accept as The Word of God these days. There are many more questionable changes in those modern translations, but as I said before, that is not what this book is about. There are many books already out there that go into great detail on this subject. If you are interested, I suggest you get one of these easy to find books on the fallacies of modern-day translations. Do you believe The Bible to be the absolute and inerrant Word of Almighty God? Well, this entire book is based on It indeed being just that. Understand that there must be a standard or foundation from which to draw from that is sure when you are stating facts. And I can think of no better standard than The Word of God. His Word is the only sure foundation from which to work from. All other writings are just opinions or commentaries. That's why I will establish nothing without giving sure scripture for it. The Word is a living Word in The Person of Jesus Christ Himself. People tell me, well, that's only your interpretation. Many people think it takes some theologian to understand what The Bible says. If that were so, you would have to take verses like these out of The Bible.

**1 John 2:26-27**
**26 These things have I written unto you concerning them that seduce you.**
**27 But the anointing which ye have received of him abideth in you, and ye need not that any man teach you: but as the same anointing teacheth you of all things, and is truth, and is no lie, and even as it hath taught you, ye shall abide in him.**

**1 Corinthians 2:7-16**
**7 But we speak the wisdom of God in a mystery, even the hidden wisdom, which God ordained before the world unto our glory:**
**8 Which none of the princes of this world knew: for had they known it, they would not have crucified the Lord of glory.**
**9 But as it is written, Eye hath not seen, nor ear heard, neither have entered into the heart of man, the things which God hath prepared for them that love him.**
**10 But God hath revealed them unto us by his Spirit: for the Spirit searcheth all things, yea, the deep things of God.**
**11 For what man knoweth the things of a man, save the spirit of man which is in him? even so the things of God knoweth no man, but the Spirit of God.**
**12 Now we have received, not the spirit of the world, but the spirit which is of God; that we might know the things that are freely given to us of God.**

**13** Which things also we speak, not in the words which man's wisdom teacheth, but which the Holy Ghost teacheth; comparing spiritual things with spiritual.

**14** But the natural man receiveth not the things of the Spirit of God: for they are foolishness unto him: neither can he know them, because they are spiritually discerned.

**15** But he that is spiritual judgeth all things, yet he himself is judged of no man.

**16** For who hath known the mind of the Lord, that he may instruct him? But we have the mind of Christ.

**1 Corinthians 1:25-29**

**25** Because the foolishness of God is wiser than men; and the weakness of God is stronger than men.

**26** For ye see your calling, brethren, how that not many wise men after the flesh, not many mighty, not many noble, are called:

**27** But God hath chosen the foolish things of the world to confound the wise; and God hath chosen the weak things of the world to confound the things which are mighty;

**28** And base things of the world, and things which are despised, hath God chosen, yea, and things which are not, to bring to nought things that are:

**29** That no flesh should glory in his presence.

Comparing spiritual things with spiritual is the key to understanding The Bible. And any saved person can do that. God chooses the weak things of the world to confound the mighty, so that no flesh should glory in His presence. And there is the answer. It is His knowledge, not ours. It is His glory, not ours. It is His interpretation when you compare His Word to His Word. The Bible says let nothing be established but by two or three witnesses. That also applies to scripture. You cannot make a doctrine out of one single scripture. A doctrine needs to have two or three witnesses of scriptures to back it up. You must also not assume what a verse means. Other scripture will verify what a verse means. You also need to find out the context of a scripture and who it is talking to. Read before and after the scripture you are trying to interpret to find out these things. God says some things, even in the New Testament, that were spoked directly to the Jews and does not apply to the Gentiles. The Gentiles were not normally participants of temple worship like the Jews were. The book of Hebrews is a prime example of this. Many things spoken in Hebrews was, at that time, spoked directly to Messianic Jewish congregations. The title of Hebrews itself tells you who it is talking to. A Hebrew is a Jew. Although, we can still glean from what it says. But if you don't acknowledge who the book of Hebrews is talking to, you could be confused in your interpretation of what it is talking about. Also, people try to spiritualize some things that are clearly literal and literalize some things that are clearly spiritual. Such as when Jesus said: "destroy this temple and in three days I will raise it up", He wasn't talking about the literal building, But He was referring to His own body.

> **John 2:19-21**
> **19 Jesus answered and said unto them, Destroy this temple,**
> **and in three days I will raise it up.**
> **20 Then said the Jews, Forty and six years was this temple**
> **in building, and wilt thou rear it up in three days?**
> **21 But he spake of the temple of his body.**

Yet people try to spiritualize Israel and say that the church is now the spiritual Israel and takes the place of the physical Israel. But clearly, God is not through with Israel and will literally turn back to them in the future. The church and Israel were never combined except the fact that Jews and Gentiles share in this age of grace together. Right now, there is neither Jew or Gentile when it comes to salvation.

> **Galatians 3:26-29**
> **26 For ye are all the children of God by faith in Christ Jesus.**

**27 For as many of you as have been baptized into Christ have put on Christ.**

**28 There is neither Jew nor Greek, there is neither bond nor free, there is neither male nor female: for ye are all one in Christ Jesus.**

**29 And if ye be Christ's, then are ye Abraham's seed, and heirs according to the promise.**

**Romans 11:25-26**

**25 For I would not, brethren, that ye should be ignorant of this mystery, lest ye should be wise in your own conceits; that blindness in part is happened to Israel, until the fulness of the Gentiles be come in.**

**26 And so all Israel shall be saved: as it is written, There shall come out of Sion the Deliverer, and shall turn away ungodliness from Jacob:**

**2 Corinthians 13:1**

**1 This is the third time I am coming to you. In the mouth of two or three witnesses shall every word be established.**

**Matthew 18:15-16**

**15 Moreover if thy brother shall trespass against thee, go and tell him his fault between thee and him alone: if he shall hear thee, thou hast gained thy brother.**

**16 But if he will not hear thee, then take with thee one or two more, that in the mouth of two or three witnesses every word may be established.**

All we have to do is read it and simply compare what is said in other parts of His Word to confirm what He is saying. It's all Him and none us. And that is all I am doing in this book. I give Him all the credit. I do have a couple of spots in this book that I give my opinion on something that isn't really clear in The Bible. But I will let you know when it is just my opinion. But God's Word is not an opinion or fable. It's absolute fact. Every single Word of It. All I ask, is for you to read the scriptures that I give you from the King James version Bible and see for yourself. Because of the widespread acceptance of this holiday today, it is important that you use a KJV Bible on this subject because other translations have softened the point-blank language that the KJV uses on direct scriptures related to Christmas. I have seen translations take Jeremiah 10: 3-4 and try to make it something other than a tree.

> **Jeremiah 10:3-4**
> **3 For the customs of the people are vain: for one cutteth a tree out of the forest, the work of the hands of the workman, with the axe.**
> **4 They deck it with silver and with gold; they fasten it with nails and with hammers, that it move not.**

Some say it is a carved image from a piece of wood, or a statue. They use verse 14 to say it was not a tree.

> **Jeremiah 10:14**
> **14 Every man is brutish in his knowledge: every founder is confounded by the graven image: for his molten image is falsehood, and there is no breath in them.**

But if you will notice, this verse is talking about a completely different idol. This one has nothing to do with a tree. It is a molten image. The one is verse 3 says it is a tree cut out of the forest and decked with silver and gold. How plain do you need it said? It even says they fasten it with nails and hammer that it move not. In other words, so it will stand up on its own. How many of you nailed boards on the bottom of the Christmas tree to make it stand upright so you could decorate it? I know today they have stands you can buy made for that with a water well in the bottom of it so the tree will last longer. But it didn't used to be that way. Back when people didn't have a lot of money, they would just take two boards and nail them to the bottom of the tree and that was it. The truth is, the idol in verse 2 is a tree. But, you know, sometimes the truth isn't very popular. However, fact is still fact, and truth is still truth no matter how anyone feels about it. What you are about to learn concerning Christmas may upset your lifestyle. It may go cross grain to everything you've learned from childhood. You may have been given some of the best memories of your life through lies and deceitfulness, springing right up from the heart of the mystery religion of Babylon. Christmas time may be your favorite time of year, and you may have lived a lifetime celebrating it faithfully every single year. But that's tradition, not Bible. Now, I'm not knocking tradition except when it conflicts with God's Word. And Christmas does exactly that; and in the worst way; by tacking The Holy Name of Jesus to a known idol. It also involves the family structure in the deceptive worship of idols. And the family structure was set up by God in the first chapter of the first Book of The Bible.

**Genesis 1:27-28**
**27 So God created man in his own image, in the image of God created he him; male and female created he them.**
**28 And God blessed them, and God said unto them, Be fruitful, and multiply, and replenish the earth, and subdue it: and have dominion over the fish of the sea, and over the fowl of the air, and over every living thing that moveth upon the earth.**

You ask: How does Christmas affect the family? The evil of Christmas is covered up with gifts, lights, and Santa Claus. But nevertheless, the destructive factor is there. And that element, as I said earlier, is tradition involving idol worship and lies.

**Colossians 2:8**
**8 Beware lest any man spoil you through philosophy and**
**vain deceit, after the tradition of men, after the rudiments**
**of the world, and not after Christ.**

Luke tells us that we must put Jesus even before family, and if celebrating the Christmas tradition means, knowingly or not, casting our Lord aside for another god simply because the whole family is doing it; then that family is involved in idol worship, working against God, causing you to stumble in idol worship before The Lord, therefore breaking down the God instituted family structure.

**Luke 14:26-27**
**26 If any man come to me, and hate not his father, and**
**mother, and wife, and children, and brethren, and sisters,**
**yea, and his own life also, he cannot be my disciple.**
**27 And whosoever doth not bear his cross, and come after**
**me, cannot be my disciple.**

Look; Christmas is fun. That's precisely why it's so hard to convince people of its evils. Come on; if people didn't really enjoy Christmas that much, I'm sure they would listen to reason with a more open mind. If something is fun, it doesn't seem to matter if it is right or wrong. Look at Halloween. Just about everyone will agree that Halloween is a high day of cult worship. At least Halloween is honest in what it claims to be. It is a time if idol worship and the pagan practice of scaring off demons with those idols (not Jesus). People know that, yet go right on celebrating it. Why? Because it's fun; that's why. They would say: I don't believe in those cults. I just do it for fun. And it's the same with Christmas. In the same sense, they would say: I don't worship the sun god of Christmas, and besides, his name has been changed from Tammuz to Jesus. So, to them, they're worshiping Jesus instead of Tammuz simply by tacking The Name of Jesus to Tammuz. Who is Tammuz, you ask? Well, I'll be glad to answer that question for you, but you're not going to like it. Let me say first that if you're celebrating Christmas, you are participating in sun worship rituals. Don't hide your face from the truth that I am about to tell you. If you don't believe me, check it out for yourself. I'm not just talking about a grey area here. There are many grey areas in life that might be sin to one person, and not to another. Like talked about in Romans

> **Romans 14:21-23**
> **21 It is good neither to eat flesh, nor to drink wine, nor any thing whereby thy brother stumbleth, or is offended, or is made weak.**
> **22 Hast thou faith? have it to thyself before God. Happy is he that condemneth not himself in that thing which he alloweth.**
> **23 And he that doubteth is damned if he eat, because he eateth not of faith: for whatsoever is not of faith is sin.**

To one, eating things sacrificed to idols was sin; to another, not. But Christmas is different. Just as God commanded us not to steel or commit adultery, He also gave us clear cut instructions on how to, and how not to worship Him; and Christmas is a how not to. I would think when you worship Jesus; you had better get it right. There are consequences for leading other people down a wrong path. All other kinds of religions other than Christianity will put you in some sort of bondage to do its rituals and works that they say you must do to be saved. Only Christianity sets you free from bondage. Christmas is linked directly to the bondage of the zodiac, which is an idol worship of the sun, the moon, the stars, the planets, the constellations and the heavens. Here, it is called: "the signs of heaven".

> **Jeremiah 10:1-2**
> **1 Hear ye the word which the Lord speaketh unto you, O house of Israel:**

**2 Thus saith the Lord, Learn not the way of the heathen, and be not dismayed at the signs of heaven; for the heathen are dismayed at them.**

But it wasn't restricted to just the heavens. It evolved into other things also. Earthly objects, animals, and the seasons, even mortal man. Those round shaped ornaments that you put on the tree. Do you know what those ornaments mean? They represent the private parts of the sun god. We will see later that these types of ornaments were used in paganism long before Jesus was born. Today, they are usually round and shiny, and reflect brilliant light depicting the brightness of the sun. The sun is the center of the zodiac. Those that believe in the zodiac look to it in the form of their horoscope for their everyday guidance, putting them in bondage to its commands, dictating to them each day what they should or shouldn't do. Satan can manipulate your daily decisions and activities through these commands of their horoscope. And yes, even today, people follow their horoscope. Some people follow this ritual religiously and the Christmas celebration is a vital part of it because it is the celebration of the winter solstice at the sign of Capricorn, the goat. The zodiac was worshiped more than two thousand years before Jesus was born. And out of It came a mother/child cult that is part of the Babylonian religion. This took place sometime after the flood. You have probably seen statues of a mother holding a child in some religions today that they claim to be Mother Mary and baby Jesus. Statues of this kind have been found in civilizations long before Jesus was born. It was an idol of the queen of heaven holding her son Tammuz, a false Christ. Jesus is no longer on the earth in the flesh. He is here in The Person of The Holy Spirit and living in believers. He is no longer a child in the manger. He grew up and is now our Lord and Savior. We do not need a natural, or secular celebration to worship Him. In fact, if you are celebrating Christmas; you are worshiping Him with a lie. December 25th is not His birthday. It's kind of an insult to try to bring Jesus back to the natural once a year, and as a baby at that.

He is no longer natural, but supernatural. He is no longer a child. He grew up. He is now The Reigning King of kings and Lord of lords. Celebrating birthdays is a man-made tradition. Nowhere in The Bible does it mention celebrating birthdays. I suppose there is nothing wrong with celebrating someone's birthday unless you involve idol worship in it like Christmas does, especially attaching The Name of Jesus to it. But even in the world, birthdays do not involve celebrating the person as if he was a newborn child again. There are candles on a birthday cake that acknowledge how old the person is. A 50-year-old person is celebrated as 50 years old. No one celebrates someone that is 50 as if he was a newborn. The world is okay with celebrating Jesus as an infant, yet they reject Him as a man and our Savior.

> **Hebrews 5:11-6:1**
> **11 Of whom we have many things to say, and hard to be uttered, seeing ye are dull of hearing.**
> **12 For when for the time ye ought to be teachers, ye have need that one teach you again which be the first principles of the oracles of God; and are become such as have need of milk, and not of strong meat.**
> **13 For every one that useth milk is unskilful in the word of righteousness: for he is a babe.**
> **14 But strong meat belongeth to them that are of full age, even those who by reason of use have their senses exercised to discern both good and evil.**
> **Ch 6-1 Therefore leaving the principles of the doctrine of Christ, let us go on unto perfection; not laying again the foundation of repentance from dead works, and of faith toward God,**
>
> **1 Corinthians 13:11**
> **11 When I was a child, I spake as a child, I understood as a child, I thought as a child: but when I became a man, I put away childish things.**

I know these two scriptures that we just read are not specifically talking about the birth of Jesus. But the consensus here is to leave behind those beginning principals and go on to perfection. I would think that would include Jesus. As glorious as it was, we are not told in The Bible to dwell on Jesus being born. We are told to remember His death burial and resurrection with the communion. The baby Jesus didn't die for our sin. The man Jesus did.

> **1 Corinthians 11:26**
> **26 For as often as ye eat this bread, and drink this cup, ye**
> **do shew the Lord's death till he come.**

Do you think it is an accident that The Bible didn't inform us of the day of Jesus birth? Why? Because He didn't want us celebrating Him as a child. He wants to be celebrated as The Reigning King. Let's worship Him that way. Supernaturally, not naturally. Him only shalt thou serve! Luke 4:8. Not a false god under any name. Anyone can call themselves by the name of Jesus, and many do now days. Most of the Christmas celebration is not in The Word of God. So, the christ of Christmas is not the right one. Let's worship only The real Jesus.

> **Acts 24:14**
> **14 But this I confess unto thee, that after the way which they**
> **call heresy, so worship I the God of my fathers, believing**
> **all things which are written in the law and in the prophets:**

He is saying here that he worships God according to the scripture, not tradition. And people call him a heretic for it. This same thing happened in the dark ages. If you didn't worship their false Christ, then you were labeled a heretic. We'll talk more about that later. But right now, let's take a look at this scripture.

**Deuteronomy 12:30-32**
**30 Take heed to thyself that thou be not snared by following**
**them, after that they be destroyed from before thee; and**
**that thou inquire not after their gods, saying, How did**
**these nations serve their gods? even so will I do likewise.**
**31 Thou shalt not do so unto the Lord thy God: for every**
**abomination to the Lord, which he hateth, have they done**
**unto their gods; for even their sons and their daughters**
**they have burnt in the fire to their gods.**
**32 What thing soever I command you, observe to do it:**
**thou shalt not add thereto, nor diminish from it.**

This is God telling the Israelites; don't worship God the same way that other religions worship their gods. I can assure you, that same thing applies to the church today. The Christmas celebration is a religious worship of a false Christ; and was converted to the worship of Jesus with very little change in form and manner with all its customs and traditions. This scripture says don't do that. It says, "Thou shalt not do so". How plain do you need it said? Yes, this verse is Old Testament and is talking to Israel. Most of the Old Testament scriptures are talking to Israel. But we Gentiles have been grafted into Abraham's seed and while we do not take the place of Israel, we can learn from what God told them in the Old Testament.

**Galatians 3:29**
**29 And if ye be Christ's, then are ye Abraham's seed, and**
**heirs according to the promise.**

**1 Corinthians 10:1-12**
**1 Moreover, brethren, I would not that ye should be**
**ignorant, how that all our fathers were under the cloud,**
**and all passed through the sea;**
**2 And were all baptized unto Moses in the cloud and**
**in the sea;**

**3 And did all eat the same spiritual meat;**

**4 And did all drink the same spiritual drink: for they drank of that spiritual Rock that followed them: and that Rock was Christ.**

**5 But with many of them God was not well pleased: for they were overthrown in the wilderness.**

**6 Now these things were our examples, to the intent we should not lust after evil things, as they also lusted.**

**7 Neither be ye idolaters, as were some of them; as it is written, The people sat down to eat and drink, and rose up to play.**

**8 Neither let us commit fornication, as some of them committed, and fell in one day three and twenty thousand.**

**9 Neither let us tempt Christ, as some of them also tempted, and were destroyed of serpents.**

**10 Neither murmur ye, as some of them also murmured, and were destroyed of the destroyer.**

**11 Now all these things happened unto them for ensamples: and they are written for our admonition, upon whom the ends of the world are come.**

**12 Wherefore let him that thinketh he standeth take heed lest he fall.**

Abram was separated from his kindred. His family was from Ur, which was about 200 miles southeast of Babylon. His father moved from Ur to Haran. After his father died, God separated Abram from the idol worship of his family and sent him to a place where He would make him a great nation. When we get saved, God separates us from the idol worship or our family also.

**Genesis 11:31-12:2**

**31 And Terah took Abram his son, and Lot the son of Haran his son's son, and Sarai his daughter in law, his son Abram's wife; and they went forth with them from Ur**

> of the Chaldees, to go into the land of Canaan; and they
> came unto Haran, and dwelt there.
> 32 And the days of Terah were two hundred and five years:
> and Terah died in Haran.
> Ch 12-1 Now the Lord had said unto Abram, Get thee
> out of thy country, and from thy kindred, and from thy
> father's house, unto a land that I will shew thee:
> 2 And I will make of thee a great nation, and I will bless thee,
> and make thy name great; and thou shalt be a blessing:

Let me tell you a little scenario that I think correctly illustrates what Jesus might think about us celebrating the idol worshiping celebration of Christmas. Let's say you are married. Imagine you are the husband. You are sitting there at home, and all the sudden your wife comes home with another man. Of course, you ask her; What are you doing my dear? And she says; Well sweetheart, this is a man that I used to love before we were married, and I used to always love to celebrate his birthday because it was always so much fun; and today is his birthday! Then you say to her; But he's not your husband darling; I am! Why do you bring this man into our house? When you married me, you promised to forsake all others! Then she says to you: Oh, but it's okay; you see; I am pretending like it's your birthday, and I am even calling him by your name, therefore it's just like he is you; so, if I convince myself that he is you, then I'm not forsaking you. Do you think he would understand? Well, I think not. I can tell you for sure that I wouldn't. Then how do you think Jesus feels when His wife, the church, brings another god home to the house of God and celebrates his birthday calling him by the name of Jesus; tossing Him, The real Jesus, aside for the Christmas season to have her personal fun with this false Christ. Our relationship with Jesus is just like that. He is a jealous God, not willing to share us with a false Christ. So, just as a husband would not be willing to share his wife with a false husband, Jesus is not willing to share His wife (the church) with a false Christ.

27

**Ephesians 5:22-24**
**22 Wives, submit yourselves unto your own husbands, as**
**unto the Lord.**
**23 For the husband is the head of the wife, even as Christ**
**is the head of the church: and he is the saviour of the body.**
**24 Therefore as the church is subject unto Christ, so let the**
**wives be to their own husbands in every thing.**

I can say as an absolute fact that December 25th is not the day of Jesus birth. I will prove that later on in this book, but it is the birthday of a false Christ named Tammuz, of whom we spoke of earlier. Let me tell you a little more about this guy. He came on the scene very early in time. Somewhere around the time of the tower of Babel. This occurred long enough after the flood for there to be a sizable population on the earth, but it was before Abraham came on the scene. It was the time of Nimrod who was Noah's great grandson, and he built the kingdom of Babel. So that can give you an idea of the timeline. Out of Nimrod's kingdom of Babel came a worship of the sun as a god. It is not clear whether this deity was Nimrod himself who became the sun god, or someone after him. Out of this false deity came a child which was the false Christ and there was a celebration honoring him on his birthday at the winter solstice which later, the Romans named Saturnalia.

**2 Corinthians 11:3-4**
**3 But I fear, lest by any means, as the serpent beguiled Eve**
**through his subtilty, so your minds should be corrupted**
**from the simplicity that is in Christ.**
**4 For if he that cometh preacheth another Jesus, whom we**
**have not preached, or if ye receive another spirit, which**
**ye have not received, or another gospel, which ye have not**
**accepted, ye might well bear with him.**

**Mark 13:5-6**
**5 And Jesus answering them began to say, Take heed lest**
**any man deceive you:**
**6 For many shall come in my name, saying, I am Christ;**
**and shall deceive many.**

Verse 6 above is talking about during the tribulation. But just like it talks about earthquakes and wars; some of this could have started before the tribulation in today's society. Saturnalia was celebrated December seventeenth through the twenty fifth, celebrating the birth of the new sun. That is the time of year that you have the shortest day of the year in the northern hemisphere and the days begin to get longer at the winter solstice, thus you have the birth of the new sun. Tammuz was said to be the child of the sun god born of a woman, who was the queen, that claimed that the sun god made her pregnant without a mortal man. Her child was said to be half man and half god and the son of the sun god and the Christ. Of course, he was a false Christ. But his birthday was December 25th. Then when Jesus arrived and the church was formed, there later came a mixing of these pagan festivals with Christianity in the church age of Pergamos in Revelation 2:14. We will talk about that later in chapter 5. True Christians wouldn't take part in this pagan festival. But Christian influence couldn't stop it. This festival was very popular. Even some Christians were okay with finding a way to keep this fun celebration. Many true Christians of that day protested against mixing this celebration with Christianity, but it meant the end of the persecution of the church and allowed Christians to take part in this popular festival, so like I said, even some Christians were okay with it. Other Christians accused those that accepted it of taking part in idolatry. The Bible points out this kind of compromise in Exodus in the story about when Moses went up on Mount Sinai to receive the law, the children of Israel built themselves a golden calf during his absence.

**Exodus Ex 32:1-5**

**1 And when the people saw that Moses delayed to come down out of the mount, the people gathered themselves together unto Aaron, and said unto him, Up, make us gods, which shall go before us; for as for this Moses, the man that brought us up out of the land of Egypt, we wot not what is become of him.**

**2 And Aaron said unto them, Break off the golden earrings, which are in the ears of your wives, of your sons, and of your daughters, and bring them unto me.**

**3 And all the people brake off the golden earrings which were in their ears, and brought them unto Aaron.**

**4 And he received them at their hand, and fashioned it with a graving tool, after he had made it a molten calf: and they said, These be thy gods, O Israel, which brought thee up out of the land of Egypt.**

**5 And when Aaron saw it, he built an altar before it; and Aaron made proclamation, and said, To morrow is a feast to the Lord.**

After this calf was molded, they planned a feast for the next day. Aaron, in an attempt to connect this celebration to God said, "Tomorrow is a feast to The Lord", mixing the idol worship of that golden calf with the worship of The Lord. Notice in this scripture that Lord is spelled with a capitol "L". This is not a false god he is talking about. It is The Lord God he was talking about when he said, let this be a feast to The Lord. If you read on, God was not impressed with that golden calf. In fact, He was quite angry. He was so angry that many died that day because of their idol worship. It didn't matter that Aaron called it a feast to The Lord because underneath it all, it was still idol worship. Is this any different than Christmas?

On another occasion, Achan took only a couple of Babylonian items from the ruins of the Babylonians that Israel had just destroyed.

They were commanded to not take any of the Babylonian items but to put the silver, gold, brass and iron in the Lord's treasury.

> **Joshua 6:18-19**
> **18 And ye, in any wise keep yourselves from the accursed thing, lest ye make yourselves accursed, when ye take of the accursed thing, and make the camp of Israel a curse, and trouble it.**
> **19 But all the silver, and gold, and vessels of brass and iron, are consecrated unto the Lord: they shall come into the treasury of the Lord.**

Achan hid the items in his tent mixing the idol worshiping items of Babylon in with the camp of Israel. God was very angry and removed the blessing from Israel resulting in Israel losing a battle with its enemy.

> **Joshua 7:5-7**
> **5 And the men of Ai smote of them about thirty and six men: for they chased them from before the gate even unto Shebarim, and smote them in the going down: wherefore the hearts of the people melted, and became as water.**
> **6 And Joshua rent his clothes, and fell to the earth upon his face before the ark of the Lord until the eventide, he and the elders of Israel, and put dust upon their heads.**
> **7 And Joshua said, Alas, O Lord God, wherefore hast thou at all brought this people over Jordan, to deliver us into the hand of the Amorites, to destroy us? would to God we had been content, and dwelt on the other side Jordan!**

> **Joshua 7:11-12**
> **11 Israel hath sinned, and they have also transgressed my covenant which I commanded them: for they have even taken of the accursed thing, and have also stolen, and**

**dissembled also, and they have put it even among their own stuff.**

**12 Therefore the children of Israel could not stand before their enemies, but turned their backs before their enemies, because they were accursed: neither will I be with you any more, except ye destroy the accursed from among you.**

Joshua didn't know about the transgression until God revealed it to him, verse 11 above. As a result of this sin, Achan and his whole family were executed and the items he took from the ruins and all his possessions and livestock and everything he owned was destroyed.

**Joshua 7:19-26**

**19 And Joshua said unto Achan, My son, give, I pray thee, glory to the Lord God of Israel, and make confession unto him; and tell me now what thou hast done; hide it not from me.**

**20 And Achan answered Joshua, and said, Indeed I have sinned against the Lord God of Israel, and thus and thus have I done:**

**21 When I saw among the spoils a goodly Babylonish garment, and two hundred shekels of silver, and a wedge of gold of fifty shekels weight, then I coveted them, and took them; and, behold, they are hid in the earth in the midst of my tent, and the silver under it.**

**22 So Joshua sent messengers, and they ran unto the tent; and, behold, it was hid in his tent, and the silver under it.**

**23 And they took them out of the midst of the tent, and brought them unto Joshua, and unto all the children of Israel, and laid them out before the Lord.**

**24 And Joshua, and all Israel with him, took Achan the son of Zerah, and the silver, and the garment, and the wedge of gold, and his sons, and his daughters, and his oxen, and**

his asses, and his sheep, and his tent, and all that he had: and they brought them unto the valley of Achor.

25 And Joshua said, Why hast thou troubled us? the Lord shall trouble thee this day. And all Israel stoned him with stones, and burned them with fire, after they had stoned them with stones.

26 And they raised over him a great heap of stones unto this day. So the Lord turned from the fierceness of his anger. Wherefore the name of that place was called, The valley of Achor, unto this day.

Now, you can take a Babylonian idol like a tree, put it in your house, and decorate it like in Jeremiah 10:2-5 and call it the birthday of Jesus; mixing idol worship with the worship of Jesus by accepting the birthday of a false Christ as the birthday of Jesus, but as for me and my house, we will choose the real Jesus, and the way that the He wants to be worshiped without idol worship mixed in.

# CHAPTER 2
# EVERYBODY'S DOING IT

Just because everyone is doing something doesn't make it okay to do it. In the story we just read about the children of Israel making a golden calf; it was everyone doing it; even Aaron, who knew better. It's hard to not participate in something everyone is doing. Turn and read Daniel 3; 1-30. It's the whole chapter, so I won't write it all here. You will note that this is the story of king Nebuchadnezzar and his experience with Shadrach, Meshach, and Abed-Nego. Babylon is the birthplace of false gods. This is the land of Nimrod, and the land where "open say's me", flying carpets, genie in the bottle, magic, snake charmers, and so on, came from. At this particular point in history, king Nebuchadnezzar, who at this time just couldn't seem to get it through his head who God really Is, has made a golden image and decreed that every man that shall hear the sound of the horn, pipe, lyre, sackbut, psaltery, and dulcimer, and all kinds of music, shall fall down and worship the golden image. And whoever doesn't fall down to worship it; that he should be cast into the midst of a burning fiery furnace. But three men, Shadrach, Meshach, and Abednego, would not bow to the image. Now, this was not a popular stand. Everyone else was doing it. Most people didn't think twice about it. But these three seen the bigger picture. If they bow down to the golden god, even for the short time required, to their God, it would be idol worship. And besides that, they chose to serve The Lord God willingly, and they stood ready to put their lives on the line in faithfulness to Him. They would rather die than to give honor to a false god.

Would that Christians of today were like minded. So, they stood alone for The Lord God, and were cast into the furnace. But The Lord God preserved them so that they didn't burn or even smell of smoke when they were brought out of the fire. Now, no doubt, the golden image must have been a beautiful thing. Accompanied by, no doubt, the best musicians in the kingdom playing skillfully and beautifully all the top 40 idol worship Babylonian hits. Probably dressed in the best Tommy Baalfiger clothes with jewels and gold and silver high fashion jewelry from the high-end jewelry store in the Babylonian mall. But all this beauty and talent and festivity was not enough to make these three men betray their God because they had enough spiritual insight to see through the beauty and talent to the core of the matter, which was compromising their faith. And they refused to do that. Christmas is a pagan festival honoring a pagan zodiac god. To celebrate it is to follow the crowd and compromise your faith by bowing down in your heart to your own golden image. Let's stand back and take a good look at Christmas a minuet. What is it? Where did it come from? Who does it honor? Does The Word of God talk about it? Serious questions that every believer should be able to give an answer. Many would, of course, say: it's the birth of Jesus. Or a time for peace on earth. Right? Maybe good will toward men??? Then, of course, you have: the tree, decorations, lights, Santa, Rudolph, exchanging gifts, stockings, snowmen, shopping, etc. Christmas time is a beautiful time of year. The beautiful decorations, all your favorite Christmas songs, all the malls and stores all decorated up with Santa inviting you in. The sights, sounds and smells of Christmas are everywhere at that time. But with all its feel-good celebration, beauty and sound, pleasing to the flesh, the eyes and the ears and your misconception of what God thinks; Christmas has another meaning that most people can't or won't see. So, let's just take it and break it down piece by piece and see if we can find the true meaning of Christmas.

1. The Bible does record the birth of Jesus but doesn't give us the date and doesn't tell us to celebrate His birth annually or

any time. But December 25th is the birthday of a false Christ in history named Tammuz.

2. The Christmas tree is in The Bible, but it is described as an idol and The Bible tells us not to put one up, Jeramiah 10:2-4. The hanging of ornaments on the tree is also described in The Bible as an idol worship practice and is involved with homosexuality, 2 Kings 23:5-7.

3. The exchanging of gifts is in The Bible, but it is not done by Christians, but by unbelievers in the future during the great tribulation when they are so glad that God's two witnesses are dead that they celebrate by exchanging gifts. Revelation 11:7-10. Nowhere in The Bible does it tell Christians to exchange gifts for any reason. Exchanging of gifts was a common practice in pagan celebrations.

4. Nowhere in The Bible is there any story of a man that allows children to come to his throne and ask him for gifts. Then he delivers those gifts from house to house on a sled pulled by flying reindeer on the eve of the birth of Jesus or for any occasion for that matter. Why would there be a person that takes the attention away from the one who's birthday it is said to be and gives gifts to each other instead of to Jesus?

5. The holly wreath is a pagan practice. The holly wreath was used by pagans to decorate buildings and places of worship with holly during their pagan feast. They would use it in their homes as protection from bad winters. It was used during the Saturnalia celebration as friendship and fertility symbols connected with the sun god. Kings and emperors made wreaths of gold and wore them on their head. Other kinds of wreaths made from a laurel tree were associated with the Greek god Zeus. The Laurel tree wreath became the symbol of victory and achievement and was later used for the victors in the Olympic games.

6. Ivy was used together with holly at pagan festivals as a symbol of male and female. The holly was the male and ivy

was the female, and they were burnt together at the pagan festival of Beltane.

7.  The mistletoe is another pagan custom. They would kiss under the mistletoe during their festival and would end up in drunken orgies. It was also used in some Druid celebrations.

8.  The Yule log was a symbol of a man becoming the sun god. It was said that a great king was buried near a dead stump or log; and overnight, a green (evergreen) tree grew out of the dead stump or log, which was said to symbolize him ascending into the sun as the sun god and that became the Yule log. They used logs like this during pagan celebrations and they were lighted to symbolize the warmth of the sun during cold winter festivals.

9.  Light in the form of candles or fires were used to dispel the darkness of the longer nights of winter and during the Saturnalia celebration. Today, electric Christmas lights are used. It was a time of feasting, giving gifts, drinking to drunkenness and sexual perversion.

The world loves Christmas, and The Bible tells us to love not what the world loves.

> **1 John 2:15**
> **15 Love not the world, neither the things that are in the world. If any man love the world, the love of the Father is not in him.**

> **Romans 12:2**
> **2 And be not conformed to this world: but be ye transformed by the renewing of your mind, that ye may prove what is that good, and acceptable, and perfect, will of God.**

Let's look at the thing most people think. Is December the 25<sup>th</sup> the birthday of Jesus? The account found in Luke chapter 2 tells us in verse 8 that shepherds were abiding in the field, keeping watch over their flock by night.

**Luke 2:7-8**
**7 And she brought forth her firstborn son, and wrapped him in swaddling clothes, and laid him in a manger; because there was no room for them in the inn.**
**8 And there were in the same country shepherds abiding in the field, keeping watch over their flock by night.**

Now, no scripture is given without significance. And this one is no exception. This one verse tells us a lot about Christmas. Not so much about when the birth of Jesus was, but when it wasn't. Israel is on a longitude line that puts it, if you put your finger on the line and follow it around the globe, about even with Texas somewhere between Houston and Texarkana, with Bethlehem being somewhat even with Waco, near Dallas. In other words, Bethlehem and Waco, Tx. are about the same distance from the North Pole and should have somewhat the same climate with only a few variables due to geographical differences. I live in Texas much further south than Waco, and I know that December the 25th would not be a good time to be out in the field at night with the flocks. Even though we, in south Texas, don't usually get the severe winters that the northern states do; it still gets very chilling cold at night and many times freezing. And there is usually a lot of rain at that time of year. The Bible says the same thing about Israel.

**Song of Solomon 2:11**
**11 For, lo, the winter is past, the rain is over and gone;**

**Ezra 10:9-13**
**9 Then all the men of Judah and Benjamin gathered themselves together unto Jerusalem within three days. It was the ninth month, on the twentieth day of the month; and all the people sat in the street of the house of God, trembling because of this matter, and for the great rain.**

**10 And Ezra the priest stood up, and said unto them, Ye have transgressed, and have taken strange wives, to increase the trespass of Israel.**

**11 Now therefore make confession unto the Lord God of your fathers, and do his pleasure: and separate yourselves from the people of the land, and from the strange wives.**

**12 Then all the congregation answered and said with a loud voice, As thou hast said, so must we do.**

**13 But the people are many, and it is a time of much rain, and we are not able to stand without, neither is this a work of one day or two: for we are many that have transgressed in this thing.**

In these verses, this time of year is described. The ninth month described here is the month of Kislev, from the religious Jewish calendar. It is the twenty fourth, nearly the end of the month. On our calendar, this would put us right into mid to late December. Ezra describes this as a time of much rain and cold in Israel, and verse 13 says that they are not even able to stand outside because of the rain, and they were trembling because they were cold, verse 9. I looked up this time of year in Israel on the internet. It said just what I told you. It's not severely cold, but it is a rainy season with cool average temperatures during the day of about 40 degrees and sometimes very cold nights, at times even below freezing. Now ask yourself, why would shepherds be abiding in the fields by night with their flocks during a time when you can't even stand outside because of the cold and rain? They wouldn't. Their flocks would be corralled for the rainy season like they always were at this time of year which was their custom. Oh, I guess there could have been a light winter with some good days that were not extremely cold where they took the flocks out to graze; But there is too much evidence that points away from December anyway. This scripture in Ezra describes a day at that time of year. For shepherds to pick that time of year to graze their flocks at night would be a stretch. Now, The Bible doesn't say at all anywhere the day when Jesus was born. A very important little fact to leave out if we were supposed to celebrate it every year. And if The Bible is our instruction book, and throughly furnishes us unto all good works, as stated in Second Timothy:

**2 Timothy 3:16-17**

**16 All scripture is given by inspiration of God, and is profitable for doctrine, for reproof, for correction, for instruction in righteousness:**

**17 That the man of God may be perfect, throughly furnished unto all good works.**

Then where are our instructions about Christmas? Don't you think it strange that so many unbelievers celebrate Christmas? I know people that don't even believe in Jesus or The Bible or any religion; but they still celebrate Christmas. Most of the world, even though only a small percentage is Christian, celebrates it. Why? Could it be that Christmas is of the world and not of Jesus? Jesus did say the world hated him. Right?

**John 7:7**

**7 The world cannot hate you; but me it hateth, because I testify of it, that the works thereof are evil.**

If the world hates Jesus, then why do they celebrate His birth??? Kinda doesn't make sense, does it? That is unless Christmas really doesn't celebrate His birth, but someone else's birth that the world loves. And that's exactly what it does. Again, check the internet or go to your local library and look up Saturnalia and see if it doesn't look like Christmas to you, and probably even compares it to Christmas.

**2 Corinthians 6:14-17**

**14 Be ye not unequally yoked together with unbelievers: for what fellowship hath righteousness with unrighteousness? and what communion hath light with darkness?**

15 And what concord hath Christ with Belial? or what part
hath he that believeth with an infidel?
16 And what agreement hath the temple of God with idols?
for ye are the temple of the living God; as God hath said,
I will dwell in them, and walk in them; and I will be their
God, and they shall be my people.
17 Wherefore come out from among them, and be ye
separate, saith the Lord, and touch not the unclean thing;
and I will receive you,

Christmas is an unholy marriage between the church and paganism.

1 Corinthians 6:15-17
15 Know ye not that your bodies are the members of
Christ? shall I then take the members of Christ, and make
them the members of an harlot? God forbid.
16 What? know ye not that he which is joined to an harlot
is one body? for two, saith he, shall be one flesh.
17 But he that is joined unto the Lord is one spirit.

Joining Christmas with Christianity is like joining the members
of the church with an idol because you are joining Tammuz with
Jesus. This happened to Solomon, David's son. It is a strange story
because Solomon was given the gift of wisdom by God Himself.

2 Chronicles 1:10-12
10 Give me now wisdom and knowledge, that I may go out
and come in before this people: for who can judge this thy
people, that is so great?
11 And God said to Solomon, Because this was in thine
heart, and thou hast not asked riches, wealth, or honour,
nor the life of thine enemies, neither yet hast asked long
life; but hast asked wisdom and knowledge for thyself, that
thou mayest judge my people, over whom I have made
thee king:

**12 Wisdom and knowledge is granted unto thee; and I will give thee riches, and wealth, and honour, such as none of the kings have had that have been before thee, neither shall there any after thee have the like.**

But when it came to women, he didn't use this wisdom very wisely. He married foreign women that were caught up in idol worship. Even though Solomon was a man of God full of wisdom, he succumbed to the idol worship that his foreign wives taught him. So, when you marry or mix a Godly man with idol worship, even if that man is full of God given wisdom like Solomon, the idol worship can overtake the man. Many, even today, think that they can marry a non-Christian mate, then convert them to Christianity. That seldom works and many times ends up in divorce.

**1 Kings 11:1-9**
**1 But king Solomon loved many strange women, together with the daughter of Pharaoh, women of the Moabites, Ammonites, Edomites, Zidonians, and Hittites;**
**2 Of the nations concerning which the Lord said unto the children of Israel, Ye shall not go in to them, neither shall they come in unto you: for surely they will turn away your heart after their gods: Solomon clave unto these in love.**
**3 And he had seven hundred wives, princesses, and three hundred concubines: and his wives turned away his heart.**
**4 For it came to pass, when Solomon was old, that his wives turned away his heart after other gods: and his heart was not perfect with the Lord his God, as was the heart of David his father.**
**5 For Solomon went after Ashtoreth the goddess of the Zidonians, and after Milcom the abomination of the Ammonites.**
**6 And Solomon did evil in the sight of the Lord, and went not fully after the Lord, as did David his father.**

**7 Then did Solomon build an high place for Chemosh, the abomination of Moab, in the hill that is before Jerusalem, and for Molech, the abomination of the children of Ammon. 8 And likewise did he for all his strange wives, which burnt incense and sacrificed unto their gods.**
**9 And the Lord was angry with Solomon, because his heart was turned from the Lord God of Israel, which had appeared unto him twice,**

Don't think that you are stronger than the idolism of Christmas. Some people succumb to Christmas even though they don't necessarily like Christmas, but they feel like they have to participate because of pressure from others that do Celebrate it. I was talking to a nurse the other day at the doctor's office, and I was telling her that I didn't celebrate Christmas because she had asked me if I had gotten all my Christmas shopping done yet. After I told her that I didn't celebrate it; she replied yes, I know how you feel; Christmas has become too commercial. She then said that the only reason she buys presents for everyone is because she feels like she has to. That is exactly the mind set of most people. They think, well, if someone buys me a present, then I must buy them a present too. And the chain reaction begins. Then you have the merchants making merchandise of Jesus. Advertising to come buy their products with Santa there luring people in their stores, all the time using The Name of Jesus to make a profit. And we wonder why kids are so materialistic today. Because it's drilled into their heads by money grubbing people that go after your kids with enticements designed for causing them to lust after their product and using The Name of Jesus to do it. The churches fill up at Christmas much to the delight of most pastors. They put on their Christmas programs to draw people in just like the stores and malls that set up huge manger scenes and Santa Claus workshops using The Name of Jesus for personal gain. The churches put on their programs to draw people in through vain deceit. This gives people that have a form of godliness an excuse to come to church twice a year for Christmas and Easter to ease their spiritual conscious.

> **2 Timothy 3:1-5**
> **1 This know also, that in the last days perilous times shall come.**
> **2 For men shall be lovers of their own selves, covetous, boasters, proud, blasphemers, disobedient to parents, unthankful, unholy,**
> **3 Without natural affection, trucebreakers, false accusers, incontinent, fierce, despisers of those that are good,**
> **4 Traitors, heady, highminded, lovers of pleasures more than lovers of God;**
> **5 Having a form of godliness, but denying the power thereof: from such turn away.**

They get their yearly fix of Jesus, then go about their own business the rest of the year, not giving another thought to Jesus. The house of prayer is turned into a merchant's dream of profit, or as Jesus said, a den of thieves.

> **Mark 11:17**
> **17 And he taught, saying unto them, Is it not written, My house shall be called of all nations the house of prayer? but ye have made it a den of thieves.**

I've got news for you; Christianity is not just a twice a year ritual. It is a permanent lifestyle. This verse in Mark is significant to talk about. Pastors that greet with open arms these people that come once or twice a year ought to rebuke them for their absence the rest of the year. They should say: This is a place to worship God. You have turned it into a place of idol worship for the Christmas season. After all, what if they really aren't saved, and only think they are because they make a yearly or bi-yearly appearance at church thinking they have fulfilled their spiritual requirements for the year? No, we are not saved by going to church. But there are people out there that think they are saved because they go to church occasionally, but they don't actually have a personal relationship with The Lord. If you let them go on thinking it's okay to just think about Jesus a couple of times a year; and let them go on thinking that Christmas is a good Christian holiday that honors Jesus; and withhold the truth about Christmas; that they are really taking part in a pagan festival rooted in idol worship; hence, not giving them space to see it for what it is; then as a result of that; they could see Christianity as an assortment of rituals and celebrations instead of an everyday lifestyle and personal relationship with Jesus Himself. Then you could be contributing to their apostasy and fall at the judgment. Do you want a person to spend an eternity in hell because you let them come twice a year to church and never told them that they should look into their salvation to make sure they are saved? I really don't think you would want that to happen. How bout lets tell people the truth instead of covering it up with a sugar-coated holiday that isn't even the truth. Are you okay with the devil dictating lies about two major events in the life of Jesus? Are you going to let the devil convince you of the day when Jesus was born and the day when He was crucified that simply are not true? Are you really going to let the devil tell you these two events are when he says they were and not when The Bible says they are? Don't you find it curious that even establishments that have kicked Jesus out the door celebrates Christmas? I was driving down the road the other day when I passed an elementary school. And lo and behold, big as you please, right up there on the school billboard, what should I see, but written the time in which their Christmas program was to be held. Even today December 15, 1989, as I write this portion of this book; my six-year-old daughter's elementary school is having their annual Christmas party. Can you imagine that? I wonder what they would do if a child wanted to get saved during their Christmas program? That would jerk a knot in their party; wouldn't it? They would be asking each other; what do we do now? With today's laws, it would be illegal for them to lead that child to The Jesus Whose birthday they are celebrating. And they even give the kids a Christmas vacation. And they do all these things in The Name of Jesus, in which they don't even acknowledge in the school system as Lord and Savior. In fact, at the time this portion of this book was written; the kids are told that a Bible isn't even allowed on a school campus, and you can't witness The Name of Jesus to a fellow student on campus. They are told they can't pray out loud to Jesus on a school campus to even say the blessing on their food. But the school celebrates Christmas? Why? What's wrong with this picture? It sounds to me like you can hold Jesus up in a false light with the lies and deceitfulness of Christmas, but you better not speak the truth of His Word on campus lest someone here it and turn to Jesus. In this third edition of this book, more than 30 years after I wrote what you just read, the courts have since deemed it legal for students to do some of the things that they were told that they couldn't do back then. Thank God. But it took a lot of those more than 30 years to deem that to be true. Meanwhile, there was a lot of years that a couple of generations of our kids grew up without God in the school system. That took a toll on our most precious commodity. Our future generation. And it is obvious that these couple of generations, that are now adults, are now making some terrible decisions as today's leaders that is turning our country away from God because our country took God away from them at a young age. But even today, the school system doesn't allow Jesus in. They were forced by the court to allow some constitutional freedoms, but they are still very limited. It seems as though the state will allow you to disgrace The Name of Jesus with a pagan tradition, which only serves to tear down Christianity. And that's okay with them. It's only when you try to honor The Name of Jesus that they get upset. The world will use The Name of Jesus at Christmas. But not in a good way. Some of the TV commercial I've seen are: A cereal company advertised a new cereal called Christmas Crunch!!! Christmas Crunch???? Can you imagine attaching the name of Christ to a cereal? We worship Christ, not church Him!!! A local telephone company advertised on

TV that peace on earth is a private phone line for your teenager!!! That's funny. I thought Peace on Earth was the peace that Jesus gives us that passes all understanding! You know; the peace that keeps our hearts and minds through Christ Jesus.

> **Philippians 4:6-7**
> **6 Be careful for nothing; but in every thing by prayer and supplication with thanksgiving let your requests be made known unto God.**
> **7 And the peace of God, which passeth all understanding, shall keep your hearts and minds through Christ Jesus.**

In a beer commercial, they used the Christmas tree. This beer advertisement tells you to come to your local store and look for the "Michelob Tree" which is a Christmas tree printed only partially on the back of each carton of beer; then if you buy all the different cartons with only a portion, but different portions of the tree; you can stack them together to form a life size Christmas tree, and they call it a "Michelob tree." They have these cartons all stacked together in the isle of the store displaying this life size Christmas tree. I wonder how many people see this and buy all those cartons so they can stack them at home to display this tree in their homes? Wouldn't Jesus be pleased? I think not!!! Remember, this is said to be a Christian holiday. So, it's the Christians that keep it going making it possible for all this to happen. Now according to Sears, this all began at Sears. As it says in their store in a local mall, year 1989: "Sears, where the magic of Christmas begins". Oh, now I get it; Mary and Joseph couldn't find a room at the inn, so they went down the street to the local Bethlehem mall, ducked into Sears, and Mary gave birth in the isle between the Craftsman tools (because Joseph was a carpenter), and the wool sweaters knitted from the sheep that the shepherds were abiding in the field. And then they would, purposely or not, say: "where the magic of Christmas begins", and lead you to think that it was magic, not God, that was in control. A Coca-Cola commercial had a young boy and presumably his grandfather walking along the road. Suddenly the grandfather picks up a pinecone and tells his grandson: "watch this". Then he took the pinecone and buried it in a spot that he knows a very large Christmas tree will be erected in a market square in two weeks. Of course, two weeks later he brings his grandson back and there is a giant Christmas tree with brilliant lights and decorations. Now the grandson looks with amazement thinking that the pinecone that grandpa planted only two weeks ago had grown into this huge majestic Christmas tree already. It would seem that in Christianity; lying is a sin; that is unless it is about Christmas; then you get a pass on lying. A Sprite commercial has a young boy carrying a sack of groceries when he passes by a snowman with a frown on his face. The boy sees that his hat had fallen off his head, so he picks it up and sits it on his head, but the frown is still there. So, he reaches in his sack and pulls out a can of Sprite and sit's it on what appears to be the snow man's hand. Can you figure out the rest? The camera focuses on the boy, and you hear in the background the can opening and someone drinking it. Then the camera focuses back on the snowman with, what??? A smile on his face and apparently an empty can of Sprite sitting on his hand. A woman on the news said that Rudolph the red nose reindeer is second in popularity at Christmas time only to Santa Claus. I guess that put's Jesus somewhere at number three or lower. A Burger King commercial said, come and get the spirit of Christmas in their burger. Does that mean when you eat their hamburger, that it contains a spirit in it? WOE!! I don't know if I want spirits jumping out of my hamburger or not. I was watching the news on channel eleven, (Houston), 12-19-1989 at noon; it was reported that most of the merchant's quit selling the Tony Alamo jackets because the owner of the company was suspected of belonging to a cult of devil worshipers. And they reported that he was also wanted by the police for suspected child abuse. But when one merchant that was still selling them was approached by a News 11 reporter to ask her why she was still selling the jacket; her response was: "good press or bad press; makes the item hotter, especially at Christmas time". So, what is Christmas to some merchants? It would seem; to make money, no matter how it tramples on Jesus. There are countless more that if I took time to say would fill a book by itself. I'm sure you have seen many Christmas commercials yourself that glorify, not Jesus, but their product. Doesn't it seem that Christmas is at the mercy of the merchant? Christmas commercials begin appearing long before even Thanksgiving; and they can't wait for Thanksgiving night to kick off the Christmas shopping season. In fact, Thanksgiving is almost overlooked for Christmas. We don't celebrate Christmas at my house as you might guess. But we do celebrate Thanksgiving. And since we don't celebrate Christmas, my wife decorates the whole house with Thanksgiving decorations at thanksgiving. But she has to be quick about buying them because the stores put Thanksgiving decorations on the shelf for only a very short time and then they move them out to make room for Christmas decorations. My wife said that this past year, it seems to her like the Thanksgiving decorations were only out for about a week, so she couldn't get very many this year. The day after thanksgiving, on Friday, is declared the biggest Christmas shopping day of the year. They call it Black Friday. Church; let me warn you; if you are celebrating Christmas; you are participating in the world's most diabolical scheme there is to get rich. And The Bible says in Matthew 6:24 that you cannot serve two masters. You cannot serve God, and mammon, or money. Because you will love one and hate the other. One of them you will hold to, and the other one you will despise.

> **Luke 16:13**
> **13 No servant can serve two masters: for either he will hate the one, and love the other; or else he will hold to the one, and despise the other. Ye cannot serve God and mammon.**

Christmas is the biggest money-making devise known to man. Merchants will tell you that Christmas time is far and away the most profitable time of year. This information is common knowledge. I know this because I used to run a music store. As manager of that store, I can tell you that we sold far more at that time than any other time of year. It wasn't even close. Just ask your local retailer yourself. People at Christmas spend more money than they have, forcing them to use credit. Usually buying presents that the person their buying for don't even need, and often times end up in the trash or a garage sale or regifting. The liquor industry profits heavily this time of year, while everyone else pays for it in the form of higher insurance rates because of all the accidents on the highways caused by drunk drivers. Not to mention the price of hospital care for the injured, and even the cost of funerals for those killed by a drunk driver. And most of all; the grief caused to the families of the victims of drunk drivers. A lot of these drunk drivers are going home from their Christmas parties. I know, because I've been there at some of those parties back when I played in a secular rock band. Christmas and New Years are the most profitable times of the year for a band. I've seen what goes on at some of those private Christmas parties. There is liquor everywhere. Some even have drugs, fornication and perversion going on. And all this in The Name of Jesus? The things I witnessed at some of those parties nauseated me, and I wasn't even a committed Christian back then. I had accepted Jesus as my savior at an early age, but I didn't live the part too well. But what I seen at some of these parties that go on in The Name of Jesus made even me, at that time, a backslidden Christian, think twice about what I was doing. I was providing music for parties like this back then, so it made me kind of an accessory to it. Playing in a secular rock band, I would often have to deal with drunks. It was pretty sickening to see slobbering drunks all night long. We often had to keep roadies near the band to protect us from drunks that would smash a beer bottle and want to cut one of our throats if we didn't play their favorite country song. The problem with that is that we were a rock band. We didn't know any country music and we were not interested in learning any. Now, that was a long time ago and I quit doing that sort of thing after I wised up and surrendered my whole life to serve The Lord. But I'm sort of glad I had those experiences because it gave me personal insight into what really goes on during those kinds of Christmas parties. I'm sure some of you have heard of or been to one of those office Christmas parties where often times married men and their secretaries' lust after one another when they get drunk. Now the church wouldn't hesitate to tell you that they are very much against the liquor industry; yet they support the instrument of its biggest profits. The liquor industry would tell you that they love Christmas because of the sales of liquor for Christmas presents and parties. Wake up church and look around you. Can't you see what's going on? It's so obvious. You know as well as I do that liquor is one of the major causes of depression, and a killer on our hi-ways, and even sometimes a prelude to drug use, gambling, adultery, homicide, and more. How many killings have taken place because someone got drunk and decided to be tough? I know people that are fine while sober, but when they get drunk, they either want to kill someone, or want to kill themselves. I believe there is a spirit associated with alcohol that takes hold of some people and tries to destroy that person, or the people and families around him. Do you think it is a coincidence that liquor is called spirits? It seems to have some kind of influence that dulls your senses and alters your thinking. This is not the actual reason it is called spirits, but to me, it fits. I believe when a person drinks, it releases this influence in his mind and effects his actions and thinking and blocks reason and rationalism. This is only my opinion, but the reason I say this is because I can recognize that same influence in most every alcoholic. In other words, there are similar traits that follow a pattern in most every alcoholic, or like the police say, they have the same M. O. or motes operandi. They operate the same. It's like they are under the same kind of spell. It is this kind of control that broke up my mother and dad's marriage. I watched my dad one day after he stayed out drinking until the bar closed at 2am, come home drunk late at night long after everyone had gone to bed, and because my mother wouldn't jump out of bed and fix him something to eat in the middle of the night, he held a gun to her head without knowing that I had earlier taken the bullets out of it. And a good thing too, because my mother said that he had already pulled the trigger several times. She also didn't know that I had taken the bullets out of it, so it was a frightening experience for her when she heard the hammer of the gun click down. It was my 22 rifle that he took out of my closet while I was asleep. I was awakened by my niece that was living with us, saying that my dad was trying to kill my mother. That's when I ran in the other room and seen him with the gun pointed at her head. I took the gun away from him but I thank God that it had no bullets in it and my mother was not killed before I could get in there. I took the bullets out because I suspected something like this could happen. I believe it was God that gave me that thought. Another time he tried to run over my sister. He was drunk and outside in the driveway about to get in the car and leave. My sister was arguing with him about his drinking because he was being very belligerent with everyone in the family. But when she confronted him about it, he got in the car and we all thought he was going to leave, but instead, he stepped on the gas pedal lunging the car toward where my sister was standing in front of the house. The driveway came all the way up to the front porch of the house where my sister was standing. My sister jumped out of the way just in time, and he hit the front porch of the house with the front of the car where she had just been standing. The car moved the wall of the porch where she had just been standing. If she hadn't jumped out of the way, she could have been killed or seriously injured being crushed between the porch and the car. My sister was a teenager at that time. This was a time when child abuse was not acted upon like it is today. Back then, it was just a family matter that was left to be dwelt with within the family. The authorities pretty much didn't get involved unless there was an actual injury caused by it. Another time, he told me I had to go to bed. It was still daylight and not even close to bedtime and my mother told me to ignore him because it was too early to go to bed. But he was drunk and got it into his head that it was bedtime. When I pointed out to him that it wasn't even close to bedtime, he got mad at me, jumped up and put his hands around my throat and tried to choke me. I was about fourteen years old and I managed to break myself free by hitting him and knocking him loose from my throat. I felt very bad about hitting him, and it still bothers me to this day, but I couldn't get loose otherwise. There are many other similar things that happened like that, but all of them happened when he was drunk. When he was sober, he was one of the nicest men you could ever meet. When he was sober, he would have never thought about hurting my mother or one of us kids. It is only when he was drunk, and that spirit took over and he became that violent person. A few years later, after I was grown and moved out on my own, he and my mother ended up getting a divorce, leaving my mother with almost nothing, and to this day very poor. She got the house, but absolutely no income. She had no job experience but found a job at a Dairy Queen hamburger joint, living off of a small salary and tips. And after working nights, she would babysit early the next morning until time to go to work again that evening. It was very hard for her for a long time. After several years of struggle, she is now drawing a small amount of social security. He is now re-married, and he has since quit drinking because of his health. The doctor told him if he took another drink, it would kill him. He, of course, didn't believe it and drank again and did almost die. This turned out to be a blessing because after that, he took the doctor serious and had no choice but to either quit drinking or die. So, he did quit drinking. The Lord had mercy on him. When he quit drinking, he began to be a normal person again. Soon after that, I'm glad to report, he received Jesus as his Savior. A happy ending for him. However, the damage was already done. My mother still lives in poverty, and all his kids, three daughters and one son, have had emotional and anxiety problems. But even back then, we knew it wasn't him doing all that bad stuff. We knew it was an addiction that he fell into with alcohol. He was a great father when he wasn't drinking. Once he conquered his addiction to alcohol, he was fine.

But, like I said, it had already done its damage. So, I know firsthand what liquor can do to a family. And I have heard lots of similar stories from other people with an alcoholic in the family. I just want to add in this third edition of this book that my mother and dad both are now gone to be with The Lord. And I have confidence that both of them made it to heaven. Before my dad died, he was very remorseful for what he had done, but he knew that we all forgave him for all of that. Not everyone in a family with an alcoholic has a good ending. Some never quit drinking and die an alcoholic. Church, if you celebrate Christmas, you're helping to keep it alive. One year at Christmas time, on my job at a local utility district; there was a supplier we used that handed out to all the employees of the district a Christmas present every year all wrapped up in Christmas paper. I opened the package that was given to me expecting it to be the usual ham that we usually got or something like that. But when I opened it; imagine that; there was the very thing that broke up my parent's marriage and crippled my family right there before my eyes. It was a bottle of whisky, and it was given to me in The Name of Jesus. I kept that bottle of whisky to this day to remind me of what it did to my family. I'm sure that there are lots of drinkers that would love to get their hands on it. It is, by now, a 40-year-old bottle of quite expensive whisky. But no one will ever get ahold of it. It is only kept as a reminder. I thought to myself; no wonder so many people are alcoholics. It's shoved in their face all the time with billboards, commercials, tons of beer joints on the side of the roads, clubs and more clubs, bars, legion halls, lodges and most restaurants serve beer and mix drinks. Then you have the music industry glorifying drinking making it cool to be drunk like it was some kind of badge of honor. And then you have the liquor industry with its best friend, Christmas. Church, you can't tell me that you don't already know that what I've just told you is true. Liquor is inseparably connected with Christmas, and you can't deny it. So why do you still support it? The liquor industry is not the only reason to not celebrate Christmas. In fact, that's only the tip of the iceberg. You see, you've been deceived church; suckered in; smooth talked; tricked; manipulated, snookered and they seen you coming. They did me too for a lot of years until I learned the truth through God's Word. Do you tell your kids that Jesus was born on December 25th? Find it in The Bible. Do you tell your kids that Santa rides in a flying sled pulled by flying reindeer? Where is the truth? There's not any. In fact, it's a bald face lie. And who is the father of lies?

> **John 8:44-45**
> **44 Ye are of your father the devil, and the lusts of your father ye will do. He was a murderer from the beginning, and abode not in the truth, because there is no truth in him. When he speaketh a lie, he speaketh of his own: for he is a liar, and the father of it.**
> **45 And because I tell you the truth, ye believe me not.**

You say there were three Kings that followed a star to the manger. You see in the movies where three kings brought gifts to baby Jesus at the manger and presented them to Him there. Where in The Bible is this scene? Can you see how tradition can confuse reality? Actually, The Bible says it was wise men, not Kings. And it doesn't say how many wise men. And Jesus was a young boy, probably approaching 2 years old by then, living in a house when they came to see him, not still at the manger.

> **Matthew 2:10-11**
> **10 When they saw the star, they rejoiced with exceeding great joy.**
> **11 And when they were come into the house, they saw the young child with Mary his mother, and fell down, and worshipped him: and when they had opened their treasures, they presented unto him gifts; gold, and frankincense, and myrrh.**

We will go over this in detail in chapter 10. Yes, Christmas seems to be a time of lies, deceitfulness, house burglaries, porch pirates, shop lifting, purse snatching, price gouging, mail fraud, drunken parties, depression, suicide, and much more. And you, Christian, keep it all going all in The Name of Jesus. Of course, you can't find where Jesus said to do it; but nevertheless; you do it anyway. Does Jesus condone lying? No! Yet we tell our kids, the most influential minds in the world, who trust us implicitly that December 25th is in fact the birthday of Jesus Christ. The truth is, it's not a fact at all, but a bald face lie. We tell them that Santa Claus leaves them gifts under a tree, and then takes off for the rest of the world to leave presents for every child in the world all in one night on his flying sled. Nothing could be further from the truth. Can't you see; it's all a big lie right before your face; a falsehood; a non-truth; a fabrication of someone's warped mind, because it's certainly not scripture and not the truth. Let's look at something a minuet. Remember we looked at 2nd Timothy 3:16-17? Well, let's examine it a little closer.

> **2 Timothy 3:16-17**
> **16 All scripture is given by inspiration of God, and is profitable for doctrine, for reproof, for correction, for instruction in righteousness:**
> **17 That the man of God may be perfect, throughly furnished unto all good works.**

First of all, it says that: "all scripture is given by inspiration of God, and is profitable for doctrine, for reproof, for correction, for instruction in righteousness". That about covers it all. The Word instructs us and corrects us. That means if The Bible says don't do it, then don't do it. It also means if The Bible says to do something, then you do it. Now I hate to get so simple with this, but it seems as though some people can't get this concept down. It definitely does not mean to do something because it feels right, or because you think it's right, or because it's fun, or because everyone else is doing it, or because it's tradition. It simply says that The Bible is our instruction book. Whether we like it or not is not the issue. Look at verse 17. "That the man of God may be perfect, thoughly furnished unto all good works.". So, since The Bible thoughly furnishes us with all good works, then anything that's not in The Bible must not be a good work, because the scripture said all good works, not most good works, not even all but one good work, but all means we are furnished with every good work, so we may be perfect. So, if The Bible furnishes us with everything we need to be perfect, especially when it comes to how to worship God, then anything not in The Bible must be imperfect, therefore making us imperfect if we do those things not found in scripture. Right? Now, I'm talking in general here. Obviously, everything today wouldn't be in The Bible written centuries ago. There are good traditions that embody Biblical standards that are fine. What I am talking about are those traditions that embody evil or idol worshiping standards that The Bible would speak against. We are fully instructed on all moral and worship issues in the instructions given to us in The Bible. So; is Christmas in The Bible? No. Absolutely not. You won't find it there. Oh yes, you will find where Jesus was born and some details about His birth. But other than that, you will find nothing about the rest of the Christmas celebration in those details that are written in The Bible. If we were supposed to celebrate this celebration; don't you think those details would have been included in The Bible? You know; sometimes we think that we are doing The Lord a service when we are really hindering His work. Like we already looked at with Aaron in Exodus 32:1-5. But we see it again when the disciples of Jesus were mistaken on who to honor in Matthew.

**Matthew 17:1-5**
**1 And after six days Jesus taketh Peter, James, and John his brother, and bringeth them up into an high mountain apart,**
**2 And was transfigured before them: and his face did shine as the sun, and his raiment was white as the light.**

> **3 And, behold, there appeared unto them Moses and Elias talking with him.**
> **4 Then answered Peter, and said unto Jesus, Lord, it is good for us to be here: if thou wilt, let us make here three tabernacles; one for thee, and one for Moses, and one for Elias.**
> **5 While he yet spake, behold, a bright cloud overshadowed them: and behold a voice out of the cloud, which said, This is my beloved Son, in whom I am well pleased; hear ye him.**

When Peter, James and John saw Jesus with Moses and Elijah. Peter wanted to build tabernacles to all three of them. But A Voice came out of a cloud and said: "This is My Beloved Son in whom I Am well pleased, hear ye Him". He thought they would be doing a good thing by building tabernacles to all three of them. But The Voice said to instead: Hear Jesus. I think that applies to us today. Stop going about trying to establish your own righteousness and hear Him. In other words, do what thus sayeth The Lord, not what thus sayeth man. In this case, Moses and Elijah represented the law and the prophets. The voice of God was telling these disciples that they need to listen to Jesus who is greater than the law and prophets. And He was also telling those disciples to listen to Jesus rather than trying to establish their own ideas. It is man's idea to set up a tree to celebrate Christmas. The Bible does not tell us to do that. In fact, The Bible tells us not to do that in Jeramiah 10. Check your nearest Bible. Find in it anywhere that it says to even celebrate the birth of Jesus every year, or at all, much less the whole pagan celebration. For that matter, find where it says when Jesus was born. It doesn't give you a date. Some Bible scalars believe that the birth of Jesus was calculated to be sometime in the Fall, not winter. And that would line up with the feast of Tabernacles, which would agree with John 2:14 that He became flesh and dwelt, (or it could say, tabernacled) among us. I realize this is probably talking about the Millennial reign of Jesus, but most major events are done on the feast of Israel. Some of these feasts could apply to more than one event. He dwelt among us while He was here when He was born into this world. Then He will dwell among us again in His millennial reign. Then Revelation 21:1-3 mentions Him dwelling with men again in the new heaven and new earth. Some historians have said that the time in history that Cyrenius became Governor and the decree went out that all the world should be taxed, would not have been done during the winter rainy season in December. It is not even logical to assume that Caesar would unreasonably issue a decree of this magnitude to take effect in the worst traveling part of the year.

> **Luke 2:1-5**
> **1 And it came to pass in those days, that there went out a decree from Caesar Augustus, that all the world should be taxed.**
> **2 (And this taxing was first made when Cyrenius was governor of Syria.)**
> **3 And all went to be taxed, every one into his own city.**
> **4 And Joseph also went up from Galilee, out of the city of Nazareth, into Judaea, unto the city of David, which is called Bethlehem; (because he was of the house and lineage of David:)**
> **5 To be taxed with Mary his espoused wife, being great with child.**

So, if you must celebrate the birth of Jesus. Wouldn't it make much better sense to at least try to get as close to the right day as possible? And no creditable Bible scholar will tell you that it is even possible that Jesus was born in December. Anyone with any sense at all would know that the shepherds in Luke 2:8 wouldn't be standing in the dead of Winter abiding with the flocks in the field by night. Most agree that it would be in the fall. Would you stand out in the cold at night to tend sheep in the dead of winter so they can eat the dead grass? Or would you corral them as was the custom at that time of year? In December, it would be bad enough in the daytime to stand outside in the cold, much less at night. If you think about it, doesn't that seem logical? We will see more proof of why it cannot be in December later in this book in chapter10, reason #18. Christmas was established on the fact that it is the Winter Solstice, when the days start getting longer again, or the birth of the new sun, or the birth of the sun god. It is a time of the zodiac sign of Capricorn, which carries with it the sign of the goat. In satanic worship, you have what is called a pentagram. A five-sided upside-down star and a circle around it. Outlined in the midst of the star is the head of a goat inside the star, with his head in the center of the star, then with his goatee filling the star's lower point pointing straight down, and his horns pointing upward within the star's upper points. Then his whiskers filling the remaining two points of the star on each side, thus the goat's head filling every part of the star. This pentagram emblem is used in satanic worship with the goat representing Satan himself. If you would like to see what one looks like, I'm sure you can find a picture of one on the internet. Just type on the subject line (sigil of Baphomet). Look at Matthew 25:31-46. What does it say about goats? Not all scripture speaks bad about goats, but many scriptures seem to indicate that the goat represents the lost or many times a person that thinks he is saved but is not. Or in the case of Satan, thinking he is a god, but he's not.

> **Matthew 25:31-34**
> **31 When the Son of man shall come in his glory, and all the holy angels with him, then shall he sit upon the throne of his glory:**
> **32 And before him shall be gathered all nations: and he shall separate them one from another, as a shepherd divideth his sheep from the goats:**
> **33 And he shall set the sheep on his right hand, but the goats on the left.**

**34 Then shall the King say unto them on his right hand, Come, ye blessed of my Father, inherit the kingdom prepared for you from the foundation of the world:**

Those that think they are saved, but are not, have a bad ending.

**Matthew 25:41**
**41 Then shall he say also unto them on the left hand, Depart from me, ye cursed, into everlasting fire, prepared for the devil and his angels:**

There are those that go about trying to establish their own righteousness and they are not saved. They think they are saved because of the so-called righteous things they do. The Bible refers to these as goats. A type of the lost that think they are saved by their works or some other means besides The Grace of God alone. The goat's head, in satanic worship, symbolizes Satan himself. The zodiac is a form of this worship, and December 25th falls under the sign of Capricorn, the goat. And according to ancient worship of the stars, this time of year when it is cold, and the sun is dying, the evil spirits are at their most powerful state of being. The tradition was that bells were rung because it was believed that a lot of noise scared off all these evil spirits. This tradition was also carried over into Christmas, hence you have the bells of Christmas. I was astonished one year at Christmas time when I seen a Christmas cartoon special. It was staring the Animated California raisins; and one of the characters in it verified the very thing I just told you almost word for word. If you see this special this year, it's a lizard looking creature narrating different Christmas songs and giving some history behind the songs. The Christmas song you hear every year on the radio with bells, that you would recognize immediately if you heard it, was the one that he was talking about, and he was describing how these bells were used to scare off those evil spirits as we just described in the pagan practices. And so, he was describing how that was carried over into the Christmas celebration. Winter begins on about the 21st of December. This begins the coldest darkest time of the year for us. And less daylight than any time in the northern hemisphere.

> **Matthew 24:12**
> **12 And because iniquity shall abound, the love of many shall wax cold.**

> **Matthew 6:23**
> **23 But if thine eye be evil, thy whole body shall be full of darkness. If therefore the light that is in thee be darkness, how great is that darkness!**

> **John 3:19-21**
> **19 And this is the condemnation, that light is come into the world, and men loved darkness rather than light, because their deeds were evil.**
> **20 For every one that doeth evil hateth the light, neither cometh to the light, lest his deeds should be reproved.**
> **21 But he that doeth truth cometh to the light, that his deeds may be made manifest, that they are wrought in God.**

> **2 Corinthians 6:14**
> **14 Be ye not unequally yoked together with unbelievers: for what fellowship hath righteousness with unrighteousness? and what communion hath light with darkness?**

And men loved darkness rather than light because their deeds were evil.

> **Ephesians 6:12**
> **12 For we wrestle not against flesh and blood, but against principalities, against powers, against the rulers of the darkness of this world, against spiritual wickedness in high places.**

Ye are all sons of light, and sons of the day; we are not of the night, nor of darkness.

**Ephesians 5:8**
**8 For ye were sometimes darkness, but now are ye light in the Lord: walk as children of light:**

**Romans 13:12**
**12 The night is far spent, the day is at hand: let us therefore cast off the works of darkness, and let us put on the armour of light.**

But this has another meaning also. Not only did they love literal darkness, but also darkness of the mind. Spiritual things are foolishness to them. Most people do evil things in the shroud of darkness. It's easier to hide in darkness. You can probably remember some things you did in darkness to shroud what you were doing, Right?

**John 1:1-5**
**1 In the beginning was the Word, and the Word was with God, and the Word was God.**
**2 The same was in the beginning with God.**
**3 All things were made by him; and without him was not any thing made that was made.**
**4 In him was life; and the life was the light of men.**
**5 And the light shineth in darkness; and the darkness comprehended it not.**

**Proverbs 2:10-15**
**10 When wisdom entereth into thine heart, and knowledge is pleasant unto thy soul;**
**11 Discretion shall preserve thee, understanding shall keep thee:**

12 To deliver thee from the way of the evil man, from the man that speaketh froward things;

13 Who leave the paths of uprightness, to walk in the ways of darkness;

14 Who rejoice to do evil, and delight in the frowardness of the wicked;

15 Whose ways are crooked, and they froward in their paths:

## 1 Corinthians 4:5-6

5 Therefore judge nothing before the time, until the Lord come, who both will bring to light the hidden things of darkness, and will make manifest the counsels of the hearts: and then shall every man have praise of God.

6 For God, who commanded the light to shine out of darkness, hath shined in our hearts, to give the light of the knowledge of the glory of God in the face of Jesus Christ.

## 1 Peter 2:9

9 But ye are a chosen generation, a royal priesthood, an holy nation, a peculiar people; that ye should shew forth the praises of him who hath called you out of darkness into his marvellous light:

## 1 John 1:6-7

6 If we say that we have fellowship with him, and walk in darkness, we lie, and do not the truth:

7 But if we walk in the light, as he is in the light, we have fellowship one with another, and the blood of Jesus Christ his Son cleanseth us from all sin.

## 1 John 2:8-11

8 Again, a new commandment I write unto you, which thing is true in him and in you: because the darkness is past, and the true light now shineth.

**9 He that saith he is in the light, and hateth his brother, is in darkness even until now.**

**10 He that loveth his brother abideth in the light, and there is none occasion of stumbling in him.**

**11 But he that hateth his brother is in darkness, and walketh in darkness, and knoweth not whither he goeth, because that darkness hath blinded his eyes.**

Don't be in the dark about Christmas. Learn the light of the truth. Someone said to me one time: "Jesus is only who you think of Him as." Meaning He can be any religious figure that has claimed to be Christ or a Christ or even a leader of another religion. He said this to me with a straight face, believing every word he said. Well, I don't know what you think; but that belief is nothing but blasphemy, and definitely false. There is only one Jesus Christ. You can try to make Him out to be anyone you want; but The one and only Jesus Christ that I worship is The one described in The Bible as The only begotten Son of God that died for my sin on a cross and The Spirit of God raised Him from the grave the third day and now sits at the right hand of the Throne of God, making intercession for the saints. And that same Bible says that He is the only way to salvation. No other name can get you there. And no other person claiming to be Jesus, but is not, can get you there either. There is only one begotten Son.

**John 3:16**

**16 For God so loved the world, that he gave his only begotten Son, that whosoever believeth in him should not perish, but have everlasting life.**

**Acts 4:10-12**

**10 Be it known unto you all, and to all the people of Israel, that by the name of Jesus Christ of Nazareth, whom ye crucified, whom God raised from the dead, even by him doth this man stand here before you whole.**

**11 This is the stone which was set at nought of you builders, which is become the head of the corner.**
**12 Neither is there salvation in any other: for there is none other name under heaven given among men, whereby we must be saved.**

Do you make Tammuz to be Jesus once a year? Because Tammuz is whose birthday December 25th really is? Christmas is the worship of Tammuz under the name of Jesus. But Tammuz is a false Christ, and Christmas is a false birthday for Jesus. And I'm not about to say Tammuz is Jesus just because the Roman/government church says so. This is a Roman holiday. It is not, and never has been a Christian holiday. If you celebrate Christmas, you are only following a Roman tradition dating back to the 4th century AD with no scriptural bases at all. Christmas is all of those things and can be proven. Do you have an ear to hear? If so, read on.

**Revelation 2:17**
**17 He that hath an ear, let him hear what the Spirit saith unto the churches; To him that overcometh will I give to eat of the hidden manna, and will give him a white stone, and in the stone a new name written, which no man knoweth saving he that receiveth it.**

# CHAPTER 3.
# DON'T LET THE SUN GO OUT

I magine one winter, as the days got shorter and shorter like they do north of the equator, from the last part of June, up until about December 21$^{st}$, that somehow, they forgot to start getting longer again. And the days just kept getting shorter and shorter until they went completely out. Of course, that sounds silly, but superstition is silly, and people that worship the sun are superstitious. There are rituals, ceremonies and sacrifices to the sun to please the sun god so he won't go out. Since the time of Nimrod, there has always, in history, been a false religious system. Sun worship was among those early cults, but really, all it takes is one error in doctrine to make a false religious system. So false religion can look quite legitimate. But even if it is 99.9% right and 0.1% false doctrine, you can have a bona fide cult. Just as you have a glass of fresh water and put only 0.1% pollutant in it, the whole glass of water becomes polluted. In fact, when I worked at a sewage treatment plant, the standard for domestic sewage is established as 99.9% water and 0.1% solids. That is standard sewer. Have you smelled sewer lately? It's only 0.1% of the bad stuff in it. That's only one tenth of one percent. But would you drink it? No, because that one tenth of one percent pollutes the whole 100%. And if drank, could give you things like Typhoid, Paratyphoid, Dysentery A & B, Cholera A & B and much more. In other words, don't drink it. It can kill you. Just that lowly 0.1%. Likewise, add a column of 100 numbers from top to bottom. Misread only one number, and no matter how many numbers you add right, your answer will still be wrong. It's the same thing with false doctrine. Let's say you believe in Jesus, but you think that you must add your own works to your salvation. You can believe everything else in The Bible correctly, and you will still die in your sin and spend eternity in hell because you cannot add anything to the finished work of Jesus to save you. Works cannot save you in any way. You must trust only in Jesus for your salvation with nothing added for it to be true salvation. Christmas is in that same category. You can say that Jesus is the reason for the season until you're blue in the face, and that won't make it true. Many cults today have been started by a person getting just one little doctrine wrong. It's like making a statement and say only one false sentence in it. Then build on that false sentence. For instance, someone ask me one day: "Have you got the Holy Ghost yet?" My response was yes. My answer was an assumption on the part of that person that I have spoken with tongues, and he began to talk with me on that basses. When I told him that I haven't spoken with tongues, he began to assume that I haven't received the Holy Ghost yet. I couldn't convince him that a person receives The Holy Spirit upon salvation and speaking in tongues has nothing to do with it. In Acts, there were gifts and fillings of The Holy Spirit that enabled them to do supernatural things including speaking with tongues. But nowhere in The Bible does it say that you haven't received The Holy Spirit unless you have spoken with tongues. In fact. The Bible tells us that if you haven't received The Spirit of Christ, which is The Holy Spirit, or sometimes called The Holy Ghost in The Bible, then you are none of His. The only way to be saved is to receive the indwelling of The Spirit of Christ.

**Romans 8:9-11**
**9 But ye are not in the flesh, but in the Spirit, if so be that the Spirit of God dwell in you. Now if any man have not the Spirit of Christ, he is none of his.**
**10 And if Christ be in you, the body is dead because of sin; but the Spirit is life because of righteousness.**

**11 But if the Spirit of him that raised up Jesus from the dead dwell in you, he that raised up Christ from the dead shall also quicken your mortal bodies by his Spirit that dwelleth in you.**

He had been indoctrinated that receiving The Holy Spirit will always be followed by the evidence of speaking with tongues. And if you didn't speak with tongues; that meant that you didn't receive the indwelling of The Holy Spirit yet. He couldn't show me how he came to that conclusion in scripture, but only that it is what his church teaches. I won't get into the tongue doctrine in this book. But that is exactly how false doctrines get started. Someone listening to man instead of The Word of God. Even if the rest of your doctrine is sound; building on a false doctrine renders the true doctrine useless. If you're interested in why I say that speaking with tongues is not a requirement to receive The Holy Spirit; get a copy of my book, "Salvation, the simple truth", which covers that subject extensively; available at Amazon.com or Barns and Noble. com. Type in the search box; "salvation the simple truth by Tommy Hale". It should come right up. I did write a book on that subject by itself. It is called "The Gift of Languages". But it hasn't been published yet. I have no backing on publishing my books and it cost a lot of money. So, that is why it isn't published yet and this book you are reading now was next in line to be published. I will eventually publish it as soon as I can. It might even be published now depending on when you are reading this book. Again, you can check online by typing "the gift of languages by Tommy Hale" in the search box of Amazon or Barnes or Noble.com. I'm not sure when I can publish it, but it will eventually be there, Lord willing. All four of my books to date are on subjects that most preachers won't touch. So, I don't have to tell you that there is not a rush at the book stores of people looking for my books. But the thing is, I would rather tell you the truth than make a lot of money. I have found that the truth is not very popular. So, people, even preachers, look for a way around the truth, but would you be an effective witness if you preached, thou shall not steal, yet you cheat on your taxes? Or you borrow more money than you can pay back and rob your creditors by filing bankruptcy, or default on a credit card or take debt settlement or write a hot check? Do you preach against adultery, yet you lust after a secretary at work, looking at her with lust and desire? Wouldn't it be pretty hard to believe you were sincere? Or even walking down the street; do you check out all the girls desiring them in lust? Or the same for women desiring men in lust. I got news for you; if you look at them desiring them in lust, you have already committed adultery in your heart without even touching them.

> **Matthew 5:27-28**
> **27 Ye have heard that it was said by them of old time, Thou shalt not commit adultery:**
> **28 But I say unto you, That whosoever looketh on a woman to lust after her hath committed adultery with her already in his heart.**

How about if you preach: don't worship idols; yet you have a known idol in your home? We have already established that the tree you call a Christmas tree is an instrument of idol worship in Jeramiah 10.

> **Jeremiah 10:3-4**
> **3 For the customs of the people are vain: for one cutteth a tree out of the forest, the work of the hands of the workman, with the axe.**
> **4 They deck it with silver and with gold; they fasten it with nails and with hammers, that it move not.**

> **2 Kings 17:16**
> **16 And they left all the commandments of the Lord their God, and made them molten images, even two calves, and**

**made a grove, and worshipped all the host of heaven, and served Baal.**

Saturnalia was a pagan festival celebrating a period of time that was from December 17th to December 24th and ended up at the Pagan Brumalia on December 25th. This festival included trees decked with silver and gold, with hangings on them. There was drunkenness, rioting, lewdness, sensuality, and exchanging of gifts. This time of year holds many such pagan celebrations in different countries, but all of one origin. It's all the worship of the zodiac that involves the worship of the sun, moon, stars, planets, and the constellations. This culminated into yearly festivals that coincided with the changing of the seasons. As we discussed, one of them was the winter solstice festival. They already worshipped the sun with that winter solstice celebration, but then there was a popular king that died and added a human touch to the worship of the sun. He was claimed by the queen to have been resurrected into the sun and became the sun god. Then because the sun god was now part man, He, as the now human/man/god was able to impregnate a mortal woman with her having his child on the day of the pagan Brumalia at the end of the winter solstice celebration. This woman was elevated to the status of the queen of heaven and her son became the false Christ, son of the sun god. There was a man in history named Nimrod who was a very popular king and he lived at a time after the flood. He is believed to be this king that died and was resurrected into the sun as the sun god, but that fact is not provable; but it is well documented in history that this was the king of Babel before they were scattered by confounding their language. So, it was likely him. He was a man that did not regard God. At the peak of his reign, Nimrod built four cities in the land of Shinar and one of them was Babel which would become known later as Babylon. A tower was built to reach up to heaven and get closer to their gods. Many believe that this tower was also built as an arrogant attempt to battle with The true God.

**Genesis 10:8-10**
**8 And Cush begat Nimrod: he began to be a mighty one**
**in the earth.**
**9 He was a mighty hunter before the Lord: wherefore it is**
**said, Even as Nimrod the mighty hunter before the Lord.**
**10 And the beginning of his kingdom was Babel, and Erech,**
**and Accad, and Calneh, in the land of Shinar.**

The Bible doesn't give us much information about Nimrod, but It does give us an acknowledgment of his existence and that he was a mighty person. The Bible indicates in that next chapter that they built a tower to rebel against God. That's where it gets a little blurry because it doesn't actually say it was Nimrod that built this tower. But since Nimrod was a mighty one; we are left to assume that he was the leader of this rebellion. The Bible doesn't actually attach his name to this tower; but we can put two and two together on it and see that it is most likely him. We know that he didn't get to finish that tower because he died an early death. But he was more that likely the king that started this endeavor and the one that was supposedly resurrected into the sun as the sun god. There are no details of how this was accomplished other than apparently the sun god chose him to resurrect into himself to be able to impregnate a mortal woman and produce a christ child. The Bible doesn't tell us a lot about it; but we are given enough information in history to put much of it together. There are many Bible dictionaries, commentaries, and topical resources available that can help put things like this together.

**Genesis 11:1-9**
**1 And the whole earth was of one language, and of**
**one speech.**
**2 And it came to pass, as they journeyed from the east,**
**that they found a plain in the land of Shinar; and they**
**dwelt there.**

**3** And they said one to another, Go to, let us make brick, and burn them throughly. And they had brick for stone, and slime had they for morter.

**4** And they said, Go to, let us build us a city and a tower, whose top may reach unto heaven; and let us make us a name, lest we be scattered abroad upon the face of the whole earth.

**5** And the Lord came down to see the city and the tower, which the children of men builded.

**6** And the Lord said, Behold, the people is one, and they have all one language; and this they begin to do: and now nothing will be restrained from them, which they have imagined to do.

**7** Go to, let us go down, and there confound their language, that they may not understand one another's speech.

**8** So the Lord scattered them abroad from thence upon the face of all the earth: and they left off to build the city.

**9** Therefore is the name of it called Babel; because the Lord did there confound the language of all the earth: and from thence did the Lord scatter them abroad upon the face of all the earth.

**Micah 5:6**

**6** And they shall waste the land of Assyria with the sword, and the land of Nimrod in the entrances thereof: thus shall he deliver us from the Assyrian, when he cometh into our land, and when he treadeth within our borders.

Other than he was a mighty hunter and built the city of Babel and some other cities in the land of Shinar, The Bible pretty much stops there on information about Nimrod. But Micah does give us insight into this when the land of Nimrod shall be defeated. This is a prophecy concerning the end times when this religious system will be defeated. and here, in Micah, it is called "the land of Nimrod". My theory on this is that The Bible is not about false religion. I believe God left the history of false religion to secular history. The whole Bible is first and foremost about Jesus Christ, and I think God didn't want to mix a lot of false religious history in with the history of The second Person of The trinity of God in the Old Testament which was The same Person that was born as The only begotten Son of God in the New Testament. So, He put enough information about this false religious system in The Bible to confirm history. And then He gave us a brain to figure out the rest in secular history. He left the bulk of the history of false religions to the secular history books. These history books are not as reliable as The Bible. That is why He left us with conformation of some of these characters of this false religious system in The Bible. And Nimrod was a major one. He was the founder of Babel which later became Babylon which later became the Mystery, Babylon the great. The tower of Babel was built in the land of Shinar which is where Nimrod established his kingdom as we just read in Genesis.

> **Genesis 10:10**
> **10 And the beginning of his kingdom was Babel, and Erech, and Accad, and Calneh, in the land of Shinar.**

Notice it says, "the beginning of his kingdom". If this is Nimrod's kingdom. Wouldn't it stand to reason that he was the king of that kingdom even though it doesn't say he was? And this was only the beginning of his kingdom. This kingdom would become the mystery talked about in Revelation called Mystery, Babylon the Great and is still here even to this day.

> **Daniel 1:1-2**
> **1 In the third year of the reign of Jehoiakim king of Judah came Nebuchadnezzar king of Babylon unto Jerusalem, and besieged it.**
> **2 And the Lord gave Jehoiakim king of Judah into his hand, with part of the vessels of the house of God: which he**

**carried into the land of Shinar to the house of his god; and he brought the vessels into the treasure house of his god.**

We can see by this scripture above that the kings of Babylon ruled from the land of Shinar where Nebuchadnezzar ruled from. In other words: Babylon. Babylon is mentioned again in Revelation. This Babylon has evolved from a place in the land of Shinar to many false religions with a major worldwide one based in Rome.

**Revelation 17:1-9**

**1 And there came one of the seven angels which had the seven vials, and talked with me, saying unto me, Come hither; I will shew unto thee the judgment of the great whore that sitteth upon many waters:**

**2 With whom the kings of the earth have committed fornication, and the inhabitants of the earth have been made drunk with the wine of her fornication.**

**3 So he carried me away in the spirit into the wilderness: and I saw a woman sit upon a scarlet coloured beast, full of names of blasphemy, having seven heads and ten horns.**

**4 And the woman was arrayed in purple and scarlet colour, and decked with gold and precious stones and pearls, having a golden cup in her hand full of abominations and filthiness of her fornication:**

**5 And upon her forehead was a name written, MYSTERY, BABYLON THE GREAT, THE MOTHER OF HARLOTS AND ABOMINATIONS OF THE EARTH.**

**6 And I saw the woman drunken with the blood of the saints, and with the blood of the martyrs of Jesus: and when I saw her, I wondered with great admiration.**

**7 And the angel said unto me, Wherefore didst thou marvel? I will tell thee the mystery of the woman, and of the beast that carrieth her, which hath the seven heads and ten horns.**

> **8 The beast that thou sawest was, and is not; and shall ascend out of the bottomless pit, and go into perdition: and they that dwell on the earth shall wonder, whose names were not written in the book of life from the foundation of the world, when they behold the beast that was, and is not, and yet is.**
>
> **9 And here is the mind which hath wisdom. The seven heads are seven mountains, on which the woman sitteth.**

We will see later how the seven mountains in verse 8 represent Rome. See how you can put things like this together with the scattered but adequate information in The Bible? There is a whole lot of history behind this mystery religion of Babylon. It is alluded to in many places in The Bible as we have seen some of them in these verses, but not explained in detail. It is referenced all throughout The Bible, but we must rely on secular history for most of the details. Out of this mystery, came the worship of the sun, the moon, the stars, the planets and the constellations of the stars, or the zodiac. Some today call it the horoscope. Yes, I've seen the internet sites that try to debunk a lot of the history written about the theory that this man became a sun god. I know that there is no absolute proof on much of this. But if it's not true, then why does The Bible allude to it with several names of these people involved easily accessed in history with accurate information that most authors, pastors and theologians on the subject agree on. including the title "queen of heaven"? If there was not a sun god, then how did this woman claim to be married to him which gave her the title of queen of heaven? And if it's not true, where did the worship of the zodiac come from? The Bible doesn't tell us that information; but it does acknowledge it with the names of the ones involved in the history of it. Nimrod, Ashtaroth, Diana, Tammuz, queen of heaven, Baal, Baalim and more. If it's not true, why are these names that are all false gods and goddesses given in The Bible?

**2 Kings 23:5**
**5 And he put down the idolatrous priests, whom the kings of Judah had ordained to burn incense in the high places in the cities of Judah, and in the places round about Jerusalem; them also that burned incense unto Baal, to the sun, and to the moon, and to the planets, and to all the host of heaven.**

**Judges 2:11-13**
**11 And the children of Israel did evil in the sight of the Lord, and served Baalim:**
**12 And they forsook the Lord God of their fathers, which brought them out of the land of Egypt, and followed other gods, of the gods of the people that were round about them, and bowed themselves unto them, and provoked the Lord to anger.**
**13 And they forsook the Lord, and served Baal and Ashtaroth.**

**Acts 19:35**
**35 And when the townclerk had appeased the people, he said, Ye men of Ephesus, what man is there that knoweth not how that the city of the Ephesians is a worshipper of the great goddess Diana, and of the image which fell down from Jupiter?**

**Ezekiel 8:14**
**14 Then he brought me to the door of the gate of the Lord's house which was toward the north; and, behold, there sat women weeping for Tammuz.**

Baal worship was the celestial worship of the sun, the moon, the stars, the planets and the constellations. In other words, as we said, the zodiac. Baal worship included the controlling of the elements; rain, sun, and conditions for a prosperous harvest along with defeating enemies and controlling your health. This was a superstitious worship of a god that could do none of those things but was used by the devil to control people that thought he could. The root word Baal is associated with Satan worship. Baal, from Baal-zebub the same meaning as Beelzebub referring to the prince of devils. In some cases, Beelzebub is referring to demons or false gods, but Satan is the prince of those demons and false gods.

**2 Kings 1:2-3**

**2 And Ahaziah fell down through a lattice in his upper chamber that was in Samaria, and was sick: and he sent messengers, and said unto them, Go, inquire of Baal-zebub the god of Ekron whether I shall recover of this disease.**
**3 But the angel of the Lord said to Elijah the Tishbite, Arise, go up to meet the messengers of the king of Samaria, and say unto them, Is it not because there is not a God in Israel, that ye go to inquire of Baal-zebub the god of Ekron?**

**2 Kings 23:4-5**

**4 And the king commanded Hilkiah the high priest, and the priests of the second order, and the keepers of the door, to bring forth out of the temple of the Lord all the vessels that were made for Baal, and for the grove, and for all the host of heaven: and he burned them without Jerusalem in the fields of Kidron, and carried the ashes of them unto Bethel.**
**5 And he put down the idolatrous priests, whom the kings of Judah had ordained to burn incense in the high places in the cities of Judah, and in the places round about Jerusalem; them also that burned incense unto Baal, to the sun, and to the moon, and to the planets, and to all the host of heaven.**

**Matthew 12:24**
**24 But when the Pharisees heard it, they said, This fellow doth not cast out devils, but by Beelzebub the prince of the devils.**

The Bible Acknowledges the woman, Ashtaroth, in a couple of verses in The Bible to give us an acknowledgement that she existed. One is above in Judges 2:13 and another in the verses below in 1 Samuel. There was not only a physical place called Babel where it all began, but it is also a Babylonian system of false religions throughout the ages, along with that major one we mentioned, headquartered in Rome, Revelation 17: 9 a couple of pages ago above. We will talk about how we know it is Rome a little later.

**1 Samuel 7:3-4**
**3 And Samuel spake unto all the house of Israel, saying, If ye do return unto the Lord with all your hearts, then put away the strange gods and Ashtaroth from among you, and prepare your hearts unto the Lord, and serve him only: and he will deliver you out of the hand of the Philistines.**
**4 Then the children of Israel did put away Baalim and Ashtaroth, and served the Lord only.**

Again, The Bible acknowledges Ashtaroth, Baal, Baalim, Diana, Nimrod and Tammuz, but not with a lot of information. But at least we can move forward knowing that The Bible does acknowledge them as existing. Now, all we have to do is see who they are in history. Ashtaroth and Diana are two references we have to this goddess in The Bible. But in history, that is enough to connect the rest of the names given to her along with the title as "the queen of heaven" and "the Mystery, Babylon the great". Her legend is extensive going in many directions, but it's all the same woman with a few male false gods mixed in. But the root of this system is this woman.

**Jeremiah 7:18**
**18 The children gather wood, and the fathers kindle the fire, and the women knead their dough, to make cakes to the queen of heaven, and to pour out drink offerings unto other gods, that they may provoke me to anger.**

**Revelation 17:5**
**5 And upon her forehead was a name written, MYSTERY, BABYLON THE GREAT, THE MOTHER OF HARLOTS AND ABOMINATIONS OF THE EARTH.**

**Revelation 17:18**
**18 And the woman which thou sawest is that great city, which reigneth over the kings of the earth.**

From this little bit of information, we can tie the rest of the names given in history to these characters added with the ones in The Bible. Nimrod, Semiramis, Beltis Tammuz, Diana, Isis, Ishtar, Venus, cupid, Horus, Osiris, Cybele, Deoius, Fortuna, Jupiterpuer, Ashtaroth, Astarte, Baal, Baalim, Madonna and more. They are all connected to each other through Babel. They are all of the same origin. All from the original Babylonian religion that started with the tower of Babel. This is all common knowledge among ministers of the gospel that have researched Christmas or the mystery of the Babylonian religion. Ask your preacher. If he is a good minister of The Word, he will have studied these religious celebrations and he will be able to tell you everything I have just told you that has been a mystery through the years, but has been revealed to us in these last days by examining the history that has happened since the time those prophecies were written back then that made no sense to them, but now, with the clarification of it by seeing the history that has happened, we are able to put it together. For example, how would they know that this mystery religion of Babylon would manifest itself when there was, at that time, no worldwide mystery religion. But now the mystery religion is clear and we have seen it develop through the years into this Roman/government church that today is would wide. But most pastors are spineless when it comes to taking a stand against this popular pagan festival for fear of emptying their church and losing their job, or popularity, or loss of church income. And he will tell you that it's true alright, but it's okay to celebrate it anyway because it has been changed to a Christian celebration. But then, he can't give you a valid scriptural basis for it being changed to Christian. If he tries to; then ask him how do you dismiss these being pagan celebrations? And, if Christmas is Biblical, where is it in The Bible? Then ask: If this is a Christian celebration, then why does the world love it so much?

> **John 15:18-19**
> **18 If the world hate you, ye know that it hated me before it hated you.**
> **19 If ye were of the world, the world would love his own: but because ye are not of the world, but I have chosen you out of the world, therefore the world hateth you.**

Ask yourself two simple questions.
1. Does the world love Christmas?
2. Does the world love Jesus?

The answer to these questions in case you don't already know are "yes" to the first one. And "no" to the second one. Can the two co-exist? No! You either love the world and hate Jesus, or you love Jesus and hate the world. Most people can think that they love Jesus, but don't. I can usually tell if that person is a true believer or a pretender by talking with them for about 5 minutes. Some are just backslidden Christians, but some are obviously not a Christian but only think they are. Those are not hard to spot. Not by judging them, but by inspecting their fruit. Christians will always show some fruit. Some Christians don't show much fruit, but all will show some.

**Matthew 6:24**
**24 No man can serve two masters: for either he will hate the one, and love the other; or else he will hold to the one, and despise the other. Ye cannot serve God and mammon.**

**1 John 2:15**
**15 Love not the world, neither the things that are in the world. If any man love the world, the love of the Father is not in him.**

People that only think they are saved, but are not, bring forth fruit also. but it is a corrupt or evil fruit.

**Matthew 7:17-21**
**17 Even so every good tree bringeth forth good fruit; but a corrupt tree bringeth forth evil fruit.**
**18 A good tree cannot bring forth evil fruit, neither can a corrupt tree bring forth good fruit.**
**19 Every tree that bringeth not forth good fruit is hewn down, and cast into the fire.**
**20 Wherefore by their fruits ye shall know them.**
**21 Not every one that saith unto me, Lord, Lord, shall enter into the kingdom of heaven; but he that doeth the will of my Father which is in heaven.**

**Matthew 13:8**
**8 But other fell into good ground, and brought forth fruit, some an hundredfold, some sixtyfold, some thirtyfold.**

Most Pastors that I confront with the question of Christmas do know the pagan aspect of it, but do nothing about it, but rather encourage it instead. Their argument is that people come to church at Christmas time, so that gives them the opportunity to preach to them and therefore they will possibly get saved. Well, on the surface, that sounds real good as if you yourself could take a trick of the devil and turn it around to good. God can do that to situations that the devil puts us in, but this is not that situation. In this situation, you are choosing to enter a trick of the devil, then expect God to turn it around for good. This would be like saying: let's put a bar in the church building and participate in drinking with the drunks so we can preach to them so they might get saved. And you forget anyway; God calls, and God saves at His time and choosing. That person can only get saved when God opens the door, and they walk through. God doesn't need a pagan holiday that is a lie like Christmas to call people to Himself. He uses the truth of the gospel, not the worlds idolatrous practices. Don't misunderstand me; God can use anything He wants to call someone. But I am just saying that normally, scripturally, He uses the truth to call a person. Pastors, can you effectively preach the Gospel to someone if you are lying to them about Christmas? Does God honor that? Don't you think you could be doing what Jesus talked about with the blind leading the blind and both fall into the ditch. This next passage is talking about religious practices that The Heavenly Father has nothing to do with.

**Romans 1:18-20**
**18 For the wrath of God is revealed from heaven against all ungodliness and unrighteousness of men, who hold the truth in unrighteousness;**
**19 Because that which may be known of God is manifest in them; for God hath shewed it unto them.**
**20 For the invisible things of him from the creation of the world are clearly seen, being understood by the things that are made, even his eternal power and Godhead; so that they are without excuse:**

**Luke 6:39**
**39 And he spake a parable unto them, Can the blind lead the blind? shall they not both fall into the ditch?**

This suggest that you are just as responsible for finding the truth as your pastor is. You are not to just blindly follow some teaching and call it truth without checking it out with The Word of God first. And I can tell you that according to The Word of God, He has nothing to do with Christmas. Another favorite excuse some pastors have for celebrating Christmas is a misinterpretation of a verse in Colossians chapter 2.

> **Colossians 2:16-17**
> **16 Let no man therefore judge you in meat, or in drink, or in respect of an holyday, or of the new moon, or of the sabbath days:**
> **17 Which are a shadow of things to come; but the body is of Christ.**

They use this to justify Christmas by saying that someone can't tell them not to celebrate Christmas because that would be judging them in a day that they consider to be a holyday. Well, any pastor that would tell you that simply doesn't know what he's talking about. First of all, the holydays referred to here are the feast days of Israel, Not Christmas. You can't just make any pagan celebration you want to be a holyday! Look at the context in verse 17. A shadow of things to come. No pagan celebrations are a prophetic shadow of things to come. God chooses the holydays, not man. There is one winter celebration called Hanukkah, sometimes called the festival of lights, and is mentioned in John as the feast of dedication. In this celebration, a menorah is used. The middle candle of nine candles is lit. The celebration last eight days in which one additional candle on the menorah is lit each night until all are lit.

> **John 10:22**
> **22 And it was at Jerusalem the feast of the dedication, and it was winter.**

Details of this feast are found in the historical book of Maccabees. It is not a commanded feast day in The Bible. It was a time when Antiochus Epiphanes, a Seleucid king who was a prototype of the antichrist came against the Jews to try to force them to worship Greek/Syrian forms of worship with pagan gods. He defiled the temple and forbade the Jews to celebrate their feast days. He killed thousands of Jews and took thousands more as slaves. He stripped the temple of anything valuable such as gold and silver and rare stones and he set up the pagan celebration of Saturnalia in the temple. He then sacrificed a pig on the alter in the temple then sprayed the pig's blood all over the walls and floors of the temple defiling the temple with that abomination. Later, the Jews revolted against him and prevailed. They had to cleanse the temple according to Jewish custom which involved a ceremonial lighting of the Memoria which took 8 days. They only had enough oil for 1 day, but the oil miraculously lasted the entire 8 days. That event became the feast of Hanukkah commemorating the rededication of the second temple after the Maccabean revolt in the 2nd century BC. Because this celebration is not described in The Bible, and not a commanded celebration from God, there are conflicting stories of it. It is said by some that Jews have used it to try to compete with Christmas using it to exchange gifts which was not originally included in the celebration. It was pretty much ignored by the Jews until the 19th century when Christmas was gaining popularity in America. The Jews as a nation don't believe in Jesus but still wanted the festival atmosphere of the winter solstice festival. So, they use Hanukkah to be able to take part in this festive time of year. It only resembles Christmas with their addition of the exchanging of gifts which was not an original part of the celebration, and it is about the same time of year as Christmas but there are no other similarities. As far as I know, there is nothing wrong with celebrating Hanukkah. But it is really not a worldwide celebration, but mostly just a Jewish celebration and not connected to Christmas in any way. And you would think that they wouldn't want Hanukkah to resemble Christmas in any way because the Seleucid king had set up the celebration of Saturnalia in their temple, desecrating the temple with this idol worshiping celebration that later became Christmas. Even though Hanukkah is not a commanded feast day in The Bible, this holyday would be included in Colossians 2:16 because it is an actual feast day of Israel. And God does acknowledge it in verse 22, above. Christmas is not and never has been declared a holyday or a feast day in The Bible or in Israel or by the Jews. Satan would like nothing more than for Jesus to come again as a peaceful infant. But He will not come again as an infant. Neither will He come peaceful. When He comes again to this earth, it will be as The Lion of the tribe of Judah. He will come as The Conquering King and Righteous Judge. It would be different if Christmas started out as a day set aside to honor Jesus. But it didn't. Many people corrupt what God has given. God gave us land to live off of and fresh air to breath, clean water to drink and good music to comfort us. Man is the one that is corrupting music with sex and drugs and alcoholism. Man is the one that is polluting the land, water and the air, making it harder and harder to find fresh air to breath, clean water to drink and a scenic place to go. It's just a blatant disregard for what God has provided for us. But corrupting that which is good is not what Christmas is. I'm talking about men that have taken something that started out evil and try to change it just enough to make it appear good on the surface so they can keep doing what they want to do. That is Christmas. It started out as idol worship. Man tried to make it appear good by attaching the Holy Name of Jesus to it. Christmas was around centuries before Jesus was born. It wasn't called Christmas, but it was still the same celebration. It is little more than a superstitious worship of the heavens. Or known today as the zodiac. Remember Jeremiah chapter 10 that we just read a couple of pages ago vividly describes something very similar to a Christmas tree? We see that they were dismayed at the signs of heaven. In other words, they worshiped the stars in heaven by fear. To be dismayed is to be afraid of, or terrified of. And they were very superstitious about the alinement of the stars to direct their daily activities. Read verse fifteen:

> **Jeremiah 10:14-15**
> **14 Every man is brutish in his knowledge: every founder is confounded by the graven image: for his molten image is falsehood, and there is no breath in them.**
> **15 They are vanity, and the work of errors: in the time of their visitation they shall perish.**

> **Jeremiah 10:2**
> **2 Thus saith the Lord, Learn not the way of the heathen, and be not dismayed at the signs of heaven; for the heathen are dismayed at them.**

I know some of you say that Paul used a false god to witness to the men of Athens on Mars hill, so that is why you use Christmas to witness to people.

> **Acts 17:23**
> **23 For as I passed by, and beheld your devotions, I found an altar with this inscription, TO THE UNKNOWN God. Whom therefore ye ignorantly worship, him declare I unto you.**

But Paul did not use the alter of Ares or Apollo and declare them to be Jesus. Paul didn't use any of the false gods of Athens. He chose the one that said to the unknown God. He was just explaining to them that he knows who the real God is that is unknown to them, therefore, the God Paul was talking about didn't used to be a Greek god. He is The real God that was unknown to them.

You may claim that people don't worship false gods today, but there is the supernatural world of idol worship that doesn't have to be a named god but rather a supernatural idea which can be a false god in itself. Some people today follow their horoscope every day to guide what they do not even realizing that it is straight out of the mystery Babylon idol worship. There are many other forms of idol worship that many people don't see as idol worship, but they let it rule their lives. I have known people that were convinced they were going to die at a certain age because a Ouija board said they would. Just the suggestion this game plants in your head can be crippling to your life and the devil can use it to put you in bondage to a false predication in your life. You could live in fear of your life for years in expectation of an event that will never happen. None of those people I knew died at the age the Ouija board told them they would. I knew one person that listened to a medium that told him he would die at the age of 51, and he believed that would happen. He lived well into his 80s and finally died of old age. Anything connected with the zodiac system that tries to direct your life through the power of suggestion by predicting your future using natural objects is the "the work of errors" and is, in fact, simply modern-day idol worship. Don't work the work of error. The whole purpose of the worship of the stars is to control your life through natural objects. The tree has always been an object of this kind of worship. We will see later that the tree plays a very large part in idol worship. You say that people today are too sophisticated to worship idols? Well, all you have to do is go and pick up most any local newspaper, and in it, you will find, in the astrology section; the position of the stars to direct your day... To tell you what to, and what not to do that day, or like we said, your horoscope. How many of you fear after breaking a mirror thinking it will bring seven years bad luck, or have a chill go up your spine when a black cat crosses your path, or are afraid of anything with the number 13 in it. When I worked as an architect, I found that there are a lot of skyscrapers that don't have a 13th floor. They simply skip the number 13 and go straight from the 12th floor to the 14th floor because no one wants to be on a 13th floor for fear of something going wrong simply because most people think the number 13 will bring them bad luck. as though the number 13 has some kind of supernatural power over your circumstances. Or you think 7 is your lucky number in which you think that the number 7 somehow has power in your favor. Or do you throw salt over your shoulder when you spill some, or carry a rabbit's foot for luck, or knock-on wood after saying something good to keep from losing the good thing you were just talking about. How many of you eat black eyed peas on New Year's Day for good luck? You have probably, without even thinking, given in at times to superstition. Perhaps silly things that you don't give a second thought to, like not stepping on a crack in the sidewalk, or blowing on dice to roll a 7, or performing rituals thinking that will cause your sports team to win, or not walking under a ladder thinking it will bring you bad luck. Although, if you are walking under a ladder, you might want to look up and make sure you don't hit your head on something or make sure nothing is going to fall on you. But that's nothing to do with luck, just common sense. But little by little, with some people, superstition can gain a foothold and soon become crippling in their mind and life with gripping fear. That is how voodoo works. To convince you that sticking pens in a doll can hurt you. It can't, unless you believe it can. The point is to avoid any kind of known idol symbolism should be the practice of every Christian. All these things I have mentioned and much more come straight out of idol worship and are practiced by millions, perhaps billions of people even today. Don't mess with it. In fact, stay far away from it. It can lead you down a dark path of bondage, destruction, and idol worship. The Bible is very clear on that point. Don't play around with it. Idol worship could creep into your life before you think about it. And that's what most people don't do; is think about it. Christmas is part of it, and is simply too dangerous to mess around with because of its ties with idol worship which we can clearly see in this book. There is another celebration at springtime when you have a spring festival in honor of the goddess of spring and rebirth. The fertility goddess. Her name is Eastre, also known as Ishtar, or in some countries, it's Astarte. That celebration is the one that we call Easter. This is the celebration of the vertical equinox and the worship of new life given to the Northern Hemisphere as spring begins. It also is nothing more than a pagan celebration. There are other days also that we celebrate in our culture that came straight out of pagan worship. The pagans worshiped the changing of the seasons and had a celebration for each them. As we said, they wanted to please their gods so they would give them rain for their crops, and easy winters, and a prosperous harvest. We need to be very careful to not take part in those pagan celebrations because we don't need those false gods for all those things. We have the one and only true God that created all the seasons and is in control of them. So, if we need rain, we should turn to Him, not some false god. For today, unless you are a farmer, it would be more like looking to Him for a good job and a prosperous income. But I know what you're thinking, you still say: "I don't worship the seasons. I just celebrate those days for fun". Well, what you are doing for fun, is an abomination to God. Think about that!

> **Deuteronomy 12:30-31**
> **30 Take heed to thyself that thou be not snared by following them, after that they be destroyed from before thee; and that thou inquire not after their gods, saying, How did these nations serve their gods? even so will I do likewise.**
> **31 Thou shalt not do so unto the LORD thy God: for every abomination to the LORD, which he hateth, have they done unto their gods; for even their sons and their daughters they have burnt in the fire to their gods.**

This next passage pretty much speaks for itself, doesn't it? God doesn't even like us to pray like the pagan nations.

> **Matthew 6:7-8**
> **7 But when ye pray, use not vain repetitions, as the heathen do: for they think that they shall be heard for their much speaking.**

**8 Be not ye therefore like unto them: for your Father knoweth what things ye have need of, before ye ask him.**

# CHAPTER 4
# HERE COMES THE SUN

In this chapter, I will tell you exactly where Christmas came from. We have already touched on some of these details in previous chapters, but I'll mention them again to clarify the subject in this chapter. It all originated way back in the beginning of Babylon when Noah's great grandson, Nimrod, built a vast Empire.

> **Genesis 10:8-12**
> **8 And Cush begat Nimrod: he began to be a mighty one in the earth.**
> **9 He was a mighty hunter before the LORD: wherefore it is said, Even as Nimrod the mighty hunter before the LORD.**
> **10 And the beginning of his kingdom was Babel, and Erech, and Accad, and Calneh, in the land of Shinar.**
> **11 Out of that land went forth Asshur, and builded Nineveh, and the city Rehoboth, and Calah,**
> **12 And Resen between Nineveh and Calah: the same is a great city.**

The great power that God gave us when He created us in His image is God like.

> **Genesis 1:26-27**
> **26 And God said, Let us make man in our image, after our likeness: and let them have dominion over the fish of the sea, and over the fowl of the air, and over the cattle,**

and over all the earth, and over every creeping thing that creepeth upon the earth.

27 So God created man in his own image, in the image of God created he him; male and female created he them.

**Genesis 3:22-23**

22 And the Lord God said, Behold, the man is become as one of us, to know good and evil: and now, lest he put forth his hand, and take also of the tree of life, and eat, and live for ever:

23 Therefore the Lord God sent him forth from the garden of Eden, to till the ground from whence he was taken.

**Genesis 2:7**

7 And the Lord God formed man of the dust of the ground, and breathed into his nostrils the breath of life; and man became a living soul.

**Genesis 11:4-9**

4 And they said, Go to, let us build us a city and a tower, whose top may reach unto heaven; and let us make us a name, lest we be scattered abroad upon the face of the whole earth.

5 And the Lord came down to see the city and the tower, which the children of men builded.

6 And the Lord said, Behold, the people is one, and they have all one language; and this they begin to do: and now nothing will be restrained from them, which they have imagined to do.

7 Go to, let us go down, and there confound their language, that they may not understand one another's speech.

8 So the Lord scattered them abroad from thence upon the face of all the earth: and they left off to build the city.

9 Therefore is the name of it called Babel; because the Lord did there confound the language of all the earth: and

**from thence did the Lord scatter them abroad upon the
face of all the earth.**

Had God not scattered them, there would have been nothing they
couldn't have done, verse 6. We are made in the image and likeness
of God, and this likeness can do unlimited things because we have
this creative likeness of The Almighty God. No, we cannot create
something from nothing. Only God can do that. But we can create
from what is here. That creative power is unlimited. Look what
man has created today. We can travel in outer space in machines
we created. We have walked on the moon, landed spacecraft on
Mars and explored the outer reaches of our galaxy with a spacecraft
called Voyager. The technology of today is growing faster and
faster every day. It is still God and not us that does it because it
is that part of God that is in us. He put that in us and we are the
only created beings that have that. You have this likeness whether
you are saved or not. All of mankind has this relationship to God
Himself that we are made in His image and likeness. That alone
will not get you into heaven. But it does give you God like creative
power. No, we are not Gods! But we have a part of God in us
giving us His likeness. This tower in verse 4 was the beginning of
a foothold on the earth that would sweep across every nation and
is still here today. It's like the small match that can burn down the
whole forest, or the small amount of leaven that leavens the whole
lump of bread. Sun worship can easily be traced straight back to
Babel. As we said in the previous chapter; they were building a
tower to reach heaven. And they wanted to make a name. I can tell
you that they were not seeking "The God" in their tower. But they
were seeking "a god". If they were seeking The Lord God Almighty,
God Almighty would not have stopped them by confounding them.
If you are seeking The true God; He will answer you.

**Matthew 7:7-8**
**7 Ask, and it shall be given you; seek, and ye shall find;
knock, and it shall be opened unto you:**

**8 For every one that asketh receiveth; and he that seeketh findeth; and to him that knocketh it shall be opened.**

It's interesting to note in Genesis 11:6, that God said nothing would be restrained from them, what they have imagined to do. So, He confounded their language to scatter them. Then at Pentecost, God gave the apostles the gift of languages to bring people together. So, in that case, there should be nothing restrained from what the church can do. Right? Well, it would be that way if the church would simply be united. The people of Babel were united in what they were doing. Why can't the church do that? In Babel, in their ignorance, they were trying to reach their gods; the sun, the moon and the stars. This was the beginnings of Baal worship that carries on all throughout The Bible and throughout time even until now. It is, right now, a worldwide false religion. Imagine what it would be like if God hadn't stopped them and scattered them by confounding their language. They were building a tower to the sun, moon, and stars to worship them. The sun, moon, and stars were worshiped all through the ages and The Bible tells of it. Alters were set up in what was called "the high places." These were places on the top of a mountain or towers built to get closer to the gods that they worshiped. I will give you a reference in Jeremiah and Ezekiel, but there are numerous references to these high places in The Bible. Too many to include all of them in this book. I suggest you reference them with your concordance and check it out for yourself.

**Jeremiah 32:32-35**
**32 Because of all the evil of the children of Israel and of the children of Judah, which they have done to provoke me to anger, they, their kings, their princes, their priests, and their prophets, and the men of Judah, and the inhabitants of Jerusalem.**
**33 And they have turned unto me the back, and not the face: though I taught them, rising up early and teaching them, yet they have not hearkened to receive instruction.**

**34 But they set their abominations in the house, which is called by my name, to defile it.**

**35 And they built the high places of Baal, which are in the valley of the son of Hinnom, to cause their sons and their daughters to pass through the fire unto Molech; which I commanded them not, neither came it into my mind, that they should do this abomination, to cause Judah to sin.**

**Ezekiel 6:6**

**6 In all your dwellingplaces the cities shall be laid waste, and the high places shall be desolate; that your altars may be laid waste and made desolate, and your idols may be broken and cease, and your images may be cut down, and your works may be abolished.**

The nations went to these high places to worship their gods, (see Deuteronomy 12:2 a couple of pages from here). And notice also under every green tree. Sound familiar? What is under every green tree at Christmas morning? Your kids. They would use trees to worship their gods, verse 3 below. Verse 2 below tells us not to do that. I know I have used this scripture several times in this book already, but read it again for yourself. This is a foundational scripture for this whole book.

**Jeremiah 10:2-5**

**2 Thus saith the LORD, Learn not the way of the heathen, and be not dismayed at the signs of heaven; for the heathen are dismayed at them.**

**3 For the customs of the people are vain: for one cutteth a tree out of the forest, the work of the hands of the workman, with the axe.**

**4 They deck it with silver and with gold; they fasten it with nails and with hammers, that it move not.**

**5 They are upright as the palm tree, but speak not: they must needs be borne, because they cannot go. Be not afraid**

**of them; for they cannot do evil, neither also is it in them
to do good.**

In verse 2, the signs of heaven are the sun, moon, and stars. And
they used this Christmas tree to represent their sun god as we
already seen. They would plant groves of these evergreen trees to
use in their idol worship. This was a common practice throughout
the Bible in the Old Testament. Do not misunderstand verse 5
when it says you don't have to be afraid of them, (the tree), that
they will do you no evil; that does not mean that you can have one
in your home. Just look back up at verse 2: "Learn not the way of
the heathen". That means don't do it. Verse 5 means that if you
happen to go into someone else's house, and there is one of these
tree idols set up in their house; you don't have to be afraid of it
and run out screaming, because it is only a piece of wood, not a
god. It can't hurt you. But it does not mean that you can have one
in your house. The tree, building a tower to the heavens and the
high places, were all part of sun worship.

**2 Kings 23:4-7**
**4 And the king commanded Hilkiah the high priest, and
the priests of the second order, and the keepers of the
door, to bring forth out of the temple of the LORD all the
vessels that were made for Baal, and for the grove, and
for all the host of heaven: and he burned them without
Jerusalem in the fields of Kidron, and carried the ashes of
them unto Bethel.**
**5 And he put down the idolatrous priests, whom the kings
of Judah had ordained to burn incense in the high places
in the cities of Judah, and in the places round about
Jerusalem; them also that burned incense unto Baal, to
the sun, and to the moon, and to the planets, and to all the
host of heaven.**
**6 And he brought out the grove from the house of the
LORD, without Jerusalem, unto the brook Kidron, and**

**burned it at the brook Kidron, and stamped it small to powder, and cast the powder thereof upon the graves of the children of the people.**

**7 And he brake down the houses of the sodomites, that were by the house of the LORD, where the women wove hangings for the grove.**

This practice of worshiping the sun, moon and stars all started at Babel. It always includes trees. As we already established, they grew special trees for their worship, much like Christmas trees are grown in tree farms today to sell for the Christmas celebration. In verse 7, they were called groves, and women in the house of the sodomites, or homosexuals, wove hangings for those trees; in other words, ornaments, verse 7 above. This was a common practice in idol worship as indicated here.

**1 Kings 14:23-24**
**23 For they also built them high places, and images, and groves, on every high hill, and under every green tree.**
**24 And there were also sodomites in the land: and they did according to all the abominations of the nations which the Lord cast out before the children of Israel.**

**2 Kings 21:3-9**
**3 For he built up again the high places which Hezekiah his father had destroyed; and he reared up altars for Baal, and made a grove, as did Ahab king of Israel; and worshipped all the host of heaven, and served them.**
**4 And he built altars in the house of the LORD, of which the LORD said, In Jerusalem will I put my name.**
**5 And he built altars for all the host of heaven in the two courts of the house of the LORD.**
**6 And he made his son pass through the fire, and observed times, and used enchantments, and dealt with familiar**

**spirits and wizards: he wrought much wickedness in the sight of the LORD, to provoke him to anger.**

**7 And he set a graven image of the grove that he had made in the house, of which the LORD said to David, and to Solomon his son, In this house, and in Jerusalem, which I have chosen out of all tribes of Israel, will I put my name for ever:**

**8 Neither will I make the feet of Israel move any more out of the land which I gave their fathers; only if they will observe to do according to all that I have commanded them, and according to all the law that my servant Moses commanded them.**

**9 But they hearkened not: and Manasseh seduced them to do more evil than did the nations whom the LORD destroyed before the children of Israel.**

Read how this is worded in verse 4: "and he built alters in the house of The Lord, of which The Lord said, in Jerusalem I will put My Name". And verse 7: "And he set a carved image of the grove that he had made in the house of which The Lord said to David, and to Solomon, his son, in this house, and in Jerusalem, which I have chosen out of all tribes of Israel, will I put My Name forever". Notice that the grove consists of trees that were associated with these idols. In this case, they made a carved image from the tree. They observed times, verse 6. One of these observances of times is the winter solstice celebration, now known today as Christmas.

**Deuteronomy 12:2-3**
**2 Ye shall utterly destroy all the places, wherein the nations which ye shall possess served their gods, upon the high mountains, and upon the hills, and under every green tree:**
**3 And ye shall overthrow their altars, and break their pillars, and burn their groves with fire; and ye shall hew down the graven images of their gods, and destroy the names of them out of that place.**

One of those names in these places was Tammuz, who was the false Christ whose birthday is December 25$^{th}$. We will see more about him in a little while. But we see that the Christian's body is now the house of The Lord, or the Temple of God. And so, trees are still in the house of The Lord, or in your heart if you have one set up in your house. Not to mention those that are set up in church buildings at Christmas all over the world. Just as Israel mixed idol worship in the temple of God, we today mix that same idol worship in our churches all over the world.

**2 Corinthians 5:1**
**1 For we know that if our earthly house of this tabernacle were dissolved, we have a building of God, an house not made with hands, eternal in the heavens.**

**2 Corinthians 6:16-17**
**16 And what agreement hath the temple of God with idols? for ye are the temple of the living God; as God hath said, I will dwell in them, and walk in them; and I will be their God, and they shall be my people.**
**17 Wherefore come out from among them, and be ye separate, saith the Lord, and touch not the unclean thing; and I will receive you,**

**Ephesians 2:19-22**
**19 Now therefore ye are no more strangers and foreigners, but fellowcitizens with the saints, and of the household of God;**
**20 And are built upon the foundation of the apostles and prophets, Jesus Christ himself being the chief corner stone;**
**21 In whom all the building fitly framed together groweth unto an holy temple in the Lord:**
**22 In whom ye also are builded together for an habitation of God through the Spirit.**

**Hebrews 3:6**
**6 But Christ as a son over his own house; whose house are we, if we hold fast the confidence and the rejoicing of the hope firm unto the end.**

**1 Peter 2:1-5**
**1 Wherefore laying aside all malice, and all guile, and hypocrisies, and envies, and all evil speakings,**
**2 As newborn babes, desire the sincere milk of the word, that ye may grow thereby:**
**3 If so be ye have tasted that the Lord is gracious.**
**4 To whom coming, as unto a living stone, disallowed indeed of men, but chosen of God, and precious,**
**5 Ye also, as lively stones, are built up a spiritual house, an holy priesthood, to offer up spiritual sacrifices, acceptable to God by Jesus Christ.**

**1 Corinthians 3:16-17**
**16 Know ye not that ye are the temple of God, and that the Spirit of God dwelleth in you?**
**17 If any man defile the temple of God, him shall God destroy; for the temple of God is holy, which temple ye are.**

I know what you're thinking. You still continue to say, "but I don't worship the tree." Well, whether you worship it or not, God said don't even set one up. Verse 22 below tells us, "Neither shalt thou set up any image; which The Lord thy God hateth". Notice it didn't ask you if you worshiped it or not. Notice also in verse 21, that this is talking about trees.

**Deuteronomy 16:21-22**
**21 Thou shalt not plant thee a grove of any trees near unto the altar of the LORD thy God, which thou shalt make thee.**
**22 Neither shalt thou set thee up any image; which the LORD thy God hateth.**

Also, as we seen a couple of pages ago in Jeremiah 10:2-5, where it says to learn not the way of the heathen; He was talking to the house of Israel who didn't worship trees, verse 1.

> **Jeremiah 10:1**
> **1 Hear ye the word which the Lord speaketh unto you, O house of Israel:**

How can you see it any other way? A tree cut down, fastened with nails and hammer; in other words, putting feet on it to stand it upright; and then decorated, is an image that God hates!!! It's all right there in black and white in the scriptures that I have clearly shown you. How can you deny it?

> **Deuteronomy 7:26:**
> **26 Neither shalt thou bring an abomination into thine house, lest thou be a cursed thing like it: but thou shalt utterly detest it, and thou shalt utterly abhor it; for it is a cursed thing.**

Now do you still believe The Bible? Or is The Bible starting to get in the way of your tradition? let's read some more of what The Word of God says.

First, the warning:

> **Deuteronomy 18:9**
> **9 When thou art come into the land which the LORD thy God giveth thee, thou shalt not learn to do after the abominations of those nations.**

We have clear warnings in The Bible about these pagan practices that I have given you throughout this book. An observer of times would include an observance of the winter solstice festival, which was an observance of the time of the old sun dying and the birth of the new sun. We just seen a couple of pages ago in Second Kings 23:7 where the women wove hangings for the grove. Remember in Deuteronomy 12:2-3, also a couple of pages ago, the grove consists of green trees. These trees had to have been evergreen trees because the celebration of the winter solstice took place December the 25th in which the only green trees available at that time of year in the northern hemisphere would be an evergreen tree. All other trees lose their leaves in winter and aren't green again until spring. We know that some of these idols were simply trees with branches, otherwise what would they hang the ornaments on that we seen in 2nd kings 23:7, above. And we know they were green trees, Deuteronomy 12:2 above. Do people put hangings on green trees at Christmas today? Yes, they do. Candles were also used in idol worship. It represented the brightness of the sun. Candles are used today at Christmas, but not on the tree. They are used today as mood setting or scented candles for those holiday smells. Electric lights instead of candles are used on the tree today. Yes, candles are used in various places Biblically. But in history, candles are often used to represent a false god with a false light. That's why you see so many candles used in many eastern religions. Even in Satanism, the candle is used to represent the brightness of their god, Satan. His original name was Lucifer, which means to bring light. He was also called "son of the morning"

**Isaiah 14:12**

**12 How art thou fallen from heaven, O Lucifer, son of the morning! how art thou cut down to the ground, which didst weaken the nations!**

**Luke 10:18**

**18 And he said unto them, I beheld Satan as lightning fall from heaven.**

**2 Corinthians 11:14**
**14 And no marvel; for Satan himself is transformed into an angel of light.**

People will always seek after light. One of the main attractions at concerts now days is their elaborate light show using bright lights and lasers. I have used a light show and flash pods many times in my concerts over the years. People are fascinated by it. The visual effect is half of the attraction of the concert. Or, if you want to draw a crowd; just put on a large fireworks display. You will have a crowd of people. Why? Because people are attracted to light. It's even an instinct of insects to fly toward a light. Turn on an outside porch light on a warm summer night and see how many insects start buzzing around it. That's how one of those bug lights work. The light lures the bug into an electrically charged wire mesh, killing the bug before it can reach the light. We ought to be careful what path we take lest we be drawn into a false light like a bug to a bug light into a path of destruction.

Secondly, Look at this:

**Jeremiah 16:11-13**
**11 Then shalt thou say unto them, Because your fathers have forsaken me, saith the LORD, and have walked after other gods, and have served them, and have worshipped them, and have forsaken me, and have not kept my law;**
**12 And ye have done worse than your fathers; for, behold, ye walk every one after the imagination of his evil heart, that they may not hearken unto me:**
**13 Therefore will I cast you out of this land into a land that ye know not, neither ye nor your fathers; and there shall ye serve other gods day and night; where I will not shew you favour.**

They walked everyone after the imagination of his evil heart and harkened not unto God. Is this any different than celebrating Christmas? Isn't Christmas nothing more than the imagination of someone, seeing that it is certainly not in Gods perfect Word? Have you forsaken The Lord God for something that you want to do like these did in verse 11 above? Have you forgotten The Lord for Baal? Verse 27 below.

> **Jeremiah 23: 26-32**
> **26 How long shall this be in the heart of the prophets that prophesy lies? yea, they are prophets of the deceit of their own heart;**
> **27 Which think to cause my people to forget my name by their dreams which they tell every man to his neighbour, as their fathers have forgotten my name for Baal.**
> **28 The prophet that hath a dream, let him tell a dream; and he that hath my word, let him speak my word faithfully. What is the chaff to the wheat? saith the LORD.**
> **29 Is not my word like as a fire? saith the LORD; and like a hammer that breaketh the rock in pieces?**
> **30 Therefore, behold, I am against the prophets, saith the LORD, that steal my words every one from his neighbour.**
> **31 Behold, I am against the prophets, saith the LORD, that use their tongues, and say, He saith.**
> **32 Behold, I am against them that prophesy false dreams, saith the LORD, and do tell them, and cause my people to err by their lies, and by their lightness; yet I sent them not, nor commanded them: therefore they shall not profit this people at all, saith the LORD.**

A couple of things here. In verse 28, the person that speaks his own word instead of God's Word is likened to the chaff of the wheat. Notice in verse 12 below, the chaff is burned up with unquenchable fire. They walked everyone after the imagination of his evil heart and hearkened not unto God. And that amounts to chaff.

**Matthew 3:11-12**

**11 I indeed baptize you with water unto repentance: but he that cometh after me is mightier than I, whose shoes I am not worthy to bear: he shall baptize you with the Holy Ghost, and with fire:**

**12 Whose fan is in his hand, and he will throughly purge his floor, and gather his wheat into the garner; but he will burn up the chaff with unquenchable fire.**

Look at what we just read in verse 29, above. "Is not my word like as a fire?" This celebration will eventually be burned up as chaff. Then in verse 30, notice it refers to stealing Gods Word from a neighbor. That is exactly what is happening at Christmas. I have found that most people think that Christmas is a scriptural celebration simply because someone told them so, like their pastor or like in verse 30, his neighbor. Then in verse 31; God is against those that say that God said this, when He really didn't. I get suspicious when I hear a preacher say: "And God told me......this or that". If what they are saying doesn't agree with The Word of God; then they are putting themselves in the place of giving new inspired revelation from God. That's what the Christmas celebration would have to be. because other than Jesus was born and a few details about his birth, Christmas is not found in The Bible. So, you would have to believe that The Bible is not yet complete. Then you would have to take out second Timothy 3:17 that says that we are throughly furnished unto all good works. And you would also have to remove a couple of scriptures below so you wouldn't receive the plagues that these scriptures says you'll receive if you add to or take away from the scriptures of that book.

**Revelation 22:18-19**

**18 For I testify unto every man that heareth the words of the prophecy of this book, If any man shall add unto these things, God shall add unto him the plagues that are written in this book:**

**19 And if any man shall take away from the words of the book of this prophecy, God shall take away his part out of the book of life, and out of the holy city, and from the things which are written in this book.**

**Deuteronomy 12:32**
**32 What thing soever I command you, observe to do it: thou shalt not add thereto, nor diminish from it.**

Then you would have to give creditability to other religious groups that have claimed to have received new revelation from God. How could you say they are wrong if you believe that God Is still giving men new inspired scripture? You will find very little information on the birth of Jesus in the scripture. The place He was born, why they were there and a few details about what happened while they were there. But that's all you will find in the scripture. You will have to make new scripture to say Jesus was born on December 25th. You will have to add to The Bible to make it say we should celebrate His birth. You would have to take many scriptures out of The Bible to be able to set up a Christmas tree in your home. You would have to add to The Bible all the things connected to the Christmas celebration like the tree, the holly wreath, the yule log, the mistletoe, the decorations, the bells, exchanging of gifts and so on.

Thirdly:

You would also have to make Christmas not quite so popular to the world.

**Luke 16:15**
**15 And he said unto them, Ye are they which justify yourselves before men; but God knoweth your hearts: for that which is highly esteemed among men is abomination in the sight of God.**

"for that which is highly esteemed among men is an abomination in the sight of God." Christmas is highly esteemed among believers and non-believers alike celebrating the same thing which, in most cases, neither one really knows that he is celebrating an abomination in the sight of God.

> **2 Corinthians 6:14-17**
> **14 Be ye not unequally yoked together with unbelievers: for what fellowship hath righteousness with unrighteousness? and what communion hath light with darkness?**
> **15 And what concord hath Christ with Belial? or what part hath he that believeth with an infidel?**
> **16 And what agreement hath the temple of God with idols? for ye are the temple of the living God; as God hath said, I will dwell in them, and walk in them; and I will be their God, and they shall be my people.**
> **17 Wherefore come out from among them, and be ye separate, saith the Lord, and touch not the unclean thing; and I will receive you,**

Be not unequally yoked together with unbelievers. Christmas does that very thing.

It says in verse 15, "What concord hath Christ with Belial?" Which means don't mix Jesus with anything that is idol worship or evil or that is against God. In verse 17, it says to come out from among them, and be ye separate, saith The Lord, and touch not the unclean thing. Is Christmas a clean thing, or an unclean thing? There is no doubt that Christmas originated as pagan idol worship, an unclean thing. Ask any pastor. Look in any good encyclopedia or on the internet. See for yourself: "go not after other gods".

> **Jeremiah 25:6**
> **6 And go not after other gods to serve them, and to worship them, and provoke me not to anger with the works of your hands; and I will do you no hurt.**

**Jeremiah 32:32-35**

32 Because of all the evil of the children of Israel and of the children of Judah, which they have done to provoke me to anger, they, their kings, their princes, their priests, and their prophets, and the men of Judah, and the inhabitants of Jerusalem.

33 And they have turned unto me the back, and not the face: though I taught them, rising up early and teaching them, yet they have not hearkened to receive instruction.

34 But they set their abominations in the house, which is called by my name, to defile it.

35 And they built the high places of Baal, which are in the valley of the son of Hinnom, to cause their sons and their daughters to pass through the fire unto Molech; which I commanded them not, neither came it into my mind, that they should do this abomination, to cause Judah to sin.

And then fourthly, does this hit home with you? Do you set any pagan idol abominations in your home like Israel and Judah did in verse 34 above?

**Jeremiah 44:15-19**

15 Then all the men which knew that their wives had burned incense unto other gods, and all the women that stood by, a great multitude, even all the people that dwelt in the land of Egypt, in Pathros, answered Jeremiah, saying,

16 As for the word that thou hast spoken unto us in the name of the Lord, we will not hearken unto thee.

17 But we will certainly do whatsoever thing goeth forth out of our own mouth, to burn incense unto the queen of heaven, and to pour out drink offerings unto her, as we have done, we, and our fathers, our kings, and our princes, in the cities of Judah, and in the streets of Jerusalem: for then had we plenty of victuals, and were well, and saw no evil.

**18 But since we left off to burn incense to the queen of heaven, and to pour out drink offerings unto her, we have wanted all things, and have been consumed by the sword and by the famine.**
**19 And when we burned incense to the queen of heaven, and poured out drink offerings unto her, did we make her cakes to worship her, and pour out drink offerings unto her, without our men?**

How many of you simply will not harken to God's Word and would say that you don't care what The Bible says, you will still celebrate Christmas anyway? The queen of heaven is the mother of Tammuz. By the way, Tammuz is not the only name given to this false Christ. Different cultures have different names for him. I use the name of Tammuz because this is the name found in The Bible for him, therefore, it is easily researched. Many, perhaps all false religions sprang off this mystery religion who is Babylon the great, or more precisely the self-proclaimed queen of heaven and her son, Tammuz. He is referred to in The Bible in Ezekiel 8:13-14, as one of the abominations set up in The Lords house.

**Ezekiel 8:13-14**
**13 He said also unto me, Turn thee yet again, and thou shalt see greater abominations that they do.**
**14 Then he brought me to the door of the gate of the Lord's house which was toward the north; and, behold, there sat women weeping for Tammuz.**

Tammuz is whose birthday Christmas really is. Do you set any abominations up in your house? Abominations like a tree decked with silver and gold. Some historians say that sometimes this tree was stripped of its bark and overlaid with silver and gold, kind of like the tree on the cover of this book. Other times, the tree was sculpted into an image. Then other times it was simply fastened on bottom to stand upright and decorated with hangings. However different though, the principal is still the same. It's still the same tree no matter how it is displayed. People today can't afford to overlay a tree with real silver and gold. But I have seen artificial Christmas trees that are completely covered with a shiny silver or gold foil. I have heard it said that at Christmas, the evergreen tree, that never loses it leaves, or needles, or it's green color like the other trees do in winter, is used to represent the everlastingness of Jesus. Sounds real good, but this comparison just doesn't line up with scripture. It really turns out to sound more like just a variation of the same tree in Jeremiah. And besides, once you cut it down and nail it with boards on the bottom of it to stand up, it doesn't stay green for long after that. Even in ancient idol worship, the evergreen tree was used to represent new life never to be cut down. That is also where the wooden cross came from. In pagan worship, it was a sign of life representing Tammuz. Throughout history there has always been an effort by Satan to get people to worship idols. Whether it was him using Balaam to get Israel to worship idols or him using Pharaoh to force idol worship and slavery on Israel, or Ahab and Jezebel who raised up alters to Baal; it's ultimately that same driving force that turns people to idols instead of to God. This driving force is the same one that caused the fall of Adam and Eve when the serpent beguiled Eve into taking of the forbidden fruit with the promise of becoming as gods. It's that original force, which is Satan, that is behind the act that is influencing them. It's the same desire that Lucifer himself had when he thought he could elevate his throne equal to the throne of God.

**Isaiah 14:12-15**
**12 How art thou fallen from heaven, O Lucifer, son of the morning! how art thou cut down to the ground, which didst weaken the nations!**
**13 For thou hast said in thine heart, I will ascend into heaven, I will exalt my throne above the stars of God: I will sit also upon the mount of the congregation, in the sides of the north:**

**14 I will ascend above the heights of the clouds; I will be like the most High.**
**15 Yet thou shalt be brought down to hell, to the sides of the pit.**

God did not create the devil. But He created Lucifer, who became the devil after the scripture we just read above. How any being created by God could think his throne could be equal with his creator puzzles me. What they don't realize is that without God, they would cease to exist. Their very existence depends on God. God could wipe this whole universe out of existence in a snap, and start all over if He wanted to. But He will not do that because of the love He has for us who are His. I'm sure Satan thought that he could relinquish control from God by taking advantage of His love for His creation by turning His creation against Him, holding them hostage. In other words, just like when man sinned and turned control of this earth that God had given him over to Satan because of his sin. Satan used that as a bargaining chip when he told Jesus in the wilderness that he would give Him all of the kingdoms of the world if He would just fall down and worship him. What arrogance and stupidity that a mere created being should tell his creator to fall down and worship him? I don't understand the reasoning behind that. Are you going to tell God, Who created you and gave you life and existence; The one and only true God that, if He wanted to, could snuff you out simply at His Word, that He should worship you???? That would be like if you were in a rowboat with only a fishing pole telling a battleship to surrender or you will destroy them with your fishing pole. Just the wake from that battleship would capsize that rowboat. And relatively speaking, God would be infinitely more powerful than that battleship would be to that rowboat.

**Matthew 4:8-10**
**8 Again, the devil taketh him up into an exceeding high mountain, and sheweth him all the kingdoms of the world, and the glory of them;**
**9 And saith unto him, All these things will I give thee, if thou wilt fall down and worship me.**
**10 Then saith Jesus unto him, Get thee hence, Satan: for it is written, Thou shalt worship the Lord thy God, and him only shalt thou serve.**

Or he may have thought he could foil a promise of God, like the promise God made to Abraham to make him a great nation, making God break His promise which would discredit Him and prove His Word flawed. The problem with created beings thinking that they can discount God's promises or control God through those He loves or trying to discredit His Word doesn't take into account God's Omniscient which would allow God to perceive a plan like that before it ever happens and prevent that kind of blackmail from a mere created being. That is exactly what Satan tried to do when Balak wanted Balaam to curse Israel, but he couldn't because they were protected by God. So then, Satan used Balaam to tell Balac that Israel could curse themselves by disobeying God. So, Balaam counseled Balak to make friends with Israel, then mix the beautiful idol worshiping women of Moab in with the men of Israel so they would commit whoredom with them which would make Israel break their covenant with God to abstain from foreign women to take as a wife or to lay with them.

**1 Kings 11:1-3**
**1 But king Solomon loved many strange women, together with the daughter of Pharaoh, women of the Moabites, Ammonites, Edomites, Zidonians, and Hittites;**
**2 Of the nations concerning which the Lord said unto the children of Israel, Ye shall not go in to them, neither shall**

**they come in unto you: for surely they will turn away your
heart after their gods: Solomon clave unto these in love.
3 And he had seven hundred wives, princesses, and three
hundred concubines: and his wives turned away his heart.**

These were more than likely beautiful women, and the men of
Israel took them as wives and lovers. As a result, Israel brought
the curse of God upon themselves for the idol worship that these
women brought in through this act. But Balak didn't count on the
saving mercy of God for those that are His. They were punished
for what they did, but they were spared because of God's promise
to Abraham to make him a great nation. God will always provide a
way of escape for His people and He will always keep a remnant of
people that remain faithful. He will not leave His own unguarded.
He watches after our soul and gives us a solution to sin. But His
people must choose to follow Him to receive His solution. But,
like I said, God will always keep for Himself a remnant that will
not bow to a false god.

**Romans 11:1
5 Even so then at this present time also there is a remnant
according to the election of grace.**

**Isaiah 7:13
13 And he said, Hear ye now, O house of David; Is it a small
thing for you to weary men, but will ye weary my God also?**

**Colossians 1:16-17
16 For by him were all things created, that are in heaven,
and that are in earth, visible and invisible, whether they
be thrones, or dominions, or principalities, or powers: all
things were created by him, and for him:
17 And he is before all things, and by him all things consist.**

**Revelation 4:11**
**11 Thou art worthy, O Lord, to receive glory and honour
and power: for thou hast created all things, and for thy
pleasure they are and were created.**

**Genesis 12:1-3**
**1 Now the Lord had said unto Abram, Get thee out of thy
country, and from thy kindred, and from thy father's
house, unto a land that I will shew thee:**
**2 And I will make of thee a great nation, and I will bless thee,
and make thy name great; and thou shalt be a blessing:**
**3 And I will bless them that bless thee, and curse him that
curseth thee: and in thee shall all families of the earth
be blessed.**

**1 John 4:10**
**10 Herein is love, not that we loved God, but that he loved
us, and sent his Son to be the propitiation for our sins.**

Getting back to the subject of Nimrod, or whoever this great leader
was ruling at the time when these false religions were established
at the tower of Babel when it was being built; he died at the peak
of his popularity and reign. His wife, who was the queen, claimed
that he was resurrected into the sun and became the sun god. She
then claimed that this sun god impregnated her with a divine child
that she claimed was her husband, the king, reincarnated in that
child therefore making him not only the king again but the son of
the sun god worthy of worship. She secretly had a man impregnate
her and claimed that she had not been with a man to produce this
child. The mother and the child gained instant fame, and statues
were made of them all over the kingdom. That mother/child cult
is still, to this day, very strong. I'm sure you've seen evidence of
it. Some religions make statues of a woman holding a child and
call them Mother Mary and baby Jesus, but they are really still the
same song, different verse. The mother\child statue of a woman

holding a child goes back long before Jesus was born. And it's the same likeness found today in some churches. But remember, like Christmas, these statues only carry the names of Mother Mary and baby Jesus. They are actually the self-proclaimed queen of heaven, and her illegitimate son, Tammuz. The names were changed by the same people that changed the name of the winter sun worship festival to Saturnalia, then renamed it again to Christmas by those same Romans. God is very clear about setting up images.

> **Deuteronomy 5:8-9**
> **8 Thou shalt not make thee any graven image, or any likeness of any thing that is in heaven above, or that is in the earth beneath, or that is in the waters beneath the earth:**
> **9 Thou shalt not bow down thyself unto them, nor serve them: for I the LORD thy God am a jealous God, visiting the iniquity of the fathers upon the children unto the third and fourth generation of them that hate me,**

No one is to make an image or statue to worship. We don't have to make statues of Jesus or set up images to represent him. He lives within us. He is with us always. The names of the woman and child that these statues represent vary in different countries, but they are all the same mother and child. Another interesting thing about this mother child duo is how they have taken over two of the main events pertaining to Jesus.

> **Matthew 12:40**
> **40 For as Jonas was three days and three nights in the whale's belly; so shall the Son of man be three days and three nights in the heart of the earth.**

> **John 2:19-22**
> **19 Jesus answered and said unto them, Destroy this temple, and in three days I will raise it up.**

**20 Then said the Jews, Forty and six years was this temple in building, and wilt thou rear it up in three days?**
**21 But he spake of the temple of his body.**
**22 When therefore he was risen from the dead, his disciples remembered that he had said this unto them; and they believed the scripture, and the word which Jesus had said.**

If Jesus was 3 days and 3 nights in the heart of the earth, then how can you get three days and three nights from Friday evening close to sundown to Sunday morning before sunrise. In John 20:1, below, says it was the 1st day of the week but it was still dark before sunrise and Jesus had already been raised from that grave because the stone was already taken away.

**Luke 23:44-46**
**44 And it was about the sixth hour, and there was a darkness over all the earth until the ninth hour.**
**45 And the sun was darkened, and the veil of the temple was rent in the midst.**
**46 And when Jesus had cried with a loud voice, he said, Father, into thy hands I commend my spirit: and having said thus, he gave up the ghost.**

**John 20:1**
**1 The first day of the week cometh Mary Magdalene early, when it was yet dark, unto the sepulchre, and seeth the stone taken away from the sepulchre.**

It was still considered the sabbath if it was yet dark, verse 1 below.

**Matthew 28:1**
**1 In the end of the sabbath, as it began to dawn toward the first day of the week, came Mary Magdalene and the other Mary to see the sepulchre.**

Yet Mark says that the sabbath was past and it was already the 1st day of the week.

> **Mark 16:1-2**
> **1 And when the sabbath was past, Mary Magdalene, and Mary the mother of James, and Salome, had bought sweet spices, that they might come and anoint him.**
> **2 And very early in the morning the first day of the week, they came unto the sepulchre at the rising of the sun.**

Luke would tend to agree with Mark.

> **Luke 23:56-24:2**
> **56 And they returned, and prepared spices and ointments; and rested the sabbath day according to the commandment.**
> **24-1 Now upon the first day of the week, very early in the morning, they came unto the sepulchre, bringing the spices which they had prepared, and certain others with them.**
> **2 And they found the stone rolled away from the sepulchre.**

Okay, Matthew says it was only dawning toward the 1st day of the week at the end of the sabbath. Mark says the sabbath was already past and it was very early on the 1st day of the week. Luke says the same thing as Mark. Then John says it was the 1st day of the week but still dark. So, how do we resolve this what seems to be a contradiction? The 1st day hadn't started yet. we know that it was very close to sunrise, yet still dark when they arrived at the sepulchre, Matthew 28:1 and John 20:1. It was still dark and the stone was already rolled away. He had already been raised from that grave when Mary arrived before sunrise. The nights were from sundown to sunrise. He had already been raised from the grave before Sunday morning at sunrise, John 20:1. Many say that because it was before sunrise and called the 1st day of the week, that proves that Sunday started at sundown Saturday. But that doesn't fit the verse where it says Mary came early the 1st day of the week. Notice at that time, He Had already been risen before sunrise.

> **Mark 16:5-6**
> **5 And entering into the sepulchre, they saw a young man sitting on the right side, clothed in a long white garment; and they were affrighted.**
> **6 And he saith unto them, Be not affrighted: Ye seek Jesus of Nazareth, which was crucified: he is risen; he is not here: behold the place where they laid him.**

The sabbath observance of no work was from sundown Friday until sundown Saturday. But that is just the observance of the law to not do any work. In actuality, the sabbath was still the sabbath until sunrise the next day, Matthew 28:1 above. If Sunday started at sundown Saturday, it wouldn't have been early. The day would have already been half over being almost 12 hours since the previous sunset, Then, Sunday would have ended Sunday evening at sundown. The Bible doesn't really associate the night with the day like we do. It is the night of that day but different from the day. The night isn't counted in hours like the day is; it is divided into watches; each watch being about 3 hours long. The 1st watch is from sunset to 9pm. The sunset and the sunrise happen at different times depending on the time of year. But the 1st watch generally started at about 6pm, and the 4th watch generally ended about 6am. The second watch is from 9pm to midnight. The third watch is from midnight to 3am. And the 4th watch from 3am to sunrise, or like we said, generally about 6am. Then at sunrise, the next day starts. So, John 20:1, Mark 16:2 above and Luke 24:1 has to be talking about the inevitability within minutes of the coming of the 1st day of the week when it is not quite here yet, or else The Bible would contradict Itself. It is made clear as we already seen by this sister verse in Matthew 28:1 where it says clearly that it was before the 1st day of the week and it was still the sabbath. Luke 23:56, where it says they rested on the sabbath before they brought the spices just means that they rested until Saturday evening at about 6pm which was when the assigned day of rest from sundown Friday to sundown Saturday was. They could have been talking about the general time it was. No matter what time you get up in the morning, even if it's before daybreak, to you, it is still the next day. You don't watch your clock and think you can't get up until straight up 6am. You get up when you get up and call it the next day. That is probably the mindset of the ones that said the 1st day of the week even though it was still a few minutes until it was actually the start of the day. There are instances with Israel's feast days and sabbath days and high sabbath days that these occasions started at sundown and lasted to the next sundown. Or in some cases, until the next morning at sunrise. But that is not the way God set up creation. In creation and throughout The Bible, God set the starting of the day at the sunrise of that day as we already seen in Matthew 28:1. This end of the sabbath was not Saturday at sunset. Notice it says as it began to dawn toward the 1st day. It wasn't the 1st day yet. It was still the sabbath but not part of the day of rest. It was only dawning toward the 1st day because it wasn't sunrise yet. This definition of when the day starts is confirmed in other places in The Bible also.

> **Genesis 19:32-34**
> **32 Come, let us make our father drink wine, and we will lie with him, that we may preserve seed of our father.**
> **33 And they made their father drink wine that night: and the firstborn went in, and lay with her father; and he perceived not when she lay down, nor when she arose.**
> **34 And it came to pass on the morrow, that the firstborn said unto the younger, Behold, I lay yesternight with my father: let us make him drink wine this night also; and go thou in, and lie with him, that we may preserve seed of our father.**

Yesternight would be the night before the next day. So that night was not part of the morrow (or the next day). For us, the day starts at midnight. So, to us, anything before midnight would be called yesterday if it was already past midnight because we don't really use the term yesternight. Therefore, to them, anything before sunrise would be called yesterday, or to them, yesternight. Yester means a time before the time you are in now such as, yesterweek is last week, or yesteryear is a past year or past years, so yesternight would be last night.

> **Leviticus 7:15-17**
> **15 And the flesh of the sacrifice of his peace offerings for thanksgiving shall be eaten the same day that it is offered; he shall not leave any of it until the morning.**
> **16 But if the sacrifice of his offering be a vow, or a voluntary offering, it shall be eaten the same day that he offereth his sacrifice: and on the morrow also the remainder of it shall be eaten:**
> **17 But the remainder of the flesh of the sacrifice on the third day shall be burnt with fire.**

The sacrifice shall be eaten the same day. Notice the next day does not start until the next morning, verse 15 above.

> **1 Samuel 19:11**
> **11 Saul also sent messengers unto David's house, to watch him, and to slay him in the morning: and Michal David's wife told him, saying, If thou save not thy life to night, to morrow thou shalt be slain.**

It was night and it wouldn't be the morrow (or tomorrow) until morning.

> **Mark 16:1-4**
> **1 And when the sabbath was past, Mary Magdalene, and Mary the mother of James, and Salome, had bought sweet spices, that they might come and anoint him.**

**2 And very early in the morning the first day of the week, they came unto the sepulchre at the rising of the sun.**
**3 And they said among themselves, Who shall roll us away the stone from the door of the sepulchre?**
**4 And when they looked, they saw that the stone was rolled away: for it was very great.**

While this would seem to contradict Matthew 28:1 which says it was still the sabbath, but the end of the sabbath, when they arrived at the sepulchre; this is probably just a general statement of the time from a different perspective from someone that perhaps got second hand information or just wasn't concerned with being as concise as Matthew was. Besides, this says in verse 1, that when the sabbath was past, they had brought sweet spices, which could mean that they had, which means that they had already brought them before the sabbath was past to have them ready to use at daybreak. You can't say one verse is true but the other false. God doesn't make mistakes. There has to be a logical explanation. God's Word says in Matthew 28:1 that the sabbath was still in effect until sunrise on the 1st day of the week. So, it wasn't Sunday until the sunrise. We can see this explained in the Passover feast in verses 3, 6, 8, 10, 12, and 14 below. They picked a lamb on the 10th day of the month and they kept it until the feast started at the evening on the 14th day of the month, verse 6, and lasted till morning, verse 10 below.

> **Exodus 12:3-14**
> **3 Speak ye unto all the congregation of Israel, saying, In the tenth day of this month they shall take to them every man a lamb, according to the house of their fathers, a lamb for an house:**
> **4 And if the household be too little for the lamb, let him and his neighbour next unto his house take it according to the number of the souls; every man according to his eating shall make your count for the lamb.**

5 Your lamb shall be without blemish, a male of the first year: ye shall take it out from the sheep, or from the goats:

6 And ye shall keep it up until the fourteenth day of the same month: and the whole assembly of the congregation of Israel shall kill it in the evening.

7 And they shall take of the blood, and strike it on the two side posts and on the upper door post of the houses, wherein they shall eat it.

8 And they shall eat the flesh in that night, roast with fire, and unleavened bread; and with bitter herbs they shall eat it.

9 Eat not of it raw, nor sodden at all with water, but roast with fire; his head with his legs, and with the purtenance thereof.

10 And ye shall let nothing of it remain until the morning; and that which remaineth of it until the morning ye shall burn with fire.

11 And thus shall ye eat it; with your loins girded, your shoes on your feet, and your staff in your hand; and ye shall eat it in haste: it is the Lord's passover.

12 For I will pass through the land of Egypt this night, and will smite all the firstborn in the land of Egypt, both man and beast; and against all the gods of Egypt I will execute judgment: I am the Lord.

13 And the blood shall be to you for a token upon the houses where ye are: and when I see the blood, I will pass over you, and the plague shall not be upon you to destroy you, when I smite the land of Egypt.

14 And this day shall be unto you for a memorial; and ye shall keep it a feast to the Lord throughout your generations; ye shall keep it a feast by an ordinance for ever.

The Passover sacrifice lasted through the night until morning.

**Numbers 33:3**
**3 And they departed from Rameses in the first month, on the fifteenth day of the first month; on the morrow after the passover the children of Israel went out with an high hand in the sight of all the Egyptians.**

**Exodus 12:41-42**
**41 And it came to pass at the end of the four hundred and thirty years, even the selfsame day it came to pass, that all the hosts of the Lord went out from the land of Egypt. 42 It is a night to be much observed unto the Lord for bringing them out from the land of Egypt: this is that night of the Lord to be observed of all the children of Israel in their generations.**

**Exodus 12:21-22**
**21 Then Moses called for all the elders of Israel, and said unto them, Draw out and take you a lamb according to your families, and kill the passover.**
**22 And ye shall take a bunch of hyssop, and dip it in the blood that is in the bason, and strike the lintel and the two side posts with the blood that is in the bason; and none of you shall go out at the door of his house until the morning.**

The 1st day of Passover was observed in the evening and lasted until morning, just as Jesus died on the cross in the evening about 3pm.

In creation, God said let there be light. After which He divided the light, first, from the darkness, second. He called the light, day, first, then secondly, He called the darkness, night. So, to complete that 1st day, the evening to the morning, or the night, was added.

**Genesis 1:4-5**
**4 And God saw the light, that it was good: and God divided the light from the darkness.**

**5 And God called the light Day, and the darkness he called Night. And the evening and the morning were the first day.**

The evening and the morning is obviously talking about from sunset to sunrise, or the night, or as we said, there were four watches. The evening and the morning is mentioned after the first day, and then consistently mentioned again each day after the day is mentioned except the 7th day. It was done the same way in days 1 through 6. Day 7 didn't receive an evening and the next morning because day 7 is never ending. This is a type of the length of time itself and how it ends. A day is as a thousand years and a thousand years is as a day.

**2 Peter 3:8**

**8 But, beloved, be not ignorant of this one thing, that one day is with the Lord as a thousand years, and a thousand years as one day.**

I believe the 7 days of creation are a type of the seven thousand years of time allotted to this world. The last thousand years is the millennial reign of Jesus and doesn't have a night to end that day because his kingdom reign will never end for that day to those that are saved. It was 2 thousand years from Adam to Abraham. It was 2 thousand years from Abraham to Jesus. It has been 2 thousand years from Jesus to now. That is the first 6 days of creation at 6 thousand years. After Jesus soon return to get His church, and after the tribulation, there will be the last or the 7th day with the thousand-year reign of Christ in His millennial kingdom reign completing the 7 thousand years of time. But after that, His kingdom will continue forever after time is done away with in the new heaven and new earth and His kingdom will never have an evening and morning because the day of His kingdom never ends and never has a night, or darkness.

**Revelation 21:9-10**
**9 And there came unto me one of the seven angels which had the seven vials full of the seven last plagues, and talked with me, saying, Come hither, I will shew thee the bride, the Lamb's wife.**
**10 And he carried me away in the spirit to a great and high mountain, and shewed me that great city, the holy Jerusalem, descending out of heaven from God,**

**Revelation 21:25**
**25 And the gates of it shall not be shut at all by day: for there shall be no night there.**

There will however, be a never-ending darkness also for those that are not saved.

**Jude 11-13**
**11 Woe unto them! for they have gone in the way of Cain, and ran greedily after the error of Balaam for reward, and perished in the gainsaying of Core.**
**12 These are spots in your feasts of charity, when they feast with you, feeding themselves without fear: clouds they are without water, carried about of winds; trees whose fruit withereth, without fruit, twice dead, plucked up by the roots;**
**13 Raging waves of the sea, foaming out their own shame; wandering stars, to whom is reserved the blackness of darkness for ever.**

Notice in verse 11, it is talking about those that have gone after the error of Balaam. We will see in the next chapter how the error of Balaam is tied directly to Christmas. But getting back to the subject of the three days and three nights, If you can't possibly get 3 days and 3 nights from Friday to the end of the sabbath, why does the world have Jesus crucified on Friday? We know that Jesus rose on Saturday, Matthew 28:1. It was still the sabbath and Jesus had already been risen, John 20:1, the stone was already taken away. So, that would be only 2 nights or perhaps only one depending when on Saturday Jesus had been risen. If He died in the evening about 3 o clock;

**Matthew 27:46-50**

**46 And about the ninth hour Jesus cried with a loud voice, saying, Eli, Eli, lama sabachthani? that is to say, My God, my God, why hast thou forsaken me?**

**47 Some of them that stood there, when they heard that, said, This man calleth for Elias.**

**48 And straightway one of them ran, and took a spunge, and filled it with vinegar, and put it on a reed, and gave him to drink.**

**49 The rest said, Let be, let us see whether Elias will come to save him.**

**50 Jesus, when he had cried again with a loud voice, yielded up the ghost.**

**then it would only stand to reason that He would have been risen three days and three nights after that at the same time He died.**

I know The Bible says that Jesus was taken off of the cross right before the sabbath.

**John 19:31-33**

**31 The Jews therefore, because it was the preparation, that the bodies should not remain upon the cross on the sabbath day, (for that sabbath day was an high day,) besought Pilate that their legs might be broken, and that they might be taken away.**

**32 Then came the soldiers, and brake the legs of the first, and of the other which was crucified with him.**

**33 But when they came to Jesus, and saw that he was dead already, they brake not his legs:**

This was not a usual Saturday sabbath. This was a high sabbath, verse 31. A high sabbath can be any day of the week. There was always a high sabbath after the day of preparation no matter what day the preparation day was. I know the regular sabbaths start Fridays at sundown. But Friday still lasted until sunrise on Saturday. Then Saturday last until sundown on Saturday as far as the day of rest goes. But the next day still doesn't start until sunrise on Sunday. The day after the preparation can be followed by a regular 7th day sabbath if the 14th of Nisan happened to be on a Friday. But this cannot be the case with this high sabbath because we already know that Jesus would rise before the start of the 1st day of the week that we call Sunday. If that were the case, the first night would have been Friday night, the second Saturday night, and the third night would have been Sunday night. But we know He had already been risen before Sunday morning.

**Matthew 28:1**
**1 In the end of the sabbath, as it began to dawn toward the first day of the week, came Mary Magdalene and the other Mary to see the sepulchre.**

And we know that Jesus had to have been in the grave three days and three nights.

**Matthew 12:40**
**40 For as Jonas was three days and three nights in the whale's belly; so shall the Son of man be three days and three nights in the heart of the earth.**

I know that some pastors try to fit three days and three nights into Friday evening to Sunday morning by saying that any part of a day in Jewish time can be counted as a whole day and night. But if that were the case, it would have said simply three days. Any time a specific day and night is mentioned together in The Bible, it is meant to account for the whole day and night.

**Genesis 7:4**
**4 For yet seven days, and I will cause it to rain upon the earth forty days and forty nights; and every living substance that I have made will I destroy from off the face of the earth.**

**Exodus 24:18**
**18 And Moses went into the midst of the cloud, and gat him up into the mount: and Moses was in the mount forty days and forty nights.**

**Acts 9:24**
**24 But their laying await was known of Saul. And they watched the gates day and night to kill him.**

**2 Corinthians 11:25**
**25 Thrice was I beaten with rods, once was I stoned, thrice I suffered shipwreck, a night and a day I have been in the deep;**

**2 Thessalonians 3:8**
**8 Neither did we eat any man's bread for nought; but wrought with labour and travail night and day, that we might not be chargeable to any of you:**

But even if you counted it like they said, you still couldn't get three days and three nights. If He was crucified on Friday, and He Had been raised before sunrise Sunday, you still couldn't count Sunday as one of the days because according to The Bible, He had already been risen before Sunday started, Matthew 28:1. So, you could count Friday as a day and night, and Saturday as a day and night, but that is the extent you could get out of it. Most pastors count Sunday as a day and night also to be able to squeeze the three days and three nights out of it because most pastors think Jesus had been risen after sunrise on Sunday morning. But like we said, it was not yet the 1st day of the week, or Sunday morning, when Jesus had been risen. So, there is no way to count the 1st day of the week in that calculation because He was already alive and had already been risen by the time the 1st day of the week started, so we can't even know how long He had been risen even before that time. We are not told what time The Spirit had raised Him. The only way you could count it that way is if He was crucified on a Thursday. That way, you could say, He was crucified Thursday evening, but count the whole day as day 1. Then, Friday would be day 2. And Saturday would be day 3. Then for the nights, you would have Thursday night, Friday night, and Saturday night as the three nights. But doing it this way knocks off almost all of Thursday day, and knocks off at least some of Saturday night because He had already been risen before the end of the 4th watch, or the end of the regular weekly 'Sabbath on Saturday. Myself, I don't think God would cheat that way. If He says Jesus was in the grave for three days and three nights, then I believe Him that it was all of three days and three nights. Knowing all of this, Jesus was likely crucified on a Wednesday, and died Wednesday evening and The Spirit raised Him Saturday evening. That way He would have been taken off of the cross and put in the grave right before sunset on Wednesday, right before the high sabbath started at sundown. This high sabbath was not a regular Saturday sabbath. A high sabbath can occur on any day of the week that would come after the preparation day on Nisan 14, which on our calendar falls on a different day every year. Then, He would have been in the grave Wednesday night, Thursday night, and Friday night as the 3 nights; then Thursday, Friday, and Saturday as the three days. I didn't use Saturday night as one of the nights because again Matthew 28:1 and John 20:1 said it was still Saturday night and He had already been risen, so that night couldn't have been counted as a full night.

We also cannot know for sure the exact time He had been risen which could have been hours before Sunday morning. It could have been Saturday evening about the same hour he died three days earlier. But we are not given this information directly in The Bible, so we can't know for sure exactly what time He had been risen other than according to Matthew 28:1, He had already been risen before sunrise Sunday morning. I know this is somewhat confusing. But this is how some people manipulate The Bible to fit their doctrines into a false narrative. The fact is, we are not told exactly what time The Spirit raised Jesus from the grave. Only that it was before the sunrise of Sunday morning which tells me that you cannot fit 3 days and 3 nights into that time frame if He was crucified Friday.

So, again, why Friday then? For that matter, why celebrate a day for the resurrection of Jesus anyway? Where in The Bible does it tell us to celebrate the day of the birth or the resurrection day of Jesus. In fact, The Bible tells us not to celebrate days like that.

> **Galatians 4:8-11**
> **8 Howbeit then, when ye knew not God, ye did service unto them which by nature are no gods.**
> **9 But now, after that ye have known God, or rather are known of God, how turn ye again to the weak and beggarly elements, whereunto ye desire again to be in bondage?**
> **10 Ye observe days, and months, and times, and years.**
> **11 I am afraid of you, lest I have bestowed upon you labour in vain.**

We observe Jesus, not with days. We observe Him with communion, prayer and worship. We don't need a couple of special days to honor Him. We honor Him every day. The observance of days is also a pagan tradition. Even the days of our week are an observance of days to honor false gods. Friday comes from the pagan naming of the days tied to Venus and the goddess of fertility where we get

Easter, from the name of the goddess Eastre or sometimes named Astarte or Ishtar. She is best known as the queen of heaven and Mystery, Babylon the great.

> **Jeremiah 7:18-20**
> **18 The children gather wood, and the fathers kindle the fire, and the women knead their dough, to make cakes to the queen of heaven, and to pour out drink offerings unto other gods, that they may provoke me to anger.**
> **19 Do they provoke me to anger? saith the Lord: do they not provoke themselves to the confusion of their own faces?**
> **20 Therefore thus saith the Lord God; Behold, mine anger and my fury shall be poured out upon this place, upon man, and upon beast, and upon the trees of the field, and upon the fruit of the ground; and it shall burn, and shall not be quenched.**

> **Revelation 17:3-5**
> **3 So he carried me away in the spirit into the wilderness: and I saw a woman sit upon a scarlet coloured beast, full of names of blasphemy, having seven heads and ten horns.**
> **4 And the woman was arrayed in purple and scarlet colour, and decked with gold and precious stones and pearls, having a golden cup in her hand full of abominations and filthiness of her fornication:**
> **5 And upon her forehead was a name written, MYSTERY, BABYLON THE GREAT, THE MOTHER OF HARLOTS AND ABOMINATIONS OF THE EARTH.**

Friday is the only day named for a goddess instead of a god. The rest of them are: Sunday: day of the Sun god. Monday: day of the Moon god. Tuesday, Tiu, the god of war named for Mars. Wednesday, Odin, the god of Mercury and considered a father to the gods. Thursday, Thor, the god of thunder and the god of Jupiter. Then as we said, Friday, the goddess of Venus, and the wife of Odin, and the goddess of fertility, also the goddess of light or spring and new birth, same as Astarte, associated with the queen of heaven, Here, her name is Frigg, but it is the same mystery, Babylon the great. Saturday is associated with the god of Saturn. So, Friday is directly associated with the queen of heaven, the mystery, Babylon the great, the great whore. So, she has associated herself with the false day of (Friday) as the death of Jesus; just as her son, Tammuz, a false Christ, is associated with the false day of the birth of Jesus on December 25th which is really the birthday of Tammuz and the birth of the new sun. The Bible says only a small amount of leaven leavens the whole lump. Just as a small amount of lie about when Jesus was born or when He was crucified can contaminate your whole doctrine. If you get these two days wrong, that opens the door for Satan to deceive you in other subtle ways.

Our calendar is set up entirely on this celestial idol worship of the stars and planets based on the earth's rotation around the sun. The Biblical calendar is based on the rotation of the moon around the earth where the months follow the cycle of the moon. You can easily see how this idol symbolism is still very much with us today, at least in vocabulary. It is interesting to note that, as we said, the Babylonian/Roman calendar is based on the earth's rotating around the sun. In other words, a lifeless body, the sun, controlling a living body, the earth, because the earth is held in orbit by the gravity of the sun, symbolizing the lifeless sun is in control of a living planet. In other words, a dead false god in control of the living like in Mystery, Babylon. Even though the false god Tammuz and the self-proclaimed queen of heaven are long dead, they still control people to this day that worship them in the form of the zodiac and the mystery religion of Babylon. But the Biblical calendar is based on the moon rotating around the earth. A living body, the earth, controlling a lifeless body, the moon, because the moon is held in orbit by earth's gravity. Just as God, the life, has power over the lifeless, (which is us in an unsaved condition), to give life to that which is dead, (which is what happens when you accept Jesus as your Savior), to quicken your mortal body and give you, who was dead in sin, life eternal by His Spirit that comes and lives in you at salvation.

### Romans 8:11

**11 But if the Spirit of him that raised up Jesus from the dead dwell in you, he that raised up Christ from the dead shall also quicken your mortal bodies by his Spirit that dwelleth in you.**

### Romans 6:4-11

**4 Therefore we are buried with him by baptism into death: that like as Christ was raised up from the dead by the glory of the Father, even so we also should walk in newness of life.**
**5 For if we have been planted together in the likeness of his death, we shall be also in the likeness of his resurrection:**
**6 Knowing this, that our old man is crucified with him, that the body of sin might be destroyed, that henceforth we should not serve sin.**
**7 For he that is dead is freed from sin.**
**8 Now if we be dead with Christ, we believe that we shall also live with him:**
**9 Knowing that Christ being raised from the dead dieth no more; death hath no more dominion over him.**
**10 For in that he died, he died unto sin once: but in that he liveth, he liveth unto God.**
**11 Likewise reckon ye also yourselves to be dead indeed unto sin, but alive unto God through Jesus Christ our Lord.**

### Ephesians 2:1-9

**1 And you hath he quickened, who were dead in trespasses and sins;**
**2 Wherein in time past ye walked according to the course of this world, according to the prince of the power of the air, the spirit that now worketh in the children of disobedience:**

**3 Among whom also we all had our conversation in times past in the lusts of our flesh, fulfilling the desires of the flesh and of the mind; and were by nature the children of wrath, even as others.**

**4 But God, who is rich in mercy, for his great love wherewith he loved us,**

**5 Even when we were dead in sins, hath quickened us together with Christ, (by grace ye are saved;)**

**6 And hath raised us up together, and made us sit together in heavenly places in Christ Jesus:**

**7 That in the ages to come he might shew the exceeding riches of his grace in his kindness toward us through Christ Jesus.**

**8 For by grace are ye saved through faith; and that not of yourselves: it is the gift of God:**

**9 Not of works, lest any man should boast.**

God gave life to us who were dead in trespasses and sins. In sun worship, that is based on the sun cycle; the sun light hits the earth leaving one side of the earth dark. In the Biblical calendar, that is based on the moon; sunlight is reflected by the moon and stars onto the dark side of the earth giving light to those in darkness. When we receive Jesus as our Savior, He gives light to us who were in darkness. The zodiac religion has the sun as the dominant ruler and leaves no hope for those in darkness. Now in no way am I giving creditability to the worship of any celestial body saying that the earth or the moon is Jesus. This is strictly a typology and symbol of light and darkness used in the Jewish calendar. This typology is like the typology in Genesis of the dream Joseph had of ruling over the sun, moon, and eleven stars, with his father and mother being the sun and the moon and the eleven stars being his eleven brothers.

**Genesis 37:9**
**9 And he dreamed yet another dream, and told it his brethren, and said, Behold, I have dreamed a dream more;**

**and, behold, the sun and the moon and the eleven stars made obeisance to me.**

In The Bible, the system of zodiac worship is called Baal worship. Baal worship varies depending on the different parts of the world it comes from, but all of them have the same premise. All of them worship the sun as a god. But like we were saying, a mighty man, most likely Nimrod, was a very popular king, and he had a wife who enjoyed her position as queen. But when this mighty and popular king was suddenly killed in the prime of his life. The people were left empty because of his death. I don't know how many of you were around when Elvis died. It left many people empty. He was in the prime of his career and suddenly died. It was a shock to the whole nation and most of the world. After his death, people wanted something to remind them of him. That is when Elvis impersonators became very popular and are still, to this day, very popular. That is the way it was with this popular king. People were willing to accept any substitute for their beloved king who was suddenly killed in the prime of his reign. The queen realized she would lose power as queen. The kingdom was in shock because their hero was dead. That's when she came up with this plan that would make her dead husband and king, a god. She claimed that when he died; he was resurrected into the sun and became the sun god. She sighted proof of this by an evergreen tree that grew out of a dead stump overnight where he was buried as a symbol of him becoming a god. This was later celebrated by cutting down an evergreen tree each year at this time, putting feet on it with nails and a hammer to make it stand upright and decking it with silver and gold at the location where this green tree first appeared out of the dead stump. Then later when their language was confounded and they left that place, they set up a green tree every year at that same time of year in their houses where they moved to. Gifts were exchanged annually to symbolize the king's ascension into the sun as the sun god. As we talked about before; this dead stump became the yule log. Before they were scattered, the Queen claimed that her husband, the king, was coming back in the form of a child by reincarnation, and that the sun god made her pregnant. Of course, she would have to say that she hadn't been with a man to get pregnant. This way she could claim that her reincarnated husband was also the christ child because he would not only be her reincarnated husband, and her son; but because she claimed she hadn't been with a man, and she claimed that the sun god got her pregnant; that would make her son the proclaimed son of god and supposedly worthy to be worshipped; and would make him a supposed eternal king because he is now proclaimed to be a god. Then, she married her own son saying that she was actually marring her reincarnated husband, who was now also the proclaimed sun god, making the child the proclaimed christ child, son of the sun god. Is that sick, or what? Just a side note here. If this child was the son of the sun god and also the son of the mortal queen; this could answer the question of where the mythical character of the half man and half god known as Hercules came from. That's not a Biblical theory. It's just a guess of mine. Anyway, this queen married her own son, therefore, she made herself not only the queen of the kingdom of Babel again because she was again married to her reincarnated husband who was the king of Babel; but because she was at the same time married to the proclaimed son of god, Tammuz; that made her the self-proclaimed queen of heaven for being married to the sun god himself. In doing this, she was elevated to a position even over her husband because she, as his wife, was in control of everything heavenly because she was married to the sun god making her the queen of heaven; and she spoke for the sun god because he couldn't speak for himself being only a spirit without a body. But then she was also in control of everything earthly because she was the mother of Tammuz, who was now the heir to the throne because he was the king's son, but he was also the proclaimed christ because he had no earthly father as king of the kingdom. Him being only a child and not able to take the throne, he was obligated to his mother/wife, the queen, to obey all that she ordered because he was only a child and could not take charge until he was old enough to rule. Therefore, according to her, she had complete control of everything earthly as queen to the reincarnated king, but yet only a child; but she also had control of everything heavenly also because she was the queen of heaven because her husband was the sun god. She could make the rules however she pleased. The only thing is, in the Roman religion, her husband/son never grew up, he mostly remained a child to the queen of heaven. That's because when they were scattered at about this same time not very long after the false Christ child was born; that was the end of this great kingdom of Babel, not counting the Babylon kingdom that would later be ruled by Nebuchadnezzar. But he did not let this queen rule for him, But, this queen and her son lived on as icons in the minds of those scattered. They took this legend with them and her kingdom lived on, not in Babylon, but all the world. Since the false Christ child was only a child when they were scattered, he remained a child, at least in the Roman religion throughout time even until now. She was made a goddess through time and was worshipped as the queen of heaven in charge of the Christ child that she had control of because he was a child in the mystery, Babylon religion. She became the mystery, Babylon the great. Over time, this duo of mother and child was adopted into the Roman church creating this adulterous mixture of Christianity with paganism which is why she is called the great whore, Revelation 17:5. This type of thinking is still alive today in the Roman church. To pray to Jesus in the Roman church, you must go through Mary. In other words, you can't pray directly to Jesus, but you must pray to Mary so she can go to Jesus with your prayer, making her in charge and the mediator between God and man. The rationale behind this type of thinking is that the scripture says you must honor and obey your father and mother.

> **Ephesians 6:1-3**
> **1 Children, obey your parents in the Lord: for this is right.**
> **2 Honour thy father and mother; (which is the first commandment with promise;)**

**3 That it may be well with thee, and thou mayest live long on the earth.**

Therefore, if you ask Mary to ask Jesus, then He must honor and obey His mother and give you your request. It's really just another false doctrine spawned by this same Babylonian religion with the self-proclaimed queen of heaven. She's been around for multiple centuries before Jesus was born. There are other versions of this same scenario throughout the world. In some of those cases, Tammuz did grow into a man, but that scenario of him growing up is almost gone today. Mostly what remains today is the mixture of the queen of heaven with her child, the false Christ child adopted by this Roman religion. But all the scenarios of him are all the same false god manifested in the sun as the sun god and having a child named Tammuz through this Babylonian queen and are all connected to Baal worship through this false religious system. And whether you see it or not; the zodiac is at the heart of this false religion. If you go by your horoscope to guide your day, you are just continuing this Baal worship that will be around until Revelation chapter 18 when this false religious system will finally fall.

**Revelation 18:2-3**
**2 And he cried mightily with a strong voice, saying, Babylon the great is fallen, is fallen, and is become the habitation of devils, and the hold of every foul spirit, and a cage of every unclean and hateful bird.**
**3 For all nations have drunk of the wine of the wrath of her fornication, and the kings of the earth have committed fornication with her, and the merchants of the earth are waxed rich through the abundance of her delicacies.**

And, yes, The Bible does acknowledge this woman and confirms her existence. She is the fallen Babylon in verse 2 above. She is also the mother of harlots, the great whore and the Mystery, Babylon the great, verse 1&5 below. This title is from mixing paganism with Christianity which was her act of adultery with the church. She is also the self-proclaimed queen of heaven, verse 19 below.

> **Revelation 17:1&5**
> **1 And there came one of the seven angels which had the seven vials, and talked with me, saying unto me, Come hither; I will shew unto thee the judgment of the great whore that sitteth upon many waters:**
> **5 And upon her forehead was a name written, MYSTERY, BABYLON THE GREAT, THE MOTHER OF HARLOTS AND ABOMINATIONS OF THE EARTH.**

> **Jeremiah 44:19**
> **19 And when we burned incense to the queen of heaven, and poured out drink offerings unto her, did we make her cakes to worship her, and pour out drink offerings unto her, without our men?**

If you think about it, this Babylonian mystery religion is the opposite of Jesus. Before Jesus was born into this world, He existed for all eternity past as God. He lowered Himself and came into this world as a child, but He grew up and He became a man and The Savior of all mankind. He was crucified and paid the price for our sin in the prime of His life after which He was raised as the firstborn from the dead and reclaimed His former glory in heaven. He will soon come back as The Reigning King over all the earth. This Babylonian self-proclaimed queen of heaven had a husband that was the reigning king of Babel first. Then he died in the prime of his life but was said to have risen into the sun and was merged with the sun god.

Therefore, he became the sun god joined with a human man, and after that, he was said to impregnate the mortal queen and come back in reincarnation as a child that this self-proclaimed queen of heaven claimed to be the Christ child. Throughout the ages, at least in the Roman version of this religion, he has remained a child with this mother/child cult that became this Babylonian mystery religion. And this self-proclaimed queen of heaven remained in control as ruler with the reincarnated king coming back as a child being just a figurehead to give power to the queen. That is why his birthday is celebrated every year as an infant. His birthday is all that honors him. He has no power as king anymore because it was transferred to his mother/wife/queen as Mother of Harlots. Even she will soon lose power as queen when Jesus returns and destroys her and her son and her false system of idol worship forever. Jesus left His childhood behind and became a man and is The King of all. His mother does not rule in His place using Him as a figurehead. Although, in the Roman religion, she does rule as Mary instead of the queen of heaven. But that is a false religion. Jesus actually rules all things Himself. He does not remain a child, so why make Him a child again every year? Why isn't his birthday celebrated as a Man and a King which He now is? He is alive right now and Is our Lord and Savior. If we are going to celebrate His birthday, wouldn't it make more sense to celebrate it with His current Self? Not acting like He Is still an infant. I can imagine Him saying, "hey, I am right here, I'm not that infant anymore. Can't you see Me? When you celebrate someone's birthday today, do you just ignore them and act like there not right there and celebrate them as an infant? NO! Then why do that to Jesus? So, to summarize up to now; a king of Babel at the time of the tower of Babel was suddenly killed. His death left his wife, the queen, without power. He was a very popular king and his wife, the queen, loved the power she had as queen but now supposed that she would lose power as queen because they would probably simply choose a new king. So, to keep power, she claimed that her husband, the king, ascended into the sun and joined with the sun god and became the sun god. The queen claimed that a green tree, probably an evergreen tree, grew out of a dead stump overnight where the king was buried to confirm his ascension into the sun as the sun god. The people were willing to accept this proclamation of the queen because of their grief over their beloved king's death. To have him back as a god was a way to keep him around. This happened at the time of the winter solstice celebration they called the birth of the new sun which was the shortest day of the year followed by the birth of longer days for the northern hemisphere. With this king who was proclaimed to have been resurrected into the sun as the sun god, and confirmed by a green tree that grew out of a dead stump; it was celebrated yearly using a green tree as a worship item commemorating the ascension of the king into the sun at the spot of the king's grave. They also exchanged gifts during this celebration. But the queen wasn't through yet; she later claimed that the sun god impregnated her with a divine child that she named Tammuz. She proclaimed him to be her dead husband, the king, who was now the sun god, reincarnated into that child. She also proclaimed the child to be the Christ child worthy to be worshiped. He would be born on December 25th at the end of the winter solstice celebration. But because she proclaimed him to also be her reincarnated dead husband, she married her own son which made her not only the queen of the kingdom again because the king was back reincarnated into this child, but also the queen of heaven because she was now married to the so-called divine christ, son of the sun god. So then, the celebration of the king being resurrected into the sun as the sun god at the winter solstice festival known as the birth of the new sun, also became the birthday celebration of Tammuz. Don't forget the day of this celebration is on December 25th which involved cutting down a green tree every year at that time, nailing boards on the bottom of it to stand it upright, and then decorating it. When God confounded their language and scattered them throughout the world, they took this tradition with them to the various places that they were scattered, and each year they cut a green tree out of the forest, nailed feet on the bottom it so it would stand upright to symbolize the tree that grew out of the dead stump, and it evolved into an elaborate celebration in which the tree was decked with silver and gold in honor of this sun god and his son, the so called christ child. Throughout history, in some cases, the queen made sure that this so called christ child remained a child and the queen retained her power as a civil and spiritual leader. Later when the Romans conquered the world, they adopted this pagan celebration in which Tammuz remained a child and they changed the name from the winter solstice festival to Saturnalia. In time, Constantine became emperor of Rome and he had an experience that convinced him to proclaim Rome as a Christian Empire. When this happened, all pagan celebrations were banned. But this action caused an uprising in the pagan population of the kingdom and a rebellion against the emperor, and even from the Roman citizens also that had grown to love the Saturnalia celebration that, by this time, was very popular. So as a compromise, he let them keep all their celebrations as long as they changed the names of the pagan gods involved to Christian names. This was an act of adultery by the emperor by accepting this great whore simply by a name change. So, Tammuz was renamed Jesus and the queen of heaven was renamed Mother Mary, and the celebration of Saturnalia was changed to Christmas, and the same thing happened to the other pagan celebration involved. Over time, a government run church was formed in Rome and these pagan celebrations renamed with Christian names were adopted by that church as Christian celebrations. This was an act of joining Christianity to paganism uniting Christianity with the great whore. This is described in Revelation as a mystery called Babylon the great because it resulted in the widespread creation of a false religious system in the world that claimed to be a Christian organization that is still here even to this day. These celebrations became mandatory by the Roman/government church for Christians to participate in and was punishable by death if you violated the order to take part in them. This started more than a thousand years of persecution from a false Christian church that would persecute the true Christian church in which an estimated 90 million true Christians were killed for not participating in the order to participate in these celebrations. Christianity was never meant to be mixed with a secular government because the church is governed by Jesus Christ Himself through The Holy Spirit. This unholy marriage of government and church and pagan celebrations was finally broken up in about the 16th century with the reformation led by Martin Luther and by the creation of translations of The Bible being made available to the general public in English. The true church was finally freed from these pagan influences in the church age of Philadelphia that we will talk more about in the next chapter of this book. But then in the next church age after that of Laodicea, that we will also see in chapter 5, something happened. The church began to celebrate these pagan festivals again on their own, this time without it being mandatory. These festivals were still led by the Roman church, but by then, they had no power to enforce a mandate on Christians like before because the Roman government had lost its power as a world Empire. Today, people have forgotten the history behind these festivals and have adopted these celebrations voluntarily into the church worldwide. Today, they are considered Christian holidays and most people don't even know the history behind them. That brings me to this book. To educate people of the history of these celebrations that includes Christmas. These celebrations are not and never have been Christian. Today, these pagan celebrations have been adopted as Christian all over the world. How people don't know about this fallacy is a mystery in itself. The evidence is abundantly clear in history. Anyone that wants to see it can easily find the truth with only a small amount of searching. I am not covering the other celebration involved (Easter) in this book. I am concentrating on the one called Christmas. But both of them are equally easy to find in history clearly showing them as pagan celebrations converted to Christian celebrations with very little change in the celebration itself other than changing the names of the pagan gods involved to Christian names.

# CHAPTER 5
# BUT THAT WAS THEN, AND THIS IS NOW! THE SEVEN CHURCHES

Many people say to me: "lighten up man, these are modern times. Things have changed since the medieval times, and the Christmas celebration has changed since the time it was a pagan celebration. All we're trying to do is honor Jesus a little extra at this time of year. It doesn't matter if it's not really His birthday. Anyway, it's the thought that counts, isn't it? It's a joyous and pleasant time of year. And besides all of that, the churches fill up on the week before Christmas, so we get a chance to witness to them while they are in church for that day. Everyone is thinking about Jesus this time of year so it's easier to be a one-on-one witness to someone that strikes up a conversation about Christmas. No one worships idols today. I think we can overlook the part of it that used to be idol worship. Besides, the Christmas celebration today is only similar to Saturnalia. There are differences. There is the stories of Joseph and Mary and what went on in Bethlehem and the story of the wise men. These two stories were never part of the Saturnalia celebration. And some of the scriptures you are giving are Old Testament, so that don't count for today." Did I cover all the excuses? probably most anyway. It doesn't matter how many excuses you can think of for celebrating Christmas. There would be only one viable one. And that is whether it is Biblically acceptable to do so or not. And I assure you; it's not. Even though parts of The true Biblical story of Jesus are used in the celebration; it is the mixture of the pagan story and The Biblical story that is unacceptable.

> **Deuteronomy 12:30-32**
> **30 Take heed to thyself that thou be not snared by following them, after that they be destroyed from before thee; and that thou inquire not after their gods, saying, How did these nations serve their gods? even so will I do likewise.**
> **31 Thou shalt not do so unto the Lord thy God: for every abomination to the Lord, which he hateth, have they done unto their gods; for even their sons and their daughters they have burnt in the fire to their gods.**
> **32 What thing soever I command you, observe to do it: thou shalt not add thereto, nor diminish from it.**

Verse 32 means do not add anything to God's Word that is not there, or don't take away from God's Word that is there. This is repeated in the New Testament in Revelation.

> **Revelation 22:18-19**
> **18 For I testify unto every man that heareth the words of the prophecy of this book, If any man shall add unto these things, God shall add unto him the plagues that are written in this book:**
> **19 And if any man shall take away from the words of the book of this prophecy, God shall take away his part out of the book of life, and out of the holy city, and from the things which are written in this book.**

But as far as the question of using Old Testament scripture; Well, all you have to do is read the New Testament Scripture in First Corinthians 10:6-15. It speaks for Itself.

**1 Corinthians 10:1-12**

**1 Moreover, brethren, I would not that ye should be ignorant, how that all our fathers were under the cloud, and all passed through the sea;**

**2 And were all baptized unto Moses in the cloud and in the sea;**

**3 And did all eat the same spiritual meat;**

**4 And did all drink the same spiritual drink: for they drank of that spiritual Rock that followed them: and that Rock was Christ.**

**5 But with many of them God was not well pleased: for they were overthrown in the wilderness.**

**6 Now these things were our examples, to the intent we should not lust after evil things, as they also lusted.**

**7 Neither be ye idolaters, as were some of them; as it is written, The people sat down to eat and drink, and rose up to play.**

**8 Neither let us commit fornication, as some of them committed, and fell in one day three and twenty thousand.**

**9 Neither let us tempt Christ, as some of them also tempted, and were destroyed of serpents.**

**10 Neither murmur ye, as some of them also murmured, and were destroyed of the destroyer.**

**11 Now all these things happened unto them for ensamples: and they are written for our admonition, upon whom the ends of the world are come.**

**12 Wherefore let him that thinketh he standeth take heed lest he fall.**

No, Christians are not under Old Testament law today. But we can use Old Testament scriptures that pertain to us today. Verse 11 is basically saying even though those things are from a past dispensation of time; they are still examples for us to learn from. Some churches today have begun to allow homosexuality as an acceptable Christian way of life, even accepting homosexual pastors and deacons. Abortion has also become accepted in some churches. There is a common practice to pass something off as acceptable on the bases that it is accepted by today's society and even the church. Many things are done this way. I have even had pastors try to turn it around and tell me that I ought to be careful because I'm working against The Lord, and that I'm causing contentions and divisions in the church. People accuse me of being with a well-known denomination that wears a white shirt and black pants that goes around knocking on your door to hand you a publication that they put out. It is well-known that this religion doesn't celebrate Christmas. They say I ought to be spending my time doing something more useful. They tell me that so much good comes from Christmas that how can it be bad? And anyone who speaks against it is seen as an extremist anyway. They tell me that I would be preventing all those people that come to church at Christmas from hearing the gospel. First of all, while, yes, that well-known denomination does not celebrate Christmas; but they have an even more serious problem than those that do celebrate it. They don't believe that Jesus is God. I could never associate myself with them in any way because of that fact. So, no, I am not, never have been and never will be associated with them in any way. And, let me be the first to tell you that idol worship does indeed apply to today; and it is talked about in The Word of God. As far as times changing; yes, Man changes with time; but not for the better. God doesn't change with the current fads. He is the same yesterday, today and forever.

**Hebrews 13:7-8**
**7 Remember them which have the rule over you, who have spoken unto you the word of God: whose faith follow, considering the end of their conversation.**
**8 Jesus Christ the same yesterday, and to day, and for ever.**

People just want to do things that they want to do, so they misinterpret The Bible to fit their agenda. So, they say that Christmas is not idol worship anymore because God has changed it to a Christian celebration. They say this so they can celebrate it with a clear conscious. But it is a false sense of security because God did not change it to a Christian celebration and you will not find in The Bible where He did.

There is another church called the church at Pergamos that thought the same way. It is talked about in Revelation 2:12-17. Now, if you will first, go back a little way to Revelation 1:4, you will see that there are seven churches in Asia mentioned here. And they are named in verse 11.

> **Revelation 1:4**
> **4 John to the seven churches which are in Asia: Grace be unto you, and peace, from him which is, and which was, and which is to come; and from the seven Spirits which are before his throne;**

> **Revelation 1:11**
> **11 Saying, I am Alpha and Omega, the first and the last: and, What thou seest, write in a book, and send it unto the seven churches which are in Asia; unto Ephesus, and unto Smyrna, and unto Pergamos, and unto Thyatira, and unto Sardis, and unto Philadelphia, and unto Laodicea.**

I could give you just the church age of Pergamos that pertains to the creation of Christmas, but I want to show you the whole picture of how these churches in Asia line up with history. Therefore, even though a lot of this gets off track of our subject, I feel it is important that you get a clear picture of how I came up with the conclusion of why Pergamos is historically connected directly to Christmas. These churches in Chapter 2 and 3 not only represent 7 churches at that time; but also represent present day churches as 7 types of churches that every church today exhibits the traits of one of these 7 churches described in Revelation. But the interesting thing is, they also represent 7 church ages that cover a 2000-year period of time since the beginning of the church in about 30 something AD until the end of the church age at the rapture of the church. And I believe the rapture of the church is very near. They represent 7 periods of time that coincide chronologically with events that happened in each of those churches as described in Revelation. This is explained in verse 19 below where it says: "hast seen", this is the past. Then: "things which are", which is the present. And finally: "things which shall be hereafter", clearly the future. It said in verse 4 above, that there are 7 Spirits. Each of these Spirits identify that church age and what sort of church each one is. And in my personal opinion, they also represent 7 types of Christians. Find out which church type you identify with.

> **Revelation 1:19-20**
> **19 Write the things which thou hast seen, and the things which are, and the things which shall be hereafter;**
> **20 The mystery of the seven stars which thou sawest in my right hand, and the seven golden candlesticks. The seven stars are the angels of the seven churches: and the seven candlesticks which thou sawest are the seven churches.**

In other words, there were 7 churches in Asia in the past that were real churches established at that time and were located in the 7 different places in verse 11 above. John wrote letters to each of these seven churches of that day. But verse 20 says there is a mystery with these seven churches. This remained a mystery until now. They could not have known this mystery at the time John had written these letters to these churches because the history of these church ages simply had not yet happened. But now we have the history that has happened over the last two thousand years of church ages to compare to what it said about these church ages. The chronological order of history seems to line up with situations that were described in each of these seven churches. I know there are theories where some Bible scholars describe this scenario. But that is not where I got this idea. I haven't read those other theories, but I have seen some of their arrangement of the dates of those church ages. I didn't base my arraignment of the dates on their writings. Some of their dates disagree with what I have come up with, but at least these other writings support the theory of this timeline of events that follow events in these 7 church ages. This is "the mystery of the seven stars" in verse 20, above. What is this mystery? We will see as I explain it in detail in this chapter. These were also 7 types of churches with different traits that identified the personality of that church. These 7 churches identify 7 personalities of churches even today. Every present-day church exhibits one of these personalities. All 7 types of these churches operate in the here and now all at the same time. The 7 churches that existed in the past are long gone. The 7 types of these churches always exist at the same time in the present no matter which present you are in. But the church ages have occurred chronologically over time starting from the beginning of the church to present day and will continue until the rapture of the church. In determining one church age to the next, you have to allow somewhat of an overlapping of the church age you are in while going to the next church age. History is the same way. You usually gradually go from one historical age to another. Jesus was about 33 ½ years old when He died on the cross and The Spirit of God raised Him from the dead, and the church was formed at that time which started this chronological timeframe of the church ages. Once a church age is over, like I said, with a possible short overlap into the next age, it will not exist in the time line again. It goes from one church age to the next with only one church age existing at a time until they end at the rapture of the church right after the last church age ends. And I believe we are close to the end of this chronological expression of these church ages. I don't know how much of a history buff you are; but these seven churches, in the order that they are in, in other words, their position in time or in chronological order, mentioned things that can be linked to events that took place at that time in the history of each church age in a space in time in the order that they are in. I believe it is quite obvious that we are in that last church age right now. These churches, and the dates that they represent in history are; Ephesus, 1st century AD. Smyrna, 2nd and 3rd century AD. Pergamos, 4th and 5th century AD. Thyatira, 6th thru 13th century AD. Sardis, 14th and 15th century AD. Philadelphia, 16th thru 19th century AD. And Laodicea, from the 20th century thru we can see it taking place right now. I based these dates on the extensive and exhaustive study I did myself of world history compared with what was said in Revelation about each one of these churches individually. I won't get into how to prove the historical placing of these different church ages because that much historical information would take a whole book by itself. Most theologians agree with me on this theory, but disagree with me on the dates. But I stand by my findings. This is not Bible fact that is provable; but it does have solid Biblical theological application. For our study on Christmas, we are going to take a close look at the third church age. The church at Pergamos. But. Like I said, so you will fully understand, I will give you a synopsis of all of them. They are:

# 1. Ephesus: 1st century AD starting at John 20 and Pentecost

**Revelation 2:1-7**

**1 Unto the angel of the church of Ephesus write; These things saith he that holdeth the seven stars in his right hand, who walketh in the midst of the seven golden candlesticks;**

**2 I know thy works, and thy labour, and thy patience, and how thou canst not bear them which are evil: and thou hast tried them which say they are apostles, and are not, and hast found them liars:**

**3 And hast borne, and hast patience, and for my name's sake hast laboured, and hast not fainted.**

**4 Nevertheless I have somewhat against thee, because thou hast left thy first love.**

**5 Remember therefore from whence thou art fallen, and repent, and do the first works; or else I will come unto thee quickly, and will remove thy candlestick out of his place, except thou repent.**

**6 But this thou hast, that thou hatest the deeds of the Nicolaitans, which I also hate.**

**7 He that hath an ear, let him hear what the Spirit saith unto the churches; To him that overcometh will I give to eat of the tree of life, which is in the midst of the paradise of God.**

Many people believe that the disciples received the Holy Spirit at Pentecost, therefore that is when the church began. This next passage says otherwise.

**John 20:21-22**

**21 Then said Jesus to them again, Peace be unto you: as my Father hath sent me, even so send I you.**

**22 And when he had said this, he breathed on them, and saith unto them, Receive ye the Holy Ghost:**

The disciples of Jesus received The Holy Spirit right here starting the church age. But actually, the church age started symbolically with Jesus being baptized by John as He went up straightway out of the water and The Spirit descended on Him like a dove which symbolized Him dying, then being raised from the dead when He went up straightway out of the water, and then The Holy Spirit descending on Him like a dove, symbolizing The Holy Spirit joining our spirit, raising us from the dead and coming to live in us in us at salvation after we die to this world and are born again into God's kingdom. But the physical church age began in John 20:21-22. When they received The Holy Spirit, they were sealed with that act and became the first church members of the 1st church age, verse 22 above.

**Matthew 3:16**
**16 And Jesus, when he was baptized, went up straightway out of the water: and, lo, the heavens were opened unto him, and he saw the Spirit of God descending like a dove, and lighting upon him:**

The 1st church age began in phases starting with the baptism of Jesus, showing symbolically how the Christian would receive The Holy Spirit, followed by His disciples receiving The Holy Spirit in John 20, above. Followed by the day of Pentecost, Acts chapter 2, when the Jews received The Holy Spirit, followed by those in Samaria receiving The Holy Spirit in Acts 8:17, followed by The Gentiles receiving The Holy Spirit the same way the Jews did, Acts 10:44, followed by the disciples of John the Baptist receive The Holy Spirit, Acts 19:6. That is the key to this church age; God living in you by you receiving The Holy Spirit into your life, giving you eternal life and direct communication with God Himself at that point. This had never happened before up to that point in time. Before that time, The Holy Spirit did not indwell and seal the believer like now. He spoke to men and filled men, but with the possible exception of the 144,000 Jews that are servants of God and are sealed by Him, as far as I can see, in The Bible, the privilege of God living in us and sealing us at salvation with His Spirit is exclusive to this church age and will be taken away at the end of this church age at the rapture of the church right before the tribulation starts.

**Revelation 7:3-4**
**3 Saying, Hurt not the earth, neither the sea, nor the trees, till we have sealed the servants of our God in their foreheads.**
**4 And I heard the number of them which were sealed: and there were sealed an hundred and forty and four thousand of all the tribes of the children of Israel.**

The Bible doesn't give us enough information about the millennial reign of Jesus to know if people that get saved during that time are sealed by The Holy Spirit upon receiving salvation at that time or not. As we said in John 20:22, the disciples got a head start on the church age to be able to usher it in at Pentecost and beyond. Then you had the newly formed church in competition with the Jewish priesthood and their animal sacrifice. Christian leaders seemingly posed some kind of threat to the religious hierarchy of Temple statuesque because of the new era of grace instead of animal sacrifice. The Jewish leadership was already in cahoots with the government. Herod the great, the Gentile king at the time Jesus was born, was called a king of the Jews. He died only a few years after the birth of Jesus at which time another Herod called Archelaus took his place, however he was only there a short time until another Herod took charge, but was never made king. He was Herod Antipas who was appointed as tetrarch. He was the Herod that was in charge when Jesus started His ministry when He was Baptized by John. Then Acts 12:1 is yet another Herod. His name was Herod Agrippa. But Herod the great took part in the renovation of the Jews second temple. Of course, Jesus is the only true King of the Jews, but back then, they served each other's purpose. Both the government and the religious Jews didn't want this new movement to gain ground. The Jewish priest joined forces with government authority to come against these Christians to try and stop this new belief before it spread too far to stop. Afterall, this new belief would do away with the Levitical Priesthood, animal sacrifice and the temple type of worship, not to mention those priests would be out of a job as priest.

**Hebrews 9:23-26**
**23 It was therefore necessary that the patterns of things in the heavens should be purified with these; but the heavenly things themselves with better sacrifices than these.**

**24** For Christ is not entered into the holy places made with hands, which are the figures of the true; but into heaven itself, now to appear in the presence of God for us:

**25** Nor yet that he should offer himself often, as the high priest entereth into the holy place every year with blood of others;

**26** For then must he often have suffered since the foundation of the world: but now once in the end of the world hath he appeared to put away sin by the sacrifice of himself.

Hebrews 10:5-12

**5** Wherefore when he cometh into the world, he saith, Sacrifice and offering thou wouldest not, but a body hast thou prepared me:

**6** In burnt offerings and sacrifices for sin thou hast had no pleasure.

**7** Then said I, Lo, I come (in the volume of the book it is written of me,) to do thy will, O God.

**8** Above when he said, Sacrifice and offering and burnt offerings and offering for sin thou wouldest not, neither hadst pleasure therein; which are offered by the law;

**9** Then said he, Lo, I come to do thy will, O God. He taketh away the first, that he may establish the second.

**10** By the which will we are sanctified through the offering of the body of Jesus Christ once for all.

**11** And every priest standeth daily ministering and offering oftentimes the same sacrifices, which can never take away sins:

**12** But this man, after he had offered one sacrifice for sins for ever, sat down on the right hand of God;

Acts 12:1-3

**1** Now about that time Herod the king stretched forth his hands to vex certain of the church.

**2** And he killed James the brother of John with the sword.

**3 And because he saw it pleased the Jews, he proceeded further to take Peter also. (Then were the days of unleavened bread.)**

This is what Saul, a Pharisee, who would later become Paul, was doing as a part of the Jews coming against Christians when Stephen, who was stoned to death for his faith and Saul was consenting unto his death.

**Acts 7:59-8:1**
**59 And they stoned Stephen, calling upon God, and saying, Lord Jesus, receive my spirit.**
**60 And he kneeled down, and cried with a loud voice, Lord, lay not this sin to their charge. And when he had said this, he fell asleep.**
**Ch 8:1 And Saul was consenting unto his death. And at that time there was a great persecution against the church which was at Jerusalem; and they were all scattered abroad throughout the regions of Judaea and Samaria, except the apostles.**

Just like Saul was consenting unto Stephen's death; this is what a lot of church leaders do today when they are consenting to some of the ungodly things that many churches take part in today. So, this first church age was a time Christians were persecuted by Rome and the religious Jews. Of course. Saul was converted and his name was changed to Paul and he served Jesus after that. It is during this church age that God turned away from the Jews and turned to the Gentiles in which Paul became an apostle out of time to the Gentiles.

**1 Corinthians 15:8**
**8 And last of all he was seen of me also, as of one born out of due time.**

This is a time before the canon of scripture was completed. As a result, there was opportunity for those to come in and corrupt the true Word. "Them which say they are apostles, and are not", verse 2. People, even today, still try to corrupt The true Word. But the difference today is, we have The completed Word that we can check out everything someone is saying to see if it lines up with that Word. But at that time, they couldn't be sure if what they were hearing was of God or some false teacher trying to make a name for himself. That's why there were temporary sign gifts in operation at that time given by God to certain Christians in this first church age to confirm The true Word He was giving to them.

> **Acts 14:3**
> **3 Long time therefore abode they speaking boldly in the Lord, which gave testimony unto the word of his grace, and granted signs and wonders to be done by their hands.**

> **Acts 2:22**
> **22 Ye men of Israel, hear these words; Jesus of Nazareth, a man approved of God among you by miracles and wonders and signs, which God did by him in the midst of you, as ye yourselves also know:**

He chose to exhibit these signs through Himself and through those He sent to establish new revelation from Him to confirm The Word that was given to them. But later, some of these sign gifts began to be abused and even faked by some that sought after the gift more than they sought after the truth, Revelation 2:2. Paul had to rebuke them for this practice.

> **Matthew 10:1**
> **1 And when he had called unto him his twelve disciples, he gave them power against unclean spirits, to cast them out, and to heal all manner of sickness and all manner of disease.**

Mark 16:15-20

15 And he said unto them, Go ye into all the world, and preach the gospel to every creature.

16 He that believeth and is baptized shall be saved; but he that believeth not shall be damned.

17 And these signs shall follow them that believe; In my name shall they cast out devils; they shall speak with new tongues;

18 They shall take up serpents; and if they drink any deadly thing, it shall not hurt them; they shall lay hands on the sick, and they shall recover.

19 So then after the Lord had spoken unto them, he was received up into heaven, and sat on the right hand of God.

20 And they went forth, and preached everywhere, the Lord working with them, and confirming the word with signs following. Amen.

1 Corinthians 12:31-13:2

31 But covet earnestly the best gifts: and yet shew I unto you a more excellent way.

Ch 13:1 Though I speak with the tongues of men and of angels, and have not charity, I am become as sounding brass, or a tinkling cymbal.

2 And though I have the gift of prophecy, and understand all mysteries, and all knowledge; and though I have all faith, so that I could remove mountains, and have not charity, I am nothing.

1 Corinthians 14:9-12

9 So likewise ye, except ye utter by the tongue words easy to be understood, how shall it be known what is spoken? for ye shall speak into the air.

10 There are, it may be, so many kinds of voices in the world, and none of them is without signification.

**11 Therefore if I know not the meaning of the voice, I shall be unto him that speaketh a barbarian, and he that speaketh shall be a barbarian unto me.**

**12 Even so ye, forasmuch as ye are zealous of spiritual gifts, seek that ye may excel to the edifying of the church.**

**Hebrews 2:3-4**

**3 How shall we escape, if we neglect so great salvation; which at the first began to be spoken by the Lord, and was confirmed unto us by them that heard him;**

**4 God also bearing them witness, both with signs and wonders, and with divers miracles, and gifts of the Holy Ghost, according to his own will?**

Many wanted to be seen as having a special gift from God more than they wanted to spread the truth. They would abuse the gifts using them to edify themselves instead of edifying the church. That is what happened with Simon the sorcerer, when he wanted to buy the power of The Holy Spirit.

**Acts 8:18-20**

**18 And when Simon saw that through laying on of the apostles' hands the Holy Ghost was given, he offered them money,**

**19 Saying, Give me also this power, that on whomsoever I lay hands, he may receive the Holy Ghost.**

**20 But Peter said unto him, Thy money perish with thee, because thou hast thought that the gift of God may be purchased with money.**

**1 Corinthians 14:12**

**12 Even so ye, forasmuch as ye are zealous of spiritual gifts, seek that ye may excel to the edifying of the church.**

**1 Corinthians 14:4**
**4 He that speaketh in an unknown tongue edifieth himself;**
**but he that prophesieth edifieth the church.**

Selfish motives always cancel out love. That's how they left their first love, as stated in verse 4. This kind of church can be found today when a person, church or pastor, gets more overzealous about their gifts, or cares more for a position in the church than for helping those that can benefit from that gift or that position. There are those that let their position go to their head and think too highly of themselves and they pound their authority over everyone's head and forget to express the love of Jesus in their presentation. I guess they forgot what Jesus said that he who wants to be great among you shall be your minister and whosoever of you will be the chiefest shall be servant of all.

**Mark 10:43-44**
**43 But so shall it not be among you: but whosoever will be great among you, shall be your minister:**
**44 And whosoever of you will be the chiefest, shall be servant of all.**

The church age of Ephesus was full of good works, and labor, and patience, and they hated evil, verse 2. But they left their first love. The church at Corinth fits that description. During this age, the church began to be divided and started splitting into different groups gathering with their preferred teachings.

**1 Corinthians 1:10-13**
**10 Now I beseech you, brethren, by the name of our Lord Jesus Christ, that ye all speak the same thing, and that there be no divisions among you; but that ye be perfectly joined together in the same mind and in the same judgment.**

**11 For it hath been declared unto me of you, my brethren, by them which are of the house of Chloe, that there are contentions among you.**
**12 Now this I say, that every one of you saith, I am of Paul; and I of Apollos; and I of Cephas; and I of Christ.**
**13 Is Christ divided? was Paul crucified for you? or were ye baptized in the name of Paul?**

You can clearly see this type of church today with all the different denominations of different beliefs. They were not united in Christ. And it's the same way today when we think we have a better way than the church down the street. This division is typical of man thinking he knows better than God because all we have to do is line up with The Word of God and just agree with what It says. This division has grown worse through the years until now we have nothing but division. But at Ephesus, with this division in the church, along with the persecution from the government and from the religious Jews; not to mention sin showing up in the church; they began to be in turmoil. The Lord is telling them to repent or He will remove their candle stick out of his place, verse 5. Also, during this church age, the friendship between the Jews and the government didn't last. The Jews finally rebelled against the government because the government wanted them to submit to their idol worship and decided to crack down on them. The Jews were declared noncitizens. The world just can't help themselves. They hate anything that pertains to God. As a result, the Romans led by Titus destroyed their temple about 70 AD. Some say that this event marks the end of the 69th week talked about in Daniel with the 70th week to resume during the soon to come tribulation.

**Daniel 9:24-27**
**24 Seventy weeks are determined upon thy people and upon thy holy city, to finish the transgression, and to make an end of sins, and to make reconciliation for iniquity, and**

to bring in everlasting righteousness, and to seal up the vision and prophecy, and to anoint the most Holy.

25 Know therefore and understand, that from the going forth of the commandment to restore and to build Jerusalem unto the Messiah the Prince shall be seven weeks, and threescore and two weeks: the street shall be built again, and the wall, even in troublous times.

26 And after threescore and two weeks shall Messiah be cut off, but not for himself: and the people of the prince that shall come shall destroy the city and the sanctuary; and the end thereof shall be with a flood, and unto the end of the war desolations are determined.

27 And he shall confirm the covenant with many for one week: and in the midst of the week he shall cause the sacrifice and the oblation to cease, and for the overspreading of abominations he shall make it desolate, even until the consummation, and that determined shall be poured upon the desolate.

It was the end of temple animal sacrifice for the Jews even to this day. Then immorality began to creep into the church.

1 Corinthians 5:1-5

1 It is reported commonly that there is fornication among you, and such fornication as is not so much as named among the Gentiles, that one should have his father's wife.

2 And ye are puffed up, and have not rather mourned, that he that hath done this deed might be taken away from among you.

3 For I verily, as absent in body, but present in spirit, have judged already, as though I were present, concerning him that hath so done this deed,

4 In the name of our Lord Jesus Christ, when ye are gathered together, and my spirit, with the power of our Lord Jesus Christ,

**5 To deliver such an one unto Satan for the destruction of the flesh, that the spirit may be saved in the day of the Lord Jesus.**

We can see this in the church today when Christians go ahead and sin, taking advantage of the Grace of God, not realizing that such behavior can lead to their death, verse 3-5 above. Paul had to discipline the Corinthian church more than once. As we said, they were beginning to put position, their gifts and freedom in Christ before love.

**1 Corinthians 6:10**
**12 All things are lawful unto me, but all things are not expedient: all things are lawful for me, but I will not be brought under the power of any.**

**1 Corinthians 13:1-3**
**1 Though I speak with the tongues of men and of angels, and have not charity, I am become as sounding brass, or a tinkling cymbal.**
**2 And though I have the gift of prophecy, and understand all mysteries, and all knowledge; and though I have all faith, so that I could remove mountains, and have not charity, I am nothing.**
**3 And though I bestow all my goods to feed the poor, and though I give my body to be burned, and have not charity, it profiteth me nothing.**

And today; this can often be the case of a new Christian not yet rooted in Christ, being easily carried off into self-absorption and strange doctrines by some feel good preacher that caters to their itching ears with a feel-good motivational sermon that is all motivation and very little Biblical substance. There are many preachers like that today that are afraid if they offend someone, that they will leave the church, so the truth is left out or exchanged for a lie in the interest of keeping everyone happy.

> **2 Timothy 4:2-4**
> **2 Preach the word; be instant in season, out of season; reprove, rebuke, exhort with all longsuffering and doctrine.**
> **3 For the time will come when they will not endure sound doctrine; but after their own lusts shall they heap to themselves teachers, having itching ears;**
> **4 And they shall turn away their ears from the truth, and shall be turned unto fables.**

A new Christian really has to learn how to not be offended by the truth of God and to be on his toes to put on love and not worry so much about how he can exalt himself in the gift God has given him, but rather how he can use that gift to help others in love.

> **1 Corinthians 4:20-21**
> **20 For the kingdom of God is not in word, but in power.**
> **21 What will ye? shall I come unto you with a rod, or in love, and in the spirit of meekness?**

> **1 Corinthians 8:1-3**
> **1 Now as touching things offered unto idols, we know that we all have knowledge. Knowledge puffeth up, but charity edifieth.**
> **2 And if any man think that he knoweth anything, he knoweth nothing yet as he ought to know.**
> **3 But if any man love God, the same is known of him.**

You must stay focused on Jesus and not your own feelings or the things and ambitions connected to your position in the church or your power and influence in this world system.

Colossians 3:1-17

1 If ye then be risen with Christ, seek those things which are above, where Christ sitteth on the right hand of God.

2 Set your affection on things above, not on things on the earth.

3 For ye are dead, and your life is hid with Christ in God.

4 When Christ, who is our life, shall appear, then shall ye also appear with him in glory.

5 Mortify therefore your members which are upon the earth; fornication, uncleanness, inordinate affection, evil concupiscence, and covetousness, which is idolatry:

6 For which things' sake the wrath of God cometh on the children of disobedience:

7 In the which ye also walked some time, when ye lived in them.

8 But now ye also put off all these; anger, wrath, malice, blasphemy, filthy communication out of your mouth.

9 Lie not one to another, seeing that ye have put off the old man with his deeds;

10 And have put on the new man, which is renewed in knowledge after the image of him that created him:

11 Where there is neither Greek nor Jew, circumcision nor uncircumcision, Barbarian, Scythian, bond nor free: but Christ is all, and in all.

12 Put on therefore, as the elect of God, holy and beloved, bowels of mercies, kindness, humbleness of mind, meekness, longsuffering;

13 Forbearing one another, and forgiving one another, if any man have a quarrel against any: even as Christ forgave you, so also do ye.

14 And above all these things put on charity, which is the bond of perfectness.

15 And let the peace of God rule in your hearts, to the which also ye are called in one body; and be ye thankful.

**16 Let the word of Christ dwell in you richly in all wisdom; teaching and admonishing one another in psalms and hymns and spiritual songs, singing with grace in your hearts to the Lord.**

**17 And whatsoever ye do in word or deed, do all in the name of the Lord Jesus, giving thanks to God and the Father by him.**

Stay grounded in The Word and be armed with the full armor of God.

**Ephesians 6:12-18**

**12 For we wrestle not against flesh and blood, but against principalities, against powers, against the rulers of the darkness of this world, against spiritual wickedness in high places.**

**13 Wherefore take unto you the whole armour of God, that ye may be able to withstand in the evil day, and having done all, to stand.**

**14 Stand therefore, having your loins girt about with truth, and having on the breastplate of righteousness;**

**15 And your feet shod with the preparation of the gospel of peace;**

**16 Above all, taking the shield of faith, wherewith ye shall be able to quench all the fiery darts of the wicked.**

**17 And take the helmet of salvation, and the sword of the Spirit, which is the word of God:**

**18 Praying always with all prayer and supplication in the Spirit, and watching thereunto with all perseverance and supplication for all saints;**

Otherwise, unfriendly forces could move in to hold hostage your mind and will.

**Ephesians 4:11-16**

**11 And he gave some, apostles; and some, prophets; and some, evangelists; and some, pastors and teachers;**

**12 For the perfecting of the saints, for the work of the ministry, for the edifying of the body of Christ:**

**13 Till we all come in the unity of the faith, and of the knowledge of the Son of God, unto a perfect man, unto the measure of the stature of the fulness of Christ:**

**14 That we henceforth be no more children, tossed to and fro, and carried about with every wind of doctrine, by the sleight of men, and cunning craftiness, whereby they lie in wait to deceive;**

**15 But speaking the truth in love, may grow up into him in all things, which is the head, even Christ:**

**16 From whom the whole body fitly joined together and compacted by that which every joint supplieth, according to the effectual working in the measure of every part, maketh increase of the body unto the edifying of itself in love.**

The type of church we learn from this 1st church age is to have a balance between love and sound doctrine. A lesson to pastors is to prove what is sound doctrine with The Word. Your opinion is not good enough in this. Then, even when you have sound doctrine proven by The Word of God, don't pound that doctrine over the heads of the people. It is your responsibility to enlighten them, not force them into submission. You are not a boss that threatens your employees with your authority. You are an equal member of the body of Christ with your particular gift of revealing the truth to the fellow members and to the lost. It's not your responsibility to straighten that person out. That is what God does. You are supposed to teach that person with love, not with a hammer over his head. Yes, you have a responsibility to exercise discipline and to keep sin or false doctrine from entering the church. But it must be done in love. Your gift as a leader is not supposed to be used to exalt yourself. It is supposed to be used to teach and exalt the church as a whole.

# 2. Smyrna: 2ⁿᵈ and 3ʳᵈ century AD.

**Revelation 2:8-11**
**8 And unto the angel of the church in Smyrna write; These things saith the first and the last, which was dead, and is alive;**
**9 I know thy works, and tribulation, and poverty, (but thou art rich) and I know the blasphemy of them which say they are Jews, and are not, but are the synagogue of Satan.**
**10 Fear none of those things which thou shalt suffer: behold, the devil shall cast some of you into prison, that ye may be tried; and ye shall have tribulation ten days: be thou faithful unto death, and I will give thee a crown of life.**
**11 He that hath an ear, let him hear what the Spirit saith unto the churches; He that overcometh shall not be hurt of the second death.**

This is the first of only two church ages that The Lord has nothing bad to say about. It is interesting that this is the second church age, and the other church age that The Lord has nothing bad to say about is the second from the last. I'm not saying that means anything. It's just interesting. In This 2ⁿᵈ church age was an attempt by the devil to get rid of the church through martyrdom. But it only served to strengthen them. Jewish leaders rebelled against the Roman authority. As a result, like we said in the last church age, the Jewish temple was destroyed around 70 AD. Then, with the Jews out of the way, the government of Rome began to come down hard on the church and even kill everyone that associated themselves with it. The apostles were all gone, and the non-Christian Jews were in turmoil. There was spiritual deception from some that said they were Jews, but were really of the synagogue of Satan, verse 9. But, in this church age, even with heavy persecution, they remained faithful. In your history books, this age starts about the second century AD and continues through the time of Diocletian, a ruler of Rome, just before the age of Pergamos. This church was heavily persecuted, verse 10. Today this relates to a Christian that the new has worn off of his Christianity and persecution and ridicule begins to set in. All was good when it was new, but now it is no fun anymore. This is where a lot of people that were not serious about salvation, but only wanted to escape hell, fall away. They were not serious about giving their whole heart to Jesus therefore they do not have the endurance of a true Christian. They say: "this ain't worth it. I didn't sign up for this kind of harassment in my life". So, they are the dog that returns to its vomit, verse 22 below. This could give us a clue why this was a church age that God had nothing bad to say about it. There were not many pretend Christians in this church age because of the severe persecution of the church. Not many people were willing to risk their life by claiming to be a Christian unless they were actually a true Christian. Therefore, there were not a lot of pretenders there to influence disobedience in the church. This harassment is especially prevalent today with the increasing hostility to anyone that expresses Christian values. Even here in the United States, Christians are accused of being haters, narrow minded and intolerant because of our Christian beliefs spelled out plainly in The Bible; and because we believe Jesus is the only way to salvation. But unlike this church age of Smyrna, people today that are not really saved stay in the church and create havoc within the church because there is no threat to their life for them to be a pretend Christian. They want to feel justified by going to church but don't want the commitment of being a true Christian. There are still today places that will kill you for being a Christian, but here in the U.S. and many other free countries, you will probably face persecution, but not to the point of death.

**2 Peter 2:20-22**

**20 For if after they have escaped the pollutions of the world through the knowledge of the Lord and Saviour Jesus Christ, they are again entangled therein, and overcome, the latter end is worse with them than the beginning.**

**21 For it had been better for them not to have known the way of righteousness, than, after they have known it, to turn from the holy commandment delivered unto them.**

**22 But it is happened unto them according to the true proverb, The dog is turned to his own vomit again; and the sow that was washed to her wallowing in the mire.**

In this age, he that overcomes is the true Christian that will stay faithful trough this trying time and he will not be hurt of the second death, verse 10. Christianity will spread across the world at an unstoppable rate because of the persecution and killing of martyrs in the church at Smyrna which, at that church age, only served to make them more determined with The Holy Spirit giving them the strength to endure and also relying on the grace, hope and assurance from The Lord in the midst of their persecution. I personally believe that God gave these gallant Christians enough extra grace to deal with the death and persecution at a time of seemingly hopelessness and despair. They endured such hardship and remained faithful to the end. Even today, there are those that say they are Christians, but are not. Most of these usually fall away when they are exposed to any persecution because they don't have The Holy Spirit to sustain them. They also cannot understand spiritual things because they are carnal. So, a separation takes place, weeding out the bad element leaving you with true Christians. I'm not saying forget the bad element. We must witness to them and try to get them to see the truth and get saved. But they must not be allowed to deceive true Christians or introduce false doctrine in the church.

**Ephesians 4:14-15**
**14 That we henceforth be no more children, tossed to and fro, and carried about with every wind of doctrine, by the sleight of men, and cunning craftiness, whereby they lie in wait to deceive;**
**15 But speaking the truth in love, may grow up into him in all things, which is the head, even Christ:**

**Ephesians 6:12**
**12 For we wrestle not against flesh and blood, but against principalities, against powers, against the rulers of the darkness of this world, against spiritual wickedness in high places.**

This persecution and time of martyrdom separated the true believers from the fake, and only served to give Christians something to fight for. That can happen to a church today, especially in this day of the government interfering with sacred institutions like marriage and beliefs on homosexuality and the sanctity of life before birth. As in every church age, there are still countries in the world that will kill you for being a Christian. A few years into the next church age; in about 306 AD; along came Constantine. But before him were ten emperors that persecuted the church very severely. This could be the ten days talked about in verse10:

> **Revelation 2:10**
> **10 Fear none of those things which thou shalt suffer: behold, the devil shall cast some of you into prison, that ye may be tried; and ye shall have tribulation ten days: be thou faithful unto death, and I will give thee a crown of life.**

And thus, is likened unto the tribulation a Christian must go through after the new wears off of his conversion. Suddenly you realize that no one in the world cares about your conversion, and you are shunned by the world. It's at this point that a dividing occurs. A true believer will remain faithful, and the pretend Christian will fall away or enter some cult or false teaching. No, they didn't lose their salvation, but some that leave were never saved in the first place or they wouldn't have left.

**1 John 2:19**
**19 They went out from us, but they were not of us; for if they had been of us, they would no doubt have continued with us: but they went out, that they might be made manifest that they were not all of us.**

**2 Timothy 4:9-10**
**9 Do thy diligence to come shortly unto me:**
**10 For Demas hath forsaken me, having loved this present world, and is departed unto Thessalonica; Crescens to Galatia, Titus unto Dalmatia.**

This is where a lot of cults and false religions get their members, because they offer an alternative to give them what they want out of religion. But it is a false sense of hope without the true conversion to a new life for true Christianity with its obedience to The Bible emphasized. And make no mistake; even though we do have security after salvation and will never lose it; there is still a requirement for obedience from us in order to avoid other kinds of trouble in our life, or to receive blessings and answered prayer and to have a long and full life and achieving the desires of our hearts and to build reward to go toward your standing at the Judgement Seat of Christ and your position in the kingdom.

**Psalms 37:4-5**
**4 Delight thyself also in the Lord; and he shall give thee the desires of thine heart.**
**5 Commit thy way unto the Lord; trust also in him; and he shall bring it to pass.**

**1 Corinthians 3:8**
8 Now he that planteth and he that watereth are one: and every man shall receive his own reward according to his own labour.

**1 Corinthians 3:11-15**
11 For other foundation can no man lay than that is laid, which is Jesus Christ.
12 Now if any man build upon this foundation gold, silver, precious stones, wood, hay, stubble;
13 Every man's work shall be made manifest: for the day shall declare it, because it shall be revealed by fire; and the fire shall try every man's work of what sort it is.
14 If any man's work abide which he hath built thereupon, he shall receive a reward.
15 If any man's work shall be burned, he shall suffer loss: but he himself shall be saved; yet so as by fire.

**Revelation 22:12**
12 And, behold, I come quickly; and my reward is with me, to give every man according as his work shall be.

**1 Corinthians 11:29-31**
29 For he that eateth and drinketh unworthily, eateth and drinketh damnation to himself, not discerning the Lord's body.
30 For this cause many are weak and sickly among you, and many sleep.
31 For if we would judge ourselves, we should not be judged.

The type of person that relates to this church age is that if you are truly saved, persecution will not turn you away from your faith or your mission. Indeed, it will empower and strengthen you instead. And this type of church will not accept a trend such as abortion or homosexuality in the church no matter how much persecution they must endure. Yet they do accept people like that who want to change. They accept the sinner, just not the sin. Just a side note: please don't think I am picking on homosexuals or people that have had an abortion in this book. Sin is sin, and we are all sinners no matter what your sin is, and we are all saved by the grace of God from our sin whether your sin is homosexuality, abortion, adultery, lying, steeling, coveting. Gossip, or any other sin. But the trouble with homosexuality and abortion is that most of the world and even much of the church today are trying to say that those are not sin but acceptable lifestyles. So, while I am not picking on the sinner, I am pointing out sin that we should, as Christians, stand against and turn away from. You have never sinned so much that God cannot save you. But you can't get rid of the sin on your own. Turn to Jesus today and let Him send you The Holy Spirit who has the power to change your life and help you to turn away from all sin.

# 3. The Church at Pergamos 4th and 5th century AD.

This brings us to our subject; Christmas, which was brought into the church through the church age of Pergamos and was clearly of pagan origin.

> **Revelation 2:12-17**
> **12 And to the angel of the church in Pergamos write; These things saith he which hath the sharp sword with two edges;**
> **13 I know thy works, and where thou dwellest, even where Satan's seat is: and thou holdest fast my name, and hast not denied my faith, even in those days wherein Antipas was my faithful martyr, who was slain among you, where Satan dwelleth.**
> **14 But I have a few things against thee, because thou hast there them that hold the doctrine of Balaam, who taught**

**Balac to cast a stumblingblock before the children of Israel, to eat things sacrificed unto idols, and to commit fornication.**

**15 So hast thou also them that hold the doctrine of the Nicolaitans, which thing I hate.**

**16 Repent; or else I will come unto thee quickly, and will fight against them with the sword of my mouth.**

**17 He that hath an ear, let him hear what the Spirit saith unto the churches; To him that overcometh will I give to eat of the hidden manna, and will give him a white stone, and in the stone a new name written, which no man knoweth saving he that receiveth it.**

This is the church age that this book is about. As we touched on already, in 306 AD, A ruler named Constantine came on the scene and became the emperor of Rome. He continued the persecution of the church like the emperors before him. Then one day, about 324 AD, he was about to enter into a critical battle that he was outnumbered and outgunned. Well, actually, they didn't have guns back then, but you know what I mean. Suddenly, he had a vision of an X with (By This Conquer) written under it. He took this as a vision from God and that it meant that he should put an X on the shields of all his soldiers. The X is the Greek symbol for Ch which means Christ. That is why many times Christmas is shortened to Xmas. So, he took this vision to mean that Christ was telling him to do this. He was not a believer in Jesus, and he was a great persecutor of those that worshiped Jesus. But this vision apparently made a big enough impact on him that he put that X on every soldier's shield and made that symbol the theme of the battle. Miraculously, he won the battle. This was the the 4th century AD; the time in history that fit's the church age of Pergamos. The church was located where Satan dwells, verse 13. In fact, at this time, this city was the capitol of paganism, and the doctrines of Balaam and the Nicolaitans were set up in that environment, verse 14 and 15. With his miraculous victory; Constantine reasoned in his mind that this was a sign that he was supposed to proclaim Christianity for everyone in Rome. In doing so, he began the process of marrying the government to the church. Christianity was adopted by the Empire. But it ended up being the Empire's version of Christianity, not The Bible's. Out of this, later, the Roman government and Christianity joined forces and grew into a government/church combo with the Roman Empire running the Church. Later a high position of dictatorship was created out of this which became known as the Pope. We have only one dictator in Christianity, and that is Jesus. And he is a righteous dictator. He is the head of the church and the church is subject only to Him. In this verse in Ephesians, below, the church is subject to Jesus just as a wife is subject, in everything, to her husband. I know the liberal/ progressives of today don't like this scripture, but God didn't ask the liberal or progressives if it was okay to put it in His Bible.

**Ephesians 5:23-24**
**23 For the husband is the head of the wife, even as Christ is the head of the church: and he is the saviour of the body. 24 Therefore as the church is subject unto Christ, so let the wives be to their own husbands in every thing.**

But when this happened with Constantine, everyone in Rome was proclaimed to be a Christian by law and all pagan activities became illegal. Pagan idol worship was widespread and very popular. A lot of Christians were happy about this because it meant the end of the persecution of the church; or at least, so they thought. On the other side, this new law sparked an uprising of protest from the pagan populace. Their pagan festivals were very popular and had been tradition for more than 2000 years. The people were not going to accept this new law without a huge uprising against this new Roman law. This concerned officials that they would lose control of such a large group of people which would complicate their leadership in Rome. So, they came up with a compromise to appease them; thus, paving the way for the name changes of their pagan gods. In other words; it became illegal to worship the pagan god Tammuz; but if you changed his name to Jesus instead of Tammuz, it was permitted. They allowed the celebration of these pagan festivals on one condition; they must change the names of these pagan gods and their celebrations to Christian names. They could keep everything else the same but only change the names to Christian names. Over time, a few Biblical details were added to these celebrations just to make them seem more legitimate. And, of course, one of these pagan festivals was Saturnalia, which was a celebration of the birth of a false Christ named Tammuz. Saturnalia suddenly became Christmas. And the object of that celebration, the December 25th birth of the false Christ named Tammuz, became known as the birthday of Jesus. Some Biblical details were mixed in like the manger scene in Bethlehem, the wise men and a few other details about what happened then. When the name changes of these festivals occurred, it threw the church into a division. Some went along with the change because it meant the end of persecution and death for them as Christians. But in doing so, it set up a scenario for a false conversion. Suddenly it was popular to be a Christian. People were Christians because the emperor said so, not because of a heart change. This drove true believers away from this government-controlled religion and set up yet another era of persecution that would last through the dark ages in which millions of Christians would be killed for not partaking in the government-controlled religion of false Christianity. Some Christians protested because they felt it compromised the purity of the church to allow pagan influence in, even under Christian names. This led to the church persecuting the church, so to speak. Only it was the false government church persecuting the true Christian church. It was like the government saying: okay, you can worship Jesus, but you must do it our way. And this was unacceptable to the true church. So, it was still the government persecuting the church; only trying to justify their action by saying that these true Christians were heretics because they undermined the government religion. This eventually evolved into the dark ages which started the worst persecution in the history of the church. And it ushered in the ages of Thyatira and Sardis, where multiple millions of faithful Christians were murdered for their faith. Now tell me, do you still want to take part in a celebration that was created by a government that killed more than 90 million Christians because these true Christians wouldn't worship Jesus according to their dictates? So, you ask, how does all of this tie in with the church age of Pergamos? This marriage of the Church to paganism is known as the doctrine of Balaam, verse 14. Remember, as the doctrine of Balaam bears out in Numbers 22; Balak, the king of Moab, wanted the prophet Balaam to put a curse on Israel, and he couldn't because Israel was blessed of God. So, in Numbers 25:1-9, at the council of Balaam, Balak made friends with Israel, then sent the daughters of Moab into the camp of Israel so that they might cause the men of Israel to commit whoredom with them. And they did. And in doing so, they brought a curse on themselves. There is too much scripture to put the whole story in this book. I will give you the highlights. You can read the entire story in Numbers chapter 22 through chapter 25.

**Numbers 22:1-7**

**1 And the children of Israel set forward, and pitched in the plains of Moab on this side Jordan by Jericho.**

**2 And Balak the son of Zippor saw all that Israel had done to the Amorites.**

**3 And Moab was sore afraid of the people, because they were many: and Moab was distressed because of the children of Israel.**

**4 And Moab said unto the elders of Midian, Now shall this company lick up all that are round about us, as the ox licketh up the grass of the field. And Balak the son of Zippor was king of the Moabites at that time.**

**5 He sent messengers therefore unto Balaam the son of Beor to Pethor, which is by the river of the land of the children of his people, to call him, saying, Behold, there is**

a people come out from Egypt: behold, they cover the face of the earth, and they abide over against me:

6 Come now therefore, I pray thee, curse me this people; for they are too mighty for me: peradventure I shall prevail, that we may smite them, and that I may drive them out of the land: for I wot that he whom thou blessest is blessed, and he whom thou cursest is cursed.

7 And the elders of Moab and the elders of Midian departed with the rewards of divination in their hand; and they came unto Balaam, and spake unto him the words of Balak.

### Numbers 22:12

12 And God said unto Balaam, Thou shalt not go with them; thou shalt not curse the people: for they are blessed.

### Numbers 31:16

16 Behold, these caused the children of Israel, through the counsel of Balaam, to commit trespass against the Lord in the matter of Peor, and there was a plague among the congregation of the Lord.

### Numbers 25:1-9

1 And Israel abode in Shittim, and the people began to commit whoredom with the daughters of Moab.

2 And they called the people unto the sacrifices of their gods: and the people did eat, and bowed down to their gods.

3 And Israel joined himself unto Baal-peor: and the anger of the Lord was kindled against Israel.

4 And the Lord said unto Moses, Take all the heads of the people, and hang them up before the Lord against the sun, that the fierce anger of the Lord may be turned away from Israel.

5 And Moses said unto the judges of Israel, Slay ye every one his men that were joined unto Baal-peor.

**6 And, behold, one of the children of Israel came and brought unto his brethren a Midianitish woman in the sight of Moses, and in the sight of all the congregation of the children of Israel, who were weeping before the door of the tabernacle of the congregation.**

**7 And when Phinehas, the son of Eleazar, the son of Aaron the priest, saw it, he rose up from among the congregation, and took a javelin in his hand;**

**8 And he went after the man of Israel into the tent, and thrust both of them through, the man of Israel, and the woman through her belly. So the plague was stayed from the children of Israel.**

**9 And those that died in the plague were twenty and four thousand.**

Not only was Israel commanded to stay pure as a nation, or a race, as it were; it was against the law for an Israelite to take a pagan or idol worshiping wife or lay with them, see above scripture. Israel was related to the Moabites through Lot. Moab was the son of Lot. But the Jewish line came through Abraham, not Lot.

**1 Kings 11:1-2**

**1 But king Solomon loved many strange women, together with the daughter of Pharaoh, women of the Moabites, Ammonites, Edomites, Zidonians, and Hittites;**

**2 Of the nations concerning which the Lord said unto the children of Israel, Ye shall not go in to them, neither shall they come in unto you: for surely they will turn away your heart after their gods: Solomon clave unto these in love.**

**Ezra 9:1-2**

**1 Now when these things were done, the princes came to me, saying, The people of Israel, and the priests, and the Levites, have not separated themselves from the people of the lands, doing according to their abominations,**

> **even of the Canaanites, the Hittites, the Perizzites, the Jebusites, the Ammonites, the Moabites, the Egyptians, and the Amorites.**
>
> **2 For they have taken of their daughters for themselves, and for their sons: so that the holy seed have mingled themselves with the people of those lands: yea, the hand of the princes and rulers hath been chief in this trespass.**

This law was to keep those pagan customs from being brought into the camp of Israel through marriage or fornication as stated in Deuteronomy and Nehemiah below, and as we seen, did happened to Solomon in 1$^{st}$ Kings above.

> **Deuteronomy 23:3**
>
> **3 An Ammonite or Moabite shall not enter into the congregation of the Lord; even to their tenth generation shall they not enter into the congregation of the Lord for ever:**

> **Nehemiah 13:22-27**
>
> **22 And I commanded the Levites that they should cleanse themselves, and that they should come and keep the gates, to sanctify the sabbath day. Remember me, O my God, concerning this also, and spare me according to the greatness of thy mercy.**
>
> **23 In those days also saw I Jews that had married wives of Ashdod, of Ammon, and of Moab:**
>
> **24 And their children spake half in the speech of Ashdod, and could not speak in the Jews' language, but according to the language of each people.**
>
> **25 And I contended with them, and cursed them, and smote certain of them, and plucked off their hair, and made them swear by God, saying, Ye shall not give your daughters unto their sons, nor take their daughters unto your sons, or for yourselves.**

**26 Did not Solomon king of Israel sin by these things? yet among many nations was there no king like him, who was beloved of his God, and God made him king over all Israel: nevertheless even him did outlandish women cause to sin. 27 Shall we then hearken unto you to do all this great evil, to transgress against our God in marrying strange wives?**

When they took these Moabite women to lie with and took them as wives, they broke that covenant with God. The women were undoubtedly beautiful, and Balak had made friends with Israel, and before you know it, the men of Israel began to lay with the women of Moab. Then the women would teach them to worship idols, thus bringing judgement upon themselves, just as Balak wanted in the first place. Satan did much the same thing in the church at Pergamos. He couldn't defeat the church from the outside during the church age of Smyrna; so, he devised a plan to deceive it from the inside in the church age of Pergamos to cause the people to sin using the mixture of Christianity to paganism and the festiveness and beauty of the celebration of Saturnalia, now called Christmas, along with other pagan celebrations. He made friends with the church and played the hero by seemingly freeing them from government oppression by Rome being proclaimed a Christian Empire. Then he joined the church and brought in his pagan celebrations causing Christians to compromise their faith by mixing it with paganism. The thing is, The Bible warns us of this deception in the scriptures we already talked about. And we have The Holy Spirit to warn us personally. But the sad thing is that a lot of people don't read The Bible and are not fine tuned in to The Holy Spirit and therefore cannot hear His warning. It's interesting to note that, as we said, they brought pagan customs into the church, and called them by Christian names. In the same sense, when the Moabite women were sent in to the Jewish camp, and they lay with the men of Israel, that constituted an act of marriage in which they and their children would have received Jewish names, just like the pagan customs have received Christian names. People see Christianity as dull and boring with rules and regulations you must keep. Idol worship is full of fun and freedom and celebration with no rules and regulations. It is a "If it feels good, do it" kind of thing. That is why people participate in those types of celebrations; so they can sin and feel justified. That's why the path to righteousness is narrow and wide is the gate that leads to destruction. Most people will choose the wide gate so they can do what they want.

> **Matthew 7:13-14**
> **13 Enter ye in at the strait gate: for wide is the gate, and broad is the way, that leadeth to destruction, and many there be which go in thereat:**
> **14 Because strait is the gate, and narrow is the way, which leadeth unto life, and few there be that find it.**

The doctrine of the Nicolaitans, verse 15, took advantage of God's grace by saying that you can live any way you want after your conversion without effecting your Christianity. And in fact, they were encouraged to sin to receive more grace. They believed that God wanted to give them more grace and was pleased when they sinned so He could exercise His grace on them. But God hates this doctrine, verse 15. This all started with Constantine and led to the setup of pagan idols in The Name of Jesus. Then articles of sun worship were introduced in the church; and that type of church today is the Roman church. Just look at the Monstrance. It is obviously a likeness of the sun. There are multiple other sun symbols in the Roman Church. The solar wheel, a statue of a woman holding a sun disc, an alter of Mary with a sun disc inside a crescent moon to name a few. The Roman church records themselves go all the way back to Constantine. Look at it; the Roman/government church is the one that originated the marriage of the church to paganism by bringing in these pagan celebrations including Christmas and Easter into the church just like it says in verse 14 where the doctrine of Balaam brought idol worshiping women into the camp of Israel to mix idol worship with the worship of God. The Roman church has statues in the church of who they say are Mother Marry and baby Jesus, but who are really the self-proclaimed queen of heaven and her son, Tammuz. Their names were changed just like all the other pagan gods. As we already seen, statues of this sort go back much farther than the birth of Jesus. The mother/child religion is one of the oldest religions in the world. I should note again that in different countries, the mother and child were called by different names. But they are all the same queen of heaven and her false Christ son.

> **Ezekiel 8:13-14**
> **13 He said also unto me, Turn thee yet again, and thou shalt see greater abominations that they do.**
> **14 Then he brought me to the door of the gate of the Lord's house which was toward the north; and, behold, there sat women weeping for Tammuz.**

The Roman/government church also adopted the cross as a symbol of Christianity which they use as a sacred symbol. But the cross is also an ancient Babylonian symbol worshiped by the pagans long before Jesus died on that cross. It was the letter that symbolized Tammuz and was put on cakes and called hot cross cakes and were baked each year for the queen of heaven. The Bible doesn't come right out and say, "hot cross cakes". In this verse, it is simply called cakes. But it is easily researched and confirmed in history that these are hot cross cakes.

> **Jeremiah 7:18**
> **18 The children gather wood, and the fathers kindle the fire, and the women knead their dough, to make cakes to the queen of heaven, and to pour out drink offerings unto other gods, that they may provoke me to anger.**

The cross was known by the pagans as the tree of life. The wood of the cross was said by the pagan religion to be wood of salvation.

It was not of course, but it was the most horrible thing that Jesus could have been nailed to because of its pagan meaning. I must note here that many scholars believe that Jesus was nailed to a tree, or a pole instead of a cross.

> **Acts 5:30**
> **30 The God of our fathers raised up Jesus, whom ye slew and hanged on a tree.**

> **Acts 10:38-39**
> **38 How God anointed Jesus of Nazareth with the Holy Ghost and with power: who went about doing good, and healing all that were oppressed of the devil; for God was with him.**
> **39 And we are witnesses of all things which he did both in the land of the Jews, and in Jerusalem; whom they slew and hanged on a tree:**

> **Galatians 3:13**
> **13 Christ hath redeemed us from the curse of the law, being made a curse for us: for it is written, Cursed is every one that hangeth on a tree:**

Even though these verses say it was a tree, I do not hold a dogmatic view that it was not a cross. This could have just been a figure of speech. There are other verses that say it was a cross.

> **John 19:19**
> **19 And Pilate wrote a title, and put it on the cross. And the writing was, JESUS OF NAZARETH THE KING OF THE JEWS.**

**John 19:25**
**25 Now there stood by the cross of Jesus his mother, and his mother's sister, Mary the wife of Cleophas, and Mary Magdalene.**

**John 19:31**
**31 The Jews therefore, because it was the preparation, that the bodies should not remain upon the cross on the sabbath day, (for that sabbath day was an high day,) besought Pilate that their legs might be broken, and that they might be taken away.**

On this, we just can't be sure. It is likely that it was a tree, and the person being crucified was nailed to a cross beam and lifted up and fastened to the tree making it appear as a cross. The fact is, anyone that was crucified on a cross, or a tree, was cursed. Why should we wear around our necks the thing that our Lord died on? I assure you; He is not still dead. He's alive! He's not on that cross or tree anymore. He has been raised from the grave! Why keep Him on that cross? I know; most people think just what you're thinking right now. Hey, don't mess with the cross. Yes, we are to take up our cross daily and follow Jesus. But where in The Bible does it say that the cross is a Christian symbol, and that we should make jewelry out of it and wear it, or display it on our church buildings or at the alter or in our homes? It is used in Hollywood movies to chase off vampires and evil spirits. The cross is used, not Jesus. I don't know what you think, but the cross doesn't rescue me from evil spirits, Jesus does. He took my sin and died on that cross, but that doesn't mean to make an idol out of it by bowing down to that cross to pray like many do today. It means to bow down to Jesus for going through the horrible torture of the cross to pay for our sin. To have a cross at the alter would be like bowing to it. I'd rather bow to the resurrected Jesus. Jesus is not on that cross anymore. He defeated death and is now very much alive. Why would you use the instrument of His execution as a symbol of Him. I realize that we are to remember that Jesus died on that cross as it says in First Corinthians 11. But nowhere in The Bible does it tell us to set a cross on the alter so we can kneel before it and pray in front of it.

> **1 Corinthians 11:23-26**
> **23 For I have received of the Lord that which also I delivered unto you, That the Lord Jesus the same night in which he was betrayed took bread:**
> **24 And when he had given thanks, he brake it, and said, Take, eat: this is my body, which is broken for you: this do in remembrance of me.**
> **25 After the same manner also he took the cup, when he had supped, saying, This cup is the new testament in my blood: this do ye, as oft as ye drink it, in remembrance of me.**
> **26 For as often as ye eat this bread, and drink this cup, ye do shew the Lord's death till he come.**

It says we are to remember Him with communion, not a cross, verse 25 above. The Roman church communion is similar to a regular communion with the exception that they believe each time you take it, the wafer and wine actually become the Body and Blood of Jesus being crucified all over again. Another thing is that; Remember, I told you that some things have been suppressed today that makes them harder to find? One of those things is the wafers that the Roman churches use in their communion. When I was writing the 1st edition of this book, I seen pictures of a round wafer with an image of the sun on it. Today, I only find a round wafer with no image on it. Somehow, the information that there used to be an image of the sun on it has disappeared. It is much harder today to find any reference to it. Like I said, in the first edition of this book, it was easy to find. I seen it myself in references back then. But I tried without success to find it now. The Roman/ government church also names their churches after people, which was a pagan practice.

1 Corinthians 1:11-17

11 For it hath been declared unto me of you, my brethren, by them which are of the house of Chloe, that there are contentions among you.

12 Now this I say, that every one of you saith, I am of Paul; and I of Apollos; and I of Cephas; and I of Christ.

13 Is Christ divided? was Paul crucified for you? or were ye baptized in the name of Paul?

14 I thank God that I baptized none of you, but Crispus and Gaius;

15 Lest any should say that I had baptized in mine own name.

16 And I baptized also the household of Stephanas: besides, I know not whether I baptized any other.

17 For Christ sent me not to baptize, but to preach the gospel: not with wisdom of words, lest the cross of Christ should be made of none effect.

We are all just Christians, or believers or people of the way.

1 Corinthians 12:13

13 For by one Spirit are we all baptized into one body, whether we be Jews or Gentiles, whether we be bond or free; and have been all made to drink into one Spirit.

Acts 11:26

26 And when he had found him, he brought him unto Antioch. And it came to pass, that a whole year they assembled themselves with the church, and taught much people. And the disciples were called Christians first in Antioch.

Acts 5:14

14 And believers were the more added to the Lord, multitudes both of men and women.)

**Acts 9:2**

2 And desired of him letters to Damascus to the synagogues, that if he found any of this way, whether they were men or women, he might bring them bound unto Jerusalem.

**Acts 19:9**

9 But when divers were hardened, and believed not, but spake evil of that way before the multitude, he departed from them, and separated the disciples, disputing daily in the school of one Tyrannus.

**Acts 24:14**

14 But this I confess unto thee, that after the way which they call heresy, so worship I the God of my fathers, believing all things which are written in the law and in the prophets:

**John 14:6**

6 Jesus saith unto him, I am the way, the truth, and the life: no man cometh unto the Father, but by me.

We should all believe alike. All we have to do is read The Bible and believe what It says. The cross spoken of, in verse 17 above, is not a piece of jewelry to wear around your neck. It is referring to the sacrifice Jesus made on the cross of Calvary. They also have a Pope that claims to be the voice of Christ on earth. Actually, we are the voice of Christ in this earth.

**Ephesians 6:19-20**

19 And for me, that utterance may be given unto me, that I may open my mouth boldly, to make known the mystery of the gospel,

20 For which I am an ambassador in bonds: that therein I may speak boldly, as I ought to speak.

**1 Peter 4:11**
**11 If any man speak, let him speak as the oracles of God; if any man minister, let him do it as of the ability which God giveth: that God in all things may be glorified through Jesus Christ, to whom be praise and dominion for ever and ever. Amen.**

They have the obelisks of pagan gods set up in Vatican square, which, by the way, many churches also use, and call them steeples, but are really a pagan symbol of a male organ, symbolizing fertility to the gods. These also are not found in The Bible so why do we have them on our churches. And like we said, they crucify Jesus over and over again with their communion during their mass in which they believe that the wafer and the wine actually turn into the flesh and blood of Jesus to atone for their sins again and again. That is where the name "Christ's mass" or shortened to "Christmas" came from. It was a mass named for the false Christ of that celebration. They also call men Father and forbid them to marry. They also have confession to a priest in which the priest pronounces a judgement on them with a task that they must do to receive forgiveness for their sin.

**Matthew 23: 9-10**
**9 And call no man your father upon the earth: for one is your Father, which is in heaven.**
**10 Neither be ye called masters: for one is your Master, even Christ.**

**1 Timothy 4:1-5**
**1 Now the Spirit speaketh expressly, that in the latter times some shall depart from the faith, giving heed to seducing spirits, and doctrines of devils;**
**2 Speaking lies in hypocrisy; having their conscience seared with a hot iron;**

**3 Forbidding to marry, and commanding to abstain from meats, which God hath created to be received with thanksgiving of them which believe and know the truth.**
**4 For every creature of God is good, and nothing to be refused, if it be received with thanksgiving:**
**5 For it is sanctified by the word of God and prayer.**

**Ephesians 2:8-9**
**8 For by grace are ye saved through faith; and that not of yourselves: it is the gift of God:**
**9 Not of works, lest any man should boast.**

**1 John 1:9**
**9 If we confess our sins, he is faithful and just to forgive us our sins, and to cleanse us from all unrighteousness.**

**1 John 2:1-2**
**1 My little children, these things write I unto you, that ye sin not. And if any man sin, we have an advocate with the Father, Jesus Christ the righteous:**
**2 And he is the propitiation for our sins: and not for ours only, but also for the sins of the whole world.**

I really hate exposing all these sacred cows that perhaps even you have. But they need to be exposed for what they are. Pagan symbols all dressed up in sheep's clothing to look Christian. All these pagan beliefs became mandatory by the Roman/government church and at one time were punishable by death if you didn't agree with them. And it was backed up by the Roman Empire. That's why the puritans fled to America. To escape from celebrations like Christmas because they knew that it was pagan. It's ironic that Thanksgiving was created by the first pilgrims to give thanks to God for this new land and freedom from kings and dictators along with freedom from Roman church dominance, including Christmas. Now, Thanksgiving kicks off the Christmas season;

the very thing we are giving thanks for being free from. People seem to be willing to be deceived by paganism disguised as church. The church of Pergamos is very much alive today with Christmas, Easter, the cross, statues, steeples, and many other things. Why do you think the Roman church puts so much emphasis on Mother Mary instead of Jesus? Nowhere in The Bible does It tell us to pray to Mother Mary. But the Mystery, Babylon the great, the queen of heaven loves being prayed to. Some who say they are Christians, compromise and choose to bow down to the idol once a year. Like in the book of Daniel, chapter 3.

> **Daniel 3:3-7**
> **3 Then the princes, the governors, and captains, the judges, the treasurers, the counsellors, the sheriffs, and all the rulers of the provinces, were gathered together unto the dedication of the image that Nebuchadnezzar the king had set up; and they stood before the image that Nebuchadnezzar had set up.**
> **4 Then an herald cried aloud, To you it is commanded, O people, nations, and languages,**
> **5 That at what time ye hear the sound of the cornet, flute, harp, sackbut, psaltery, dulcimer, and all kinds of musick, ye fall down and worship the golden image that Nebuchadnezzar the king hath set up:**
> **6 And whoso falleth not down and worshippeth shall the same hour be cast into the midst of a burning fiery furnace.**
> **7 Therefore at that time, when all the people heard the sound of the cornet, flute, harp, sackbut, psaltery, and all kinds of musick, all the people, the nations, and the languages, fell down and worshipped the golden image that Nebuchadnezzar the king had set up.**

Let me pause here a minuet to add this. While the Roman church I am speaking of is somewhat different today than the Roman/government church of the dark ages; and they have begun to change some of their doctrines and beliefs to conform to a less pagan doctrine. And most of these Roman churches, no doubt, do a lot of good things. They help a lot of people in times of need and people in need in general. No one disputes the good works that This Roman church does. I have seen them help churches of other denominations that had suffered a disaster of a fire or other destruction. They feed the poor and help people with nowhere else to turn. Despite all of this, they still represent that government/church combo that killed millions of true Christians during the dark ages. I also know that no one in that church today does or condones the killing of true Christians that this church took part in in the past. But they still, to this day, apply all of the pagan celebrations to Christian names. They still pray to Mary and still use a non-Biblical priesthood that was never established in The Bible for the church except for Jesus being our High Priest and us being called a holy or royal priesthood in 1st Peter. But not a priesthood like the Levitical priesthood or a priesthood where we call the priest Father.

**Matthew 23:4**
**9 And call no man your father upon the earth: for one is your Father, which is in heaven.**

**1 Peter 2:5**
**5 Ye also, as lively stones, are built up a spiritual house, an holy priesthood, to offer up spiritual sacrifices, acceptable to God by Jesus Christ.**

**1 Peter 2:9**
**9 But ye are a chosen generation, a royal priesthood, an holy nation, a peculiar people; that ye should shew forth the praises of him who hath called you out of darkness into his marvellous light:**

Because of this, I must still take a stand against their false doctrines and pagan celebrations. I'm sorry if you are a member of this Roman church and are offended by what I am saying. But I must tell you the truth or I would be delinquent in my stewardship. I do believe there could be a lot of people in this church that are saved. I know about some priest in this church that do not follow the ridged Roman teachings anymore. Some even pray to Jesus instead of Mother Mary. But overall, this church is still a long way from Biblical teachings. Also, this church is not the only organization connected to this false religious system. There are many cults and religions that are just as connected to this Babylonian mystery religion as the Roman church is. I use this church in this book because it is the part of this Babylonian mystery religion that is connected directly to creating the Christmas celebration. But there are many others out there that are just as connected to the mystery religion as they are and all of them will come together during the tribulation as a one world religion and pledge allegiance to the antichrist. But about the passage in Daniel, we just read; as we discussed in chapter 2 of this book; in Daniel chapter 3, Shadrach, Meshach, and Abednego refused to bow down to the golden image that Nebuchadnezzar had made. It was easy for everyone to bow down to the image simply because everyone was doing it. No one could see much wrong with it. It was only a small thing for a moment, then you could go on about your own business. But these three men refused on only one premise. They were not willing to compromise their worship of God with this idol worship, even if it meant death. We already looked at this story, so you know that God protected them in the furnace. But don't you think it would be worth a little investigation of Christmas before you commit yourself any further to it? What if it really is idol worship? How do you think you'll fare at the judgment seat of Christ if you find out that you have been honoring the adversary and have been a hindrance to the cause of Jesus? Is it worth the risk of celebrating something you can't find in The Bible? So, is it of God? Not according to my Bible. Millions of faithful Christians were tortured and killed during the dark ages because they wouldn't accept this false religious system. The true Christians saw the flaw in the Empire's version of a false Christianity mixed with paganism and controlled by the Roman government. Christmas was at the center of that religious system. Do you want to be a part of it too? That false religion is still going strong today with a church that is called by a name that we would all recognize immediately. In this book, I have chosen to call it the Roman/government church. or just the Roman church for today. That church is no longer controlled by the Roman government today, but it is still the same church that adopted the pagan celebrations in the 4th century AD. I didn't want to single them out by their proper name that they use because they are only one of many that belong to the great whore, this Mystery, Babylon the great in Revelation 17:5. So, it wouldn't be fair to single them out by name and leave out all the other names of churches that belong to this same gigantic worldwide religious system. This religious system didn't start with them or with Constantine. It goes back much further. Even to the Tower of Babel. For that matter, even to the garden of Eden with the serpent tempting Eve that her an Adam could be as gods. That is the biggest trick of the devil. To diminish The Authority of God and lift you up to a god like status. He tells you that you don't have to follow all those rules of God. He tells you that you can be your own god and make your own rules. The biggest commandment in the satanic bible is "do what thou will". But the tower of Babel is where this religious system started getting organized with the pagan celebrations to the sun, moon, stars and planets that became the zodiac. This is the same religious system that was adopted into the Roman/government church that followed the actions of Constantine and those emperors after him. This marriage is noted in The Bible as an act of fornication committed by the kings of the earth as we just read in Revelation 17:1-2, and will eventually become the false religious system led by the false prophet during the tribulation. There are two names in the book of Revelation written in large print. One is found in chapter 19:16,

**Revelation 19:16**
**16 And he hath on his vesture and on his thigh a name written, KING OF KINGS, AND LORD OF LORDS.**

The other is found in chapter 17:5.

**Revelation 17:5**
**5 And upon her forehead was a name written, MYSTERY, BABYLON THE GREAT, THE MOTHER OF HARLOTS AND ABOMINATIONS OF THE EARTH.**

These two names are not a comparison to each other. There is a yin and yang in a false eastern religion that says good and evil are equal, and one cannot exist without the other so as to balance the universe with these two concepts. There is a popular neckless you can buy that represents this concept and is round with an infinity sign dividing it into two equal halves. And those two halves are cut along the infinity line in the neckless to make two separate but equal pieces that fit together perfectly if you hold them up together. Many people buy them and give half of the symbol to a girlfriend or a girl would give it to a boyfriend and wear the other half themselves to symbolize the two of them as only halves, but together, equaling a whole, completing the circle. Half of this neckless is black and the other half is white, divided by that infinity symbol. In this eastern religion, it symbolizes that good and evil coexist equally, the white half of the neckless representing good, and the black representing evil, but both being equal to each other. That is a false narrative taken from false religion. God is alone in His righteousness. He doesn't need evil to exist. God can create the evil of war as punishment for those that work against Him. But He can keep you from it if you rest in Him. If you look at the context of verse 7 below, He makes peace and creates evil, which in that context means He can create peace or war which ever suites His purpose. Light and darkness, peace and war.

**Isaiah 45:5-7**
**5 I am the Lord, and there is none else, there is no God beside me: I girded thee, though thou hast not known me: 6 That they may know from the rising of the sun, and from the west, that there is none beside me. I am the Lord, and there is none else.**
**7 I form the light, and create darkness: I make peace, and create evil: I the Lord do all these things.**

**2 Thessalonians 3:3**
**3 But the Lord is faithful, who shall stablish you, and keep you from evil.**

God has no evil in Him, but He can use evil as a tool for His glory. Satan is the one that evil indwells with his rebellion against God. But he was only able to do that by the permission of God allowing it in His eternal plan. God existed for eternity before evil came along, and He will still exist for eternity after He no longer needs evil and it is extinguished. He is so far above evil that He can't even be compared to it. God cannot be compared to anyone or anything. He is so far above everyone and everything else that there is nothing to compare Him to. Think about it. He is all powerful. God is not opposite of anything. He just Is because He Is.

**Exodus 3:14**
**14 And God said unto Moses, I AM THAT I AM: and he said, Thus shalt thou say unto the children of Israel, I AM hath sent me unto you.**

**Matthew 28:18**
**18 And Jesus came and spake unto them, saying, All power is given unto me in heaven and in earth.**

There is no power but of God. Any power given to man or angel was given to them by God. It all still belongs to God. Without Him, you have nothing in existence. He has unlimited power. Did you hear me? unlimited power! That's a lot of power! All power is His! Let that sink in for a minute. All power! What could you do with all power? Anything! Just be thankful that The One that has all power is The loving, caring and righteous God. Be thankful that some evil force doesn't have this kind of power. The One that has all power is Love because God is Love.

> **1 John 4:8**
> **8 He that loveth not knoweth not God; for God is love.**

> **1 John 4:16**
> **16 And we have known and believed the love that God hath to us. God is love; and he that dwelleth in love dwelleth in God, and God in him.**

> **Colossians 1:12-17**
> **12 Giving thanks unto the Father, which hath made us meet to be partakers of the inheritance of the saints in light:**
> **13 Who hath delivered us from the power of darkness, and hath translated us into the kingdom of his dear Son:**
> **14 In whom we have redemption through his blood, even the forgiveness of sins:**
> **15 Who is the image of the invisible God, the firstborn of every creature:**
> **16 For by him were all things created, that are in heaven, and that are in earth, visible and invisible, whether they be thrones, or dominions, or principalities, or powers: all things were created by him, and for him:**
> **17 And he is before all things, and by him all things consist.**

Nothing or no one compares to The one and only all-powerful, all knowing, Almighty God. You might as well try to compare your living room to the universe. God is the only reason anything is here. He created it all, He controls it all, He owns it all, He rules it all.

For anything or anyone to think they can affect even one thing that God does through their own power would be like an ant thinking he can attach a chain to a 100-car freight train loaded with cargo, then put the chain around his neck and pull that loaded freight train up to the top of Mount Everest. As for this mother of harlots, God is only allowing her to exist in the here and now for His own purpose. He will judge this great whore of Babylon later and she will be completely and utterly eliminated.

> **Revelation 19:1-2**
> **1 And after these things I heard a great voice of much people in heaven, saying, Alleluia; Salvation, and glory, and honour, and power, unto the Lord our God:**
> **2 For true and righteous are his judgments: for he hath judged the great whore, which did corrupt the earth with her fornication, and hath avenged the blood of his servants at her hand.**

The question would be; who is this woman?

> **Revelation 17:7-9**
> **7 And the angel said unto me, Wherefore didst thou marvel? I will tell thee the mystery of the woman, and of the beast that carrieth her, which hath the seven heads and ten horns.**
> **8 The beast that thou sawest was, and is not; and shall ascend out of the bottomless pit, and go into perdition: and they that dwell on the earth shall wonder, whose names were not written in the book of life from the foundation of the world, when they behold the beast that was, and is not, and yet is.**
> **9 And here is the mind which hath wisdom. The seven heads are seven mountains, on which the woman sitteth.**

This woman in history is now long ago dead. But Satan set her memory up as an idol. Today, Satan uses this woman as the false religious system that covers the entire world. The false prophet will use this religious system during the tribulation. Where are these seven mountains? Rome sits on seven hills, or you can call them mountains. I don't know where else this could be talking about, so why didn't The Bible just come right out and say it was Rome? I know some think these seven mountains are the seven kings talked about in the next verse.

> **Revelation 17:10**
> **10 And there are seven kings: five are fallen, and one is, and the other is not yet come; and when he cometh, he must continue a short space.**

But this verse says, "and there are seven kings". It doesn't say that the seven mountains are the seven kings. Therefore, I think this is taking about two different things. This is hidden manna. Some things God makes us look for or makes us study to find the hidden things of God. There is reward for doing that. A lot of theologians agree that these are the seven Roman hills. All throughout history, Rome is called the city on seven hills. The hills even have names: Aventine Hill, Caelian Hill, Capitoline Hill, Esquiline Hill, Palatine Hill, Quirinal Hill and Viminal Hill. And the headquarters of this Babylonian system is located in Vatican square in Rome. If The Bible came right out and said the name of this church, there wouldn't be many people join themselves to it. But God wants people that think for themselves and take the time to search out these things and seek God with their whole heart no matter how it messes with things they want to do. Of the two names in capital letters; the one in chapter 19:16 is The true Lord and Savior, Jesus Christ. The one in chapter 17:5 is the false religious system of Babylon. As I said; these two titles are not equal or opposites to each other. Nothing can compare to God and nothing is equal to God. It says of this false religious system that it reigns over the kings of the earth. Not that Rome reigns over the kings of the earth today. But it once did. And it will again during the tribulation when what has been called, the holy Roman Empire, will be re-established. We see this in the statue that king Nebuchadnezzar had a dream of that Daniel interpreted for him.

> **Daniel 2:1**
> **1 And in the second year of the reign of Nebuchadnezzar Nebuchadnezzar dreamed dreams, wherewith his spirit was troubled, and his sleep brake from him.**

His dream was of a statue with a head of gold, a silver chest, a brass waste, iron legs and feet and toes of iron mixed with clay.

> **Daniel 2:32-34**
> **32 This image's head was of fine gold, his breast and his arms of silver, his belly and his thighs of brass,**
> **33 His legs of iron, his feet part of iron and part of clay.**
> **34 Thou sawest till that a stone was cut out without hands, which smote the image upon his feet that were of iron and clay, and brake them to pieces.**

If you read on in this chapter, you will find that all these metals are different kingdoms through time. The legs of iron represented the Roman Empire. But then the feet and toes were iron mixed with clay which represents the re-born Roman Empire in the end times. Iron mixed with clay is not as strong as iron alone which symbolized Rome at the peak of its rule. But this false religious system weakened the iron and will eventually cause it to crumble when it is struck by the Chief Corner Stone as we seen in Daniel 2:34 above.

> **Ephesians 2:20**
> **20 And are built upon the foundation of the apostles and prophets, Jesus Christ himself being the chief corner stone;**

**Daniel 2:40-44**

**40 And the fourth kingdom shall be strong as iron: forasmuch as iron breaketh in pieces and subdueth all things: and as iron that breaketh all these, shall it break in pieces and bruise.**

**41 And whereas thou sawest the feet and toes, part of potters' clay, and part of iron, the kingdom shall be divided; but there shall be in it of the strength of the iron, forasmuch as thou sawest the iron mixed with miry clay.**

**42 And as the toes of the feet were part of iron, and part of clay, so the kingdom shall be partly strong, and partly broken.**

**43 And whereas thou sawest iron mixed with miry clay, they shall mingle themselves with the seed of men: but they shall not cleave one to another, even as iron is not mixed with clay.**

**44 And in the days of these kings shall the God of heaven set up a kingdom, which shall never be destroyed: and the kingdom shall not be left to other people, but it shall break in pieces and consume all these kingdoms, and it shall stand for ever.**

I don't have time in this book to show you this theory. But even now, Rome itself may not reign over the earth, but this religious Babylonian system reigns over the kings of the earth through this Roman religion.

**Revelation 17:17-18**

**17 For God hath put in their hearts to fulfil his will, and to agree, and give their kingdom unto the beast, until the words of God shall be fulfilled.**

**18 And the woman which thou sawest is that great city, which reigneth over the kings of the earth.**

This describes the attachment of this religious system to the world.

**Revelation 18:1-3**

1 And after these things I saw another angel come down from heaven, having great power; and the earth was lightened with his glory.

2 And he cried mightily with a strong voice, saying, Babylon the great is fallen, is fallen, and is become the habitation of devils, and the hold of every foul spirit, and a cage of every unclean and hateful bird.

3 For all nations have drunk of the wine of the wrath of her fornication, and the kings of the earth have committed fornication with her, and the merchants of the earth are waxed rich through the abundance of her delicacies.

**Revelation 18:9-19**

9 And the kings of the earth, who have committed fornication and lived deliciously with her, shall bewail her, and lament for her, when they shall see the smoke of her burning,

10 Standing afar off for the fear of her torment, saying, Alas, alas, that great city Babylon, that mighty city! for in one hour is thy judgment come.

11 And the merchants of the earth shall weep and mourn over her; for no man buyeth their merchandise any more:

12 The merchandise of gold, and silver, and precious stones, and of pearls, and fine linen, and purple, and silk, and scarlet, and all thyine wood, and all manner vessels of ivory, and all manner vessels of most precious wood, and of brass, and iron, and marble,

13 And cinnamon, and odours, and ointments, and frankincense, and wine, and oil, and fine flour, and wheat, and beasts, and sheep, and horses, and chariots, and slaves, and souls of men.

14 And the fruits that thy soul lusted after are departed from thee, and all things which were dainty and goodly are departed from thee, and thou shalt find them no more at all.

**15 The merchants of these things, which were made rich by her, shall stand afar off for the fear of her torment, weeping and wailing,**

**16 And saying, Alas, alas, that great city, that was clothed in fine linen, and purple, and scarlet, and decked with gold, and precious stones, and pearls!**

**17 For in one hour so great riches is come to nought. And every shipmaster, and all the company in ships, and sailors, and as many as trade by sea, stood afar off,**

**18 And cried when they saw the smoke of her burning, saying, What city is like unto this great city!**

**19 And they cast dust on their heads, and cried, weeping and wailing, saying, Alas, alas, that great city, wherein were made rich all that had ships in the sea by reason of her costliness! for in one hour is she made desolate.**

Christmas is part of this financial Empire that doesn't rule with guns, but with money and financial dominance. This system will fall, verse 2 above, and verses 20-21 below

**Revelation 18:20-21**

**20 Rejoice over her, thou heaven, and ye holy apostles and prophets; for God hath avenged you on her.**

**21 And a mighty angel took up a stone like a great millstone, and cast it into the sea, saying, Thus with violence shall that great city Babylon be thrown down, and shall be found no more at all.**

This is the same religious system that started with Babel in Genesis. And that kingdom is still here today in one form as this Roman Church that we have been talking about. It all ties in with the doctrine of Balaam, and the marriage of Christianity to paganism.

**Revelation 2:14**
**14 But I have a few things against thee, because thou hast**
**there them that hold the doctrine of Balaam, who taught**
**Balac to cast a stumblingblock**
**before the children of Israel, to eat things sacrificed unto**
**idols, and to commit fornication.**

As we already said, to find out what verses 14 above is talking about, you must read Numbers chapter 22 through chapter 31 which is too much to put in this book, so you can read it for yourself. As we already seen, the doctrine of Balaam is how Balac cursed Israel by making friends with them and sending Moabite women into the camp of Israel so that the men of Israel would curse themselves by breaking their covenant of purity with God by mixing Israel with idol worship, committing fornication with these idol worshiping women which was the advice that Balaam had given to the Balac, the king. In the church at Pergamos, this is called, the doctrine of Balaam in verse 14. This is the same kind of mixing of church and paganism that happened when Rome married paganism to the church in the 4th century AD. This explains the connection of the church age of Pergamos with Constantine. and the marriage of that church to the queen of heaven, and to the Babylonian system of false religion and idol worship. This is an unholy adulteress union that should never have taken place. Back then, when it happened, they had only limited access to The Word of God to show them the way. They had to depend on their religious leaders to present The Word of God to them. But that excuse did not excuse their falling into idol worship because even though The Word of God wasn't widely available, they still had the Holy Spirit to guide them away from false doctrine and idol worship. Even at that, many of those religious leaders still fell into the claws of the Babylonian religion, and they began to teach on that basis. But there were true men of God that didn't fall for it. They listened to The Holy Spirit in their lives. They were labeled as heretics by the government church and they were hunted, and many killed for standing against the government's religion. Today, at least in America, we have no excuse at all. We have a complete Word of God readily available to us in unlimited supply. We are supposed to read It to find out for ourselves what is of God or not. The reward for overcoming this false religious system is the revealing of this hidden manna to you. And later at the Judgement Seat of Christ to give you a white stone, and in that white stone a new name, verse 17. If you don't do that; then you could fall into the same trap that Pergamos did and be thrown into trouble like the next two church ages, Thyatira and eventually like Sardis. This Pergamos type of church today is a church that compromises with the things of this world and calls it Christian. It's the same thing for this type of person. Yes, they want to be a Christian, but they want to hang on to the things of this world also. and so, they compromise with the idol worship of the world. To hide the idol worship of it, they bent it and shape it so they can call it Christian.

# 4. Thyatira: 6th through the 13th century AD.

This age of martyrdom and persecution was without a doubt the longest church age of the 7, being 8 centuries long. This was a time when The Bible was a complete book. The problem is, there wasn't a lot of translations and it wasn't available in English or to the general public. The only ones that had a complete canon of scripture were the Roman priest, and they added their own interpretation to what they taught because no one else could read the Latin versions that these priests used to teach out of. So the people had to rely on those that knew how to read Latin, which was the dominant translation used at that time. The true church had copies of the apostle's letters, but they didn't have a lot of access to a complete canon of scripture and no one had access to their own personal copies of these apostles' letters. Many Christians compromised their faith by attending the Roman church because they were concerned with losing their life for being associated with the true church, and they allowed themselves to be deceived into believing that it wasn't that big of a deal to just go along with this false system. This is the difference in the persecution of the church age at Smyrna and this church age. In the age of Smyrna, they were willing to stay faithful even unto death. In this church age, they were given an alternative to death which was to accept this mixture of paganism in the church given during the church age of Pergamos. And many took that alternative rather than die. They thought that at least they were worshipping God in Name. Then there were many that were not Christians at all but thought they were Christians simply because the emperor said they were. So, they didn't care as long as the government left them alone. It was during this church age of Thyatira that the government church took this mixture of church and paganism to a new level and this pagan mixture became very dominant throughout the world driving the true church underground having to worship God in hiding places to keep from being killed because of these pagan celebrations that became law and punishable by death if you disagreed with them. The true church sometimes had only a portion of scripture to read from, but they cherished whatever small portion they had. It wasn't until the 14th century AD that English translations began to spring up led by John Wycliffe with The Bible being translated into English. But he died before he could finish the work. Others completed it, but it just wasn't within reach of the common person to have their own access to The Word of God yet. It wasn't widely available to the general public until the Tyndale Bible kicked off a rash of English translations in the 16th century. And look what happened when the common person gained access to God's Word. This began the great reformation of the 16th century AD that led to the creation of the famed Authorized version of The Bible in the 17th century AD that is still here today as the King James version of 1611. But most of that happens in the church age of Philadelphia that we will go over later. During this age of Thyatira, they had to primarily depend on those Latin versions that only a few could even read. This gave the Roman priest opportunity to corrupt The true

Word of God through 8 long centuries of controlling the narrative their way and suppressing the true believers. But God always has a remnant of true believers that remain true to His Word and I'm sure God made sure that they had access to The scriptures and someone that could read them. But there are those that counterfeit Gods Word with misinterpretations and purposely alter His Word, like Jezebel, in verse 20, who was a type of the evil queen of heaven. Seems like any time the name Jezebel is mentioned in The Bible, it is an evil woman. Take heart if your name is Jezebel and don't believe you are evil simply because you have that name. Your name doesn't affect accepting Jesus as your Savior. There were many in this church age that had love for each other and served each other and had faith and patients and did many good works, verse 19. But because of this false religious system brought in through the church age of Pergamos, there were a lot of Christians that fell for the adulterous doctrines of the government church. Like I said before; no one denies the good works that this Roman church does even today. But salvation is not based upon works at all. Only faith in Jesus. But then you must have The right Jesus. You can't believe in a false Christ and be saved. Now, there is a fine line here. If someone is sincere about wanting to accept Jesus as their Savior; and because they don't know anything about The Bible and what It says about Jesus; so, they can't know that this is a false religion, but their heart is in the right place; perhaps God will save them and then show them the right path through The Holy Spirit to get them out of that cult. But there are some that do know The Bible or have been told about Jesus, they have no excuse. They willingly choose to follow this false religion even though they have heard the truth. These will end up lost and in hell if they refuse to see the right way, because God will always show us the right way. The problem is, they will listen to man and not God. There is a religion out there that doesn't believe that Jesus is God. Even though those people believe that they are saved by that Jesus; a Jesus that isn't God cannot save you.

**Jude 24-25**

24 Now unto him that is able to keep you from falling, and to present you faultless before the presence of his glory with exceeding joy,

25 To the only wise God our Saviour, be glory and majesty, dominion and power, both now and ever. Amen.

**Revelation 2:18-29:**

18 And unto the angel of the church in Thyatira write; These things saith the Son of God, who hath his eyes like unto a flame of fire, and his feet are like fine brass;

19 I know thy works, and charity, and service, and faith, and thy patience, and thy works; and the last to be more than the first.

20 Notwithstanding I have a few things against thee, because thou sufferest that woman Jezebel, which calleth herself a prophetess, to teach and to seduce my servants to commit fornication, and to eat things sacrificed unto idols.

21 And I gave her space to repent of her fornication; and she repented not.

22 Behold, I will cast her into a bed, and them that commit adultery with her into great tribulation, except they repent of their deeds.

23 And I will kill her children with death; and all the churches shall know that I am he which searcheth the reins and hearts: and I will give unto every one of you according to your works.

24 But unto you I say, and unto the rest in Thyatira, as many as have not this doctrine, and which have not known the depths of Satan, as they speak; I will put upon you none other burden.

25 But that which ye have already hold fast till I come.

26 And he that overcometh, and keepeth my works unto the end, to him will I give power over the nations:

**27 And he shall rule them with a rod of iron; as the vessels of a potter shall they be broken to shivers: even as I received of my Father.**

**28 And I will give him the morning star.**

**29 He that hath an ear, let him hear what the Spirit saith unto the churches.**

In the church at Thyatira, the subject is adultery, verse 22. And that is what happened after the government religion married paganism to Christianity at the church age of Pergamos that we already went over. Those Christians that submitted to this unholy marriage were committing adultery with paganism when they should have been faithful to Jesus by rejecting this false religion. Like I said, in verse 20, Jezebel is a type and picture of that religious system that deceives the nations. Satan couldn't get rid of the Christians by killing them as in the church age of Smyrna. So, he took advantage of the government religion to kill the true Christians. He doesn't mind a false religious system being here because he can control and manipulate that system with his deception. The Thyatirian church age enters the beginnings of the dark ages and the progression of the Roman/government church. The queen of heaven is not the only false religious system in this world that was brought into being by Satan. There are many others. But all of them originated at Babel. Satan corrupted the church at Thyatira with his deception of paganism. He is still hard at work today appearing to be a good Christian, but all the while deceiving whole nations and peoples. Are you one of those people? He tells you he comes in The Name of The Lord, but really, he comes to destroy you.

**Matthew 7:15:**
**15 Beware of false prophets, which come to you in sheep's clothing, but inwardly they are ravening wolves.**

**Mark 13:5-6**
**5 And Jesus answering them began to say, Take heed lest
any man deceive you:**
**6 For many shall come in my name, saying, I am Christ;
and shall deceive many.**

Also, in this church age, the devil's aim is to keep you from learning
the truth because he knows that the truth will make you free. This
is very relevant today because most people don't read their Bibles
and are ignorant to the devices the devil uses to deceive them.
This next scripture gives us a hint of who this influence is with
their forbidding to marry. What church today forbids their priest to
marry? And they even abstain from certain meats on Friday. You
probably didn't know that vegetarianism is a doctrine of devils,
did you? Read it for yourself.

**1 Timothy 4:1-3**
**1 Now the Spirit speaketh expressly, that in the latter times
some shall depart from the faith, giving heed to seducing
spirits, and doctrines of devils;**
**2 Speaking lies in hypocrisy; having their conscience
seared with a hot iron;**
**3 Forbidding to marry, and commanding to abstain
from meats, which God hath created to be received with
thanksgiving of them which believe and know the truth.**

But really, it's not just this Roman church. It's a worldwide
religious system that can infiltrate any church anytime with only
the slightest of influence that can grow into a controlling factor.
One of those slight influences is Christmas. If you are celebrating
Christmas, you are one of those participants in this false religious
system. If you love the party of Christmas so much that you are
blinded to its true meaning; then you too are participating in idol
worship. As Christians, we can't just pick and choose religious
practices like from a buffet. Christianity as the main course, with

a little paganism as a side dish, then a glass full of false religion, then a little idolism for dessert. There is only one thing we should have on our plate; and that is the manna of The Word of God. There is no paganism or false religions or idolism on the table of The Word of God.

> **1 Corinthians 10:21**
> **21 Ye cannot drink the cup of the Lord, and the cup of devils: ye cannot be partakers of the Lord's table, and of the table of devils.**

Looks can be very deceiving. People don't look beyond the surface. All they see is the outward appearance.

> **Matthew 23:27-28:**
> **27 Woe unto you, scribes and Pharisees, hypocrites! for ye are like unto whited sepulchres, which indeed appear beautiful outward, but are within full of dead men's bones, and of all uncleanness.**
> **28 Even so ye also outwardly appear righteous unto men, but within ye are full of hypocrisy and iniquity.**

The outward appearance can keep you from learning the truth. I know from the experience of trying to sell a car now and then, that you can take a car that is in perfect running condition but the body is a little rough; and you will have a hard time selling that car for any kind of money. However, someone can take a clunker, and fix up the body with a new paint job, and make it look great, and they can make some money off that car even though the motor or transmission may be shot. People don't look beyond the surface. By the way, I never sold a car with that kind of deception, but I have seen it done. But all people see is the outward appearance. It's like we just read in Matthew where the whited sepulcher looks good on the outside; but the inside is full of dead men's bones. Many marriages have ended in divorce because a man seen a beautiful woman, or a girl seen a handsome man, only to find out that after marrying them; they were really ugly on the inside and they couldn't stand each other. So, let's look at the external beauty of Christmas. A Christmas tree all decked out, all the lights, and decorations, the snow scenes with the one horse slay, Santa Claus all dressed in bright red and white, all the people filling the department stores and malls. The joy of Christmas morning, getting out of bed to open presents and gather with families and having a family Christmas meal and celebrating the birth of The Savior. What could possibly be wrong with that? That is what most people see when they look at Christmas. But that's only the external beauty. The whited sepulchres. But those whited sepulchres are full of dead men's bones that were murdered by this Roman/government church, verse 27 above. But let's look at the deeper meaning. The inner obscurity, the deceitfulness of Christmas. First, it is not the birthday of our Savior. There is no doubt that Christmas and its symbols came straight out of paganism. You need to understand that people are willing to be deceived if it suits their desires. It was a day of idol worship in which some pagan customs were to pass their children through the fire to their god.

**Deuteronomy 12:31**
**31 Thou shalt not do so unto the Lord thy God: for every abomination to the Lord, which he hateth, have they done unto their gods; for even their sons and their daughters they have burnt in the fire to their gods.**

**Deuteronomy 18:9-14**
**9 When thou art come into the land which the Lord thy God giveth thee, thou shalt not learn to do after the abominations of those nations.**
**10 There shall not be found among you any one that maketh his son or his daughter to pass through the fire, or that useth divination, or an observer of times, or an enchanter, or a witch,**

**11 Or a charmer, or a consulter with familiar spirits, or a wizard, or a necromancer.**

**12 For all that do these things are an abomination unto the Lord: and because of these abominations the Lord thy God doth drive them out from before thee.**

**13 Thou shalt be perfect with the Lord thy God.**

**14 For these nations, which thou shalt possess, hearkened unto observers of times, and unto diviners: but as for thee, the Lord thy God hath not suffered thee so to do.**

**Deuteronomy 12:1-4**

**1 These are the statutes and judgments, which ye shall observe to do in the land, which the Lord God of thy fathers giveth thee to possess it, all the days that ye live upon the earth.**

**2 Ye shall utterly destroy all the places, wherein the nations which ye shall possess served their gods, upon the high mountains, and upon the hills, and under every green tree:**

**3 And ye shall overthrow their altars, and break their pillars, and burn their groves with fire; and ye shall hew down the graven images of their gods, and destroy the names of them out of that place.**

**4 Ye shall not do so unto the Lord your God.**

You say: I don't pass my children through the fire to a false god. But ask yourself; who is the god of Christmas? I can tell you, it's not Jesus. The question is, who is the Christmas celebration geared toward? You may not pass your kids through the fire to these false gods, but you are setting a pattern of a false narrative that could lead to a pattern of accepting worship of a false god that could lead to tolerance of other religions that don't believe who Jesus is which could ultimately cast your child in the fire of hell if he or she accepts one of those false narratives that prevents them from seeing the truth about that false religion causing them to fall short of true salvation. If your child believes it's okay to take part in a worship that is not scriptural and that can't be justified by The Bible; then that opens the door to accepting other things that are not scriptural that cannot be backed up in The Bible. In Deuteronomy 18:10 that we just read; the custom of those idol worshipers was to observe times. Christmas started out as an observance of time at the winter solstice. It was also the custom of this people to set up a tree that they cut down and nailed boards on the bottom so it would stand upright, then decorated it, as we seen in Jeremiah 10:4:5. The tree was the focal point of the idol worship. Sound familiar? Now, The Bible doesn't come out and say: "The holiday known as Christmas is bad." But to read The Bible, you must connect what is being talked about with what is happening. For instance, we know by the signs of the times that these are the last days because of what The Bible says to look for in the last days. I know The Bible said we were in the last days even at Pentecost 2000 years ago. But I'm talking about The Bible indicating that these are the last of the last days, possibly the last generation before the rapture of the church. Things have happened that tells us that this could be the case, like the regathering of Israel, which began in 1948 when Israel was recognized as a nation again. And even recently when President Trump recognized Jerusalem as the capital of Israel and moved our embassy there.

> **Matthew 24:32-34**
> **32 Now learn a parable of the fig tree; When his branch is yet tender, and putteth forth leaves, ye know that summer is nigh:**
> **33 So likewise ye, when ye shall see all these things, know that it is near, even at the doors.**
> **34 Verily I say unto you, This generation shall not pass, till all these things be fulfilled.**

I know most theologians think that this passage in Matthew 24 is talking about 70 AD, when the temple was destroyed. This is only a type of what will happen during the seven-year tribulation at the end of the age. There was another event that typifies that event also. It is when a ruler named Antiochus Epiphanies, who set up an abomination in the Temple in the second century BC. But that is yet just another typology and doesn't fit the narrative of the scripture in the context of the chapter.

> **Matthew 24:15**
> **15 When ye therefore shall see the abomination of desolation, spoken of by Daniel the prophet, stand in the holy place, (whoso readeth, let him understand:)**

The abomination of desolation happens in the middle of a seven-year treaty that the antichrist will make with Israel in which the antichrist will break that treaty in the middle of the seven years which is when the abomination of desolation takes place. This time is known as the 7-year tribulation.

> **Matthew 24:21**
> **21 For then shall be great tribulation, such as was not since the beginning of the world to this time, no, nor ever shall be.**

> **Daniel 12:11**
> **11 And from the time that the daily sacrifice shall be taken away, and the abomination that maketh desolate set up, there shall be a thousand two hundred and ninety days.**

> **Daniel 9:27**
> **27 And he shall confirm the covenant with many for one week: and in the midst of the week he shall cause the sacrifice and the oblation to cease, and for the overspreading of abominations he shall make it desolate, even until the consummation, and that determined shall be poured upon the desolate.**

Verse 21, above, says great tribulation, such as was not since the beginning of the world to this time, no, nor ever shall be. If you have read Revelation, you know that there is no equal, no, not even close to the tribulation that comes during the 7-year tribulation after the church is raptured. And that is yet to come. Far more tribulation than those other two events we described. Then verse 27, below, describes the second coming of The Lord. And verses 29 through 31, below, describes the end of the tribulation when angels shall gather together Israel from the four winds and even from heaven.

> **Matthew 24:27**
> **27 For as the lightning cometh out of the east, and shineth even unto the west; so shall also the coming of the Son of man be.**

> **Matthew 24:29-31**
> **29 Immediately after the tribulation of those days shall the sun be darkened, and the moon shall not give her light, and the stars shall fall from heaven, and the powers of the heavens shall be shaken:**
> **30 And then shall appear the sign of the Son of man in heaven: and then shall all the tribes of the earth mourn, and they shall see the Son of man coming in the clouds of heaven with power and great glory.**
> **31 And he shall send his angels with a great sound of a trumpet, and they shall gather together his elect from the four winds, from one end of heaven to the other.**

Verse 31, above, has not happened yet. This is not the rapture of the church. The rapture happens 7 years before this verse. Verse 31 is the second coming of Jesus to this earth after the 7-year tribulation. Like we said, this has not happened yet. And this scripture below says that the antichrist will not be revealed until the beginning of the 7-year tribulation after the church is gone.

**2 Thessalonians 2:1-10**

1 Now we beseech you, brethren, by the coming of our Lord Jesus Christ, and by our gathering together unto him,

2 That ye be not soon shaken in mind, or be troubled, neither by spirit, nor by word, nor by letter as from us, as that the day of Christ is at hand.

3 Let no man deceive you by any means: for that day shall not come, except there come a falling away first, and that man of sin be revealed, the son of perdition;

4 Who opposeth and exalteth himself above all that is called God, or that is worshipped; so that he as God sitteth in the temple of God, shewing himself that he is God.

5 Remember ye not, that, when I was yet with you, I told you these things?

6 And now ye know what withholdeth that he might be revealed in his time.

7 For the mystery of iniquity doth already work: only he who now letteth will let, until he be taken out of the way.

8 And then shall that Wicked be revealed, whom the Lord shall consume with the spirit of his mouth, and shall destroy with the brightness of his coming:

9 Even him, whose coming is after the working of Satan with all power and signs and lying wonders,

10 And with all deceivableness of unrighteousness in them that perish; because they received not the love of the truth, that they might be saved.

This is when we, the church, who letteth, or holds back, shall be taken out of the way, in other words, raptured. With us out of the way, the antichrist will do his thing without us hindering him. This will mark the beginning of the 7-year tribulation.

**Revelation 13:1-8**

1 And I stood upon the sand of the sea, and saw a beast rise up out of the sea, having seven heads and ten horns, and

upon his horns ten crowns, and upon his heads the name of blasphemy.

2 And the beast which I saw was like unto a leopard, and his feet were as the feet of a bear, and his mouth as the mouth of a lion: and the dragon gave him his power, and his seat, and great authority.

3 And I saw one of his heads as it were wounded to death; and his deadly wound was healed: and all the world wondered after the beast.

4 And they worshipped the dragon which gave power unto the beast: and they worshipped the beast, saying, Who is like unto the beast? who is able to make war with him?

5 And there was given unto him a mouth speaking great things and blasphemies; and power was given unto him to continue forty and two months.

6 And he opened his mouth in blasphemy against God, to blaspheme his name, and his tabernacle, and them that dwell in heaven.

7 And it was given unto him to make war with the saints, and to overcome them: and power was given him over all kindreds, and tongues, and nations.

8 And all that dwell upon the earth shall worship him, whose names are not written in the book of life of the Lamb slain from the foundation of the world.

Revelation 13:13-15

13 And he doeth great wonders, so that he maketh fire come down from heaven on the earth in the sight of men,

14 And deceiveth them that dwell on the earth by the means of those miracles which he had power to do in the sight of the beast; saying to them that dwell on the earth, that they should make an image to the beast, which had the wound by a sword, and did live.

15 And he had power to give life unto the image of the beast, that the image of the beast should both speak, and

cause that as many as would not worship the image of the beast should be killed.

There will be no doubt when the final antichrist will come on the scene, as we see in the scripture above. So, the fig tree, below, is Israel gathered back into their land, which happened in 1948.

Matthew 24:32-34

32 Now learn a parable of the fig tree; When his branch is yet tender, and putteth forth leaves, ye know that summer is nigh:

33 So likewise ye, when ye shall see all these things, know that it is near, even at the doors.

34 Verily I say unto you, This generation shall not pass, till all these things be fulfilled.

Hosea 9:10

10 I found Israel like grapes in the wilderness; I saw your fathers as the firstripe in the fig tree at her first time: but they went to Baal-peor, and separated themselves unto that shame; and their abominations were according as they loved.

Jeremiah 29:16-17

16 Know that thus saith the Lord of the king that sitteth upon the throne of David, and of all the people that dwelleth in this city, and of your brethren that are not gone forth with you into captivity;

17 Thus saith the Lord of hosts; Behold, I will send upon them the sword, the famine, and the pestilence, and will make them like vile figs, that cannot be eaten, they are so evil.

**Jeremiah 24:1-10**

**1 The Lord shewed me, and, behold, two baskets of figs were set before the temple of the Lord, after that Nebuchadrezzar king of Babylon had carried away captive Jeconiah the son of Jehoiakim king of Judah, and the princes of Judah, with the carpenters and smiths, from Jerusalem, and had brought them to Babylon.**

**2 One basket had very good figs, even like the figs that are first ripe: and the other basket had very naughty figs, which could not be eaten, they were so bad.**

**3 Then said the Lord unto me, What seest thou, Jeremiah? And I said, Figs; the good figs, very good; and the evil, very evil, that cannot be eaten, they are so evil.**

**4 Again the word of the Lord came unto me, saying,**

**5 Thus saith the Lord, the God of Israel; Like these good figs, so will I acknowledge them that are carried away captive of Judah, whom I have sent out of this place into the land of the Chaldeans for their good.**

**6 For I will set mine eyes upon them for good, and I will bring them again to this land: and I will build them, and not pull them down; and I will plant them, and not pluck them up.**

**7 And I will give them an heart to know me, that I am the Lord: and they shall be my people, and I will be their God: for they shall return unto me with their whole heart.**

**8 And as the evil figs, which cannot be eaten, they are so evil; surely thus saith the Lord, So will I give Zedekiah the king of Judah, and his princes, and the residue of Jerusalem, that remain in this land, and them that dwell in the land of Egypt:**

**9 And I will deliver them to be removed into all the kingdoms of the earth for their hurt, to be a reproach and a proverb, a taunt and a curse, in all places whither I shall drive them.**

**10 And I will send the sword, the famine, and the pestilence, among them, till they be consumed from off the land that I gave unto them and to their fathers.**

In Romans, below, Israel is called the natural branches of an olive tree being grafted back into the olive tree in the coming tribulation time when all of Israel shall be saved.

> **Romans 11:24-27**
> **24 For if thou wert cut out of the olive tree which is wild by nature, and wert graffed contrary to nature into a good olive tree: how much more shall these, which be the natural branches, be graffed into their own olive tree?**
> **25 For I would not, brethren, that ye should be ignorant of this mystery, lest ye should be wise in your own conceits; that blindness in part is happened to Israel, until the fulness of the Gentiles be come in.**
> **26 And so all Israel shall be saved: as it is written, There shall come out of Sion the Deliverer, and shall turn away ungodliness from Jacob:**
> **27 For this is my covenant unto them, when I shall take away their sins.**

This is the regathering of Israel that will only happen in the last of the last days of the church right before the rapture. Matthew 24:34, above, says that generation shall not pass till all things are fulfilled. That same chapter in Matthew talks about wars and rumors of wars and earthquakes. Then Revelation describes a lining up of the European nations, and so on; all things that The Bible said would happen in the last days right before Jesus returns. The Bible doesn't say, "in the beginning of the 21st century, you will be in the last days". But we don't have to know the year to know that the last days are here. And as we said, we also know that a world ruler known as the antichrist will come on the scene during the tribulation. We don't know his name and the church will already be raptured out of here before the antichrist is made known. But for a person that knows The Bible; the antichrist wouldn't be hard to spot because of the things The Bible says he will do. Well, it's the same thing with Christmas, The Bible doesn't say: "There will be a holiday come along called Christmas, and it will deceive many people into celebrating a pagan festival, and they will think they are celebrating the birth of Jesus." Nevertheless, we can read The Bible, and look at history, or even the morning news, and see that The Bible foretold things that are taking place right now, and is still foretelling what will take place in the future. So, if you will look at history; at the time of Constantine and after, you will find, with very little trouble, the way that paganism was adopted into the church. And you will also find, with very little trouble, that Christmas was copied from the pagan winter festival of that time. We are in a period of time similar to the time when Jesus was here walking the earth. The Jews rejected Jesus because they didn't recognize Him as The Messiah. They didn't know the scripture well enough to see who He Is.

**Luke 4:16-30**

**16 And he came to Nazareth, where he had been brought up: and, as his custom was, he went into the synagogue on the sabbath day, and stood up for to read.**

**17 And there was delivered unto him the book of the prophet Esaias. And when he had opened the book, he found the place where it was written,**

**18 The Spirit of the Lord is upon me, because he hath anointed me to preach the gospel to the poor; he hath sent me to heal the brokenhearted, to preach deliverance to the captives, and recovering of sight to the blind, to set at liberty them that are bruised,**

**19 To preach the acceptable year of the Lord.**

**20 And he closed the book, and he gave it again to the minister, and sat down. And the eyes of all them that were in the synagogue were fastened on him.**

21 And he began to say unto them, This day is this scripture fulfilled in your ears.

22 And all bare him witness, and wondered at the gracious words which proceeded out of his mouth. And they said, Is not this Joseph's son?

23 And he said unto them, Ye will surely say unto me this proverb, Physician, heal thyself: whatsoever we have heard done in Capernaum, do also here in thy country.

24 And he said, Verily I say unto you, No prophet is accepted in his own country.

25 But I tell you of a truth, many widows were in Israel in the days of Elias, when the heaven was shut up three years and six months, when great famine was throughout all the land;

26 But unto none of them was Elias sent, save unto Sarepta, a city of Sidon, unto a woman that was a widow.

27 And many lepers were in Israel in the time of Eliseus the prophet; and none of them was cleansed, saving Naaman the Syrian.

28 And all they in the synagogue, when they heard these things, were filled with wrath,

29 And rose up, and thrust him out of the city, and led him unto the brow of the hill whereon their city was built, that they might cast him down headlong.

30 But he passing through the midst of them went his way,

They were shrouded in tradition and couldn't see through their tradition to recognize their own Messiah.

**John 1:10-11**

10 He was in the world, and the world was made by him, and the world knew him not.

11 He came unto his own, and his own received him not.

Today, it seems like people can't see who He isn't. He is not the christ of Christmas. People are willing to be deceived rather than believe the truth because of their tradition. We are warned about this in Colossians.

> **Colossians 2:8**
> **8 Beware lest any man spoil you through philosophy and vain deceit, after the tradition of men, after the rudiments of the world, and not after Christ.**

Very few people know enough about the scripture to even have a Biblical opinion. Most people will let their Pastor tell them about the scripture without even checking it out for themselves. That's why we are told that every person should be able to rightly divide The Word of Truth whether you are a pastor or just a common person in the congregation, verse 15 below. We are responsible to get the right information for ourselves by checking everything out with the completed Word of God so we will not believe a lie. The Bible doesn't tell us to seek out the truth from a pastor or Bible teacher. It tells us to study The Bible for ourselves. There is a point you can reach in studying The Bible that you can clearly know what It says without a preacher having to tell you. Every Christian should reach this point over time so they will know for themselves how to discern God's Word. There are far too many false doctrines out there because people just accept what they're being told as fact and they haven't even checked it out for themselves in The Word of God. Most people don't realize what a privilege it is to have God's Word available to us in our language to everyone who wants It. What an awesome thing; to have The spoken Words of God Himself right here in our hands. If you don't take advantage of that; you have squandered the greatest opportunity that there is in life.

2 Timothy 2:15-18

**15 Study to shew thyself approved unto God, a workman that needeth not to be ashamed, rightly dividing the word of truth.**

**16 But shun profane and vain babblings: for they will increase unto more ungodliness.**

**17 And their word will eat as doth a canker: of whom is Hymenaeus and Philetus;**

**18 Who concerning the truth have erred, saying that the resurrection is past already; and overthrow the faith of some.**

The Bible tells us not to be carried off by the sleight of men that lie in wait to deceive. We don't need any man to teach us. We are all equipped with The Holy Spirit in our life to lead us to the truth. But you must read His Word to find the truth to be able to know it.

1 John 2:26-27

**26 These things have I written unto you concerning them that seduce you.**

**27 But the anointing which ye have received of him abideth in you, and ye need not that any man teach you: but as the same anointing teacheth you of all things, and is truth, and is no lie, and even as it hath taught you, ye shall abide in him.**

Ephesians 4:14

**14 That we henceforth be no more children, tossed to and fro, and carried about with every wind of doctrine, by the sleight of men, and cunning craftiness, whereby they lie in wait to deceive;**

Unbelievers can't help but believe a lie because they can't discern spiritual things. But believers have no excuse.

**1 Corinthians 2:14-16**
**14 But the natural man receiveth not the things of the Spirit of God: for they are foolishness unto him: neither can he know them, because they are spiritually discerned.**
**15 But he that is spiritual judgeth all things, yet he himself is judged of no man.**
**16 For who hath known the mind of the Lord, that he may instruct him? But we have the mind of Christ.**

This type of church age today is people that love tradition more than they love the truth. In other words; deception. Like I said, at least they had the excuse that they didn't have much personal access to God's Word, but they didn't listen to the leading of The Holy Spirit to reveal the truth to them. Today, especially in America, we have free and total unfettered access to God's Word. But unfortunately, many don't read it. And there are still those today that are not tuned into The Holy Spirit and His instruction on things. Why would anyone with such access want to add something to God's Word that is not there when it is so easy to verify if it is Biblical or not? This type of church goes ahead and commits adultery with the world either out of ignorance or just going along with the crowd or simply wanting to participate in it no matter what The Bible has to say about it. Some of them believe that God's morals change with the times. And so they think they are now permitted to do things that The Bible speaks against simply because now everyone is doing it and saying it is now permitted because public opinion has changed about it. The pastor usually goes along with it out of fear for his job or fear of chasing off members. The person of this type doesn't study The Bible for himself. He is okay with just going along with whatever the trend is as long as it is accepted by the church or most of society. He thinks that if the pastor preaches in favor of it, then it must be okay. At least this church age did have some good qualities in its favor. Verse 19. But it also had some bad things that eventually sent the church into a tailspin in the next church age.

**Romans 1:22-25**

22 Professing themselves to be wise, they became fools,

23 And changed the glory of the uncorruptible God into an image made like to corruptible man, and to birds, and fourfooted beasts, and creeping things.

24 Wherefore God also gave them up to uncleanness through the lusts of their own hearts, to dishonour their own bodies between themselves:

25 Who changed the truth of God into a lie, and worshipped and served the creature more than the Creator, who is blessed for ever. Amen.

# 5. Sardis: 14th and 15th century AD.

**Revelation 3:1-6**

1 And unto the angel of the church in Sardis write; These things saith he that hath the seven Spirits of God, and the seven stars; I know thy works, that thou hast a name that thou livest, and art dead.

2 Be watchful, and strengthen the things which remain, that are ready to die: for I have not found thy works perfect before God.

3 Remember therefore how thou hast received and heard, and hold fast, and repent. If therefore thou shalt not watch, I will come on thee as a thief, and thou shalt not know what hour I will come upon thee.

4 Thou hast a few names even in Sardis which have not defiled their garments; and they shall walk with me in white: for they are worthy.

5 He that overcometh, the same shall be clothed in white raiment; and I will not blot out his name out of the book of life, but I will confess his name before my Father, and before his angels.

**6 He that hath an ear, let him hear what the Spirit saith unto the churches.**

As I said, the church at Thyatira led the church into the dark ages. By the time we get to Sardis; it's nothing but dark ages. This is probably the darkest church age of all as far as the church ages go. This church is almost dead, barely hanging on to life with only a handful of true believers, verse 4. It's a good thing this age of Sardis is only about 2 centuries long or the church might have completely fell. But God wouldn't let that happen. God will always keep to Himself a remnant of faithful believers that will not defile their garments with idolism and compromise, verse 4. But then and even today, there are those that think they are saved through the Roman/ government church, or today, the Roman religion, or through some other religion, but will ultimately find their name blotted out of the book of life when they fall short of true salvation, verse 5. In this church age of Sardis, the Roman/government church is in control and the true Christian is labeled as a heretic for not following the dictates of this government church. This was a very hard time to be a Christian. They were killed for their faith. Most people just submitted to the government run church rather than face the death penalty of being an outspoken true Christian. Do you see now why mixing Christianity with paganism is so dangerous? The church at Sardis here is almost dead because of it. You can't play around with paganism. It may seem like a small thing to you to celebrate this Babylonish holiday, but just look what happened to the church in this church age because of this small thing. There is not a lot to say about this church age that is good. In fact, this is one of only two church ages that God had nothing good to say about other than He said He had a few in this age that haven't defiled their garments, verse 4. This is the result of letting paganism and idol worship infiltrate the church. We have God on our side. We should stand up against anything not of God entering the church. The world doesn't stand a chance against a united church that stands against worldly influences. Thank God that there were a few that didn't participate and stain their garments with these worldly celebrations. I believe the same thing is happening in this type of church age in our present church age. There is an increasing falling away of true committed believers even today that holds back many great things that the church could accomplish if we would only be united and unwavering in what we do; but without playing in the world's backyard with its painted-up traditions and celebrations. Even the godless people of Babel were united, and it was unrestrained in what they could have done if God had not confounded their language.

**Genesis 11:6**
**6 And the Lord said, Behold, the people is one, and they have all one language; and this they begin to do: and now nothing will be restrained from them, which they have imagined to do.**

If it is unrestrained what some united godless people could have done if God hadn't stopped them, imagine what the church could do if we would just be united in what we do. And God wouldn't stop us like he did the godless people of Babel; but He would help us and provide us with the power and wisdom to do those things. But the church today is not united. Therefore, we can't get anything done. Much of the church today compromises with the world and mixes the work of God with idol worship. I'm afraid that much of the church today is a Sardis type church, just going along with vain traditions and with teachings not found in The Bible. This type of church today can be a mega church. They can have thousands of members but have no truth in their teachings. This type of person loves tradition more than they love the truth of The Word of God. They are lost in vain tradition and make no attempt to search for the truth. Other than some Christian Jewish congregations, I don't know of any church today that exposes the Christmas lie. And I don't know but a handful of Christians that make any attempt to study their Bibles to find these truths. Yes, the Sardis type of church is very much with us today.

# 6. Philadelphia: 16ᵗʰ through the 19ᵗʰ century AD.

**Revelation 3:7-13**
**7 And to the angel of the church in Philadelphia write; These things saith he that is holy, he that is true, he that hath the key of David, he that openeth, and no man shutteth; and shutteth, and no man openeth;**
**8 I know thy works: behold, I have set before thee an open door, and no man can shut it: for thou hast a little strength, and hast kept my word, and hast not denied my name.**
**9 Behold, I will make them of the synagogue of Satan, which say they are Jews, and are not, but do lie; behold, I will make them to come and worship before thy feet, and to know that I have loved thee.**
**10 Because thou hast kept the word of my patience, I also will keep thee from the hour of temptation, which shall come upon all the world, to try them that dwell upon the earth.**
**11 Behold, I come quickly: hold that fast which thou hast, that no man take thy crown.**
**12 Him that overcometh will I make a pillar in the temple of my God, and he shall go no more out: and I will write upon him the name of my God, and the name of the city of my God, which is new Jerusalem, which cometh down out of heaven from my God: and I will write upon him my new name.**
**13 He that hath an ear, let him hear what the Spirit saith unto the churches.**

This is kinda like going from the worst to the best. Actually, the persecution of the church at Sardis strengthened the handful of true Christians. And out of that persecution grew a movement that would crush the dominant hold that the Roman/government church had on Christians. This is when the time of reformation began, when several bold Christians took a stand and exposed the lies of the government run church. The beginning of this Philadelphian church age is when The Word of God became widely available to the general public and people began to see the flaw in what was being taught. This is the time when Martin Luther nailed his ninety-five theses to the door of the church and changed everything. Now, I don't' agree with everything Martin Luther believed. And of course, he wasn't the only one that took part in that great reformation. But he pretty much kicked it off with that bold act. In the age of Philadelphia, the Roman church split, and England formed a separate English church away from the mother church at Rome. Don't misunderstand me, this English church was not freedom of religion. They still adhered to all the Roman celebrations and customs. They were simply separating from Rome and giving an alternative for Englanders to keep their finances in the church at home. There were a few doctrinal differences that they used as an excuse to break away from the mother church at Rome but that is not what this book is about. If you want to know these differences, I suggest you look up "church of England" on the internet. However, this act did weaken the Roman/government church substantially and contributed greatly to the release of the chokehold that the Roman church had on world religion. This happened in about 1534 AD, sometime after the reformation with Martin Luther and some other bold Christians that challenged the Roman church teachings. Then, at the same time, The Word of God suddenly became available in English to the common everyday person. This was all part of the breakup of the hold that the Roman church had on the world. Then our ancestors braved the trip over here to this new land of America to be able to be a Christian without compromising it with pagan festivals. It is the Philadelphian church age that would usher in a time of freedom of religion for many and put an end to the Roman/government church dominance that had lasted over a thousand years. It was the end of the dark ages and a bright new day for Christianity. The storm was over and the skies have cleared. This church age is recent enough that we have ample evidence of the dramatic change that occurred with its arrival. The Sardinian church age was the darkest time for the church and was followed by the brightest time for the church. This is the only other church age besides Smyrna that God had nothing bad to say about. But the context was different. Smyrna stayed faithful despite deep persecution and martyrdom. Philadelphia was faithful in the end of persecution and martyrdom with profound freedom for the church. Actually, there was still persecution in some places. That will always be the case in every church age until Jesus comes. But this church age marked the end of the worldwide Roman dominance in the church and a beginning of religious freedom in a lot of the world. This is the church age of the birth of the United States of America that was founded on religious freedom and became a beacon and a refuge for those that wanted an escape from the mandates of the Roman/government church and its pagan rituals. So again, we went from the darkest day to the brightest day.... But it wouldn't last. The church enjoyed four centuries of this church age with profound freedom in the church and good times seemingly never ending. The Philadelphian type of person is one that knows the truth and studies The Bible for his answers. He stays away from pagan influences and frees himself from worldly influences and stands firm for The Word of truth. We seen this type of church in the recent past that puts God first and shuns vain traditions and actually lives by The Word of God. Unfortunitally, today, it has died out and the next church age has taken over.

# 7. Laodicean: The 20th century through Now AD.

**Revelation 3:14-22**

**14 And unto the angel of the church of the Laodiceans write; These things saith the Amen, the faithful and true witness, the beginning of the creation of God;**

**15 I know thy works, that thou art neither cold nor hot: I would thou wert cold or hot.**

**16 So then because thou art lukewarm, and neither cold nor hot, I will spue thee out of my mouth.**

**17 Because thou sayest, I am rich, and increased with goods, and have need of nothing; and knowest not that thou art wretched, and miserable, and poor, and blind, and naked:**

**18 I counsel thee to buy of me gold tried in the fire, that thou mayest be rich; and white raiment, that thou mayest be clothed, and that the shame of thy nakedness do not appear; and anoint thine eyes with eyesalve, that thou mayest see.**

**19 As many as I love, I rebuke and chasten: be zealous therefore, and repent.**

**20 Behold, I stand at the door, and knock: if any man hear my voice, and open the door, I will come in to him, and will sup with him, and he with me.**

**21 To him that overcometh will I grant to sit with me in my throne, even as I also overcame, and am set down with my Father in his throne.**

**22 He that hath an ear, let him hear what the Spirit saith unto the churches.**

This church age probably started or overlapped with the Philadelphian age in the late 1800s. That is when you began to see the return of the Roman church mixture of paganism with Christianity, cold with hot equals lukewarm. The hot Philadelphian church began to accept the cold pagan traditions again ushering in the lukewarm Laodicean church. This time, without the Roman government to enforce their doctrines. Those pagan rituals have been brought back into the church willingly this time because of widespread deception of what it is. It slowly made its way back with the United States making it a national holiday in 1870. Before that time, Christmas was not much of an issue. But then the church began to adopt these pagan traditions again when the popularity of it became notable. This time, it was voluntary. There was no government telling them that they had to do this. They did it willingly to be able to participate in the fun celebration of the holiday even though it wasn't Christian. It had been long enough that people forgot that these were even pagan festivals and thought that they were Biblical celebrations. They forgot the Roman aggression connected to these celebrations. They forgot how these compromises brought in through the church age of Pergamos led to the dark ages of the church age of Thyatira, and then into the almost dead church age of Sardis. The church age of Philadelphia brought the church out of that decline by breaking away from that corrupt mixture of church and paganism. But now it seems like we are falling right back into the trap. That is why I am writing this book. To inform the uninformed. This reinstating of these celebrations was probably most responsible for kicking off the Laodicean church age. The church began to mix with the world bringing on the lukewarm characteristic described in verse 16. It was the beginning of the modern western age and the beginning of the moral decline of the modern age. This church age was the beginning of the age of invention. From the beginning of this age until now, we went from getting around on horse and buggy to landing a man on the moon. You had the age of music coming on the scene with the advent of Jazz becoming very popular. That, along with the invention of radio, set off a rash of new music that is still going on today. The Philadelphian church kind of overlapped into the Laodicean church age and created kind of a mixture of good and bad, hot and cold, again equaling lukewarm. There was the great revival of the late 1800s when a lot of the hymns that we know today were written. Then you had the birth of the charismatic movement in the early 1900s where many Pentecostal type churches were born. Then came World War I that would be the start of a series of wars in the 20th century. Then the popularity of Jazz brought in the roaring twenties which began the relaxing of morals. After that was World War II that brought in the industrial age. After that, Billy Graham came on the scene sparking the great stadium revivals of his day and sparking a rash of large stadium evangelist coming on the scene. More recently, we have seen the birth of the great Christian networks with Pat Robison, Jim Baker, Paul Crouch and his son Matt Crouch and Christian networks such as CBN, TBN, Daystar and more. This was a great evangelistic tool, but many times, the message began to be watered down, lukewarm, with a mixture of the world added in. You began to see the mega church age come to pass with several large congregations in which some of them also watered down the message and became a motivational institute instead of a church with Biblical substance. Itching ears were scratched, and again, the lukewarm description. You had the Brownsville revival in 1995 but with controversial questions being raised about some of the practices of that revival. With a lot of these evangelistic events of the 20th century, there were elements of it that were controversial that divided some of the church and raised doctrinal questions. With the advent of the charismatic movement in the early 1900s, there were serious questions raised about what The Bible says about women in leadership roles in the church and the use of tongues as a requirement for receiving The Holy Spirit, both of which exacerbated the lukewarm issue. These questions are still an issue in dividing the church even to this day into lukewarmness. Also, most all of the prominent preachers and evangelist of this church age accepted the Christmas celebration as a Christian celebration. Other movements have come and gone with some raising more questions. But at least some of these movements did somehow result in people getting saved. Even though doctrinal questions divided a lot of these churches, God still used these movements to save people. Through all the division, Jesus was still preached and there is power in that Name. But we have seen the end of it now. There has been a spiritual vacuum for several years now which, I believe, verifies that we are in the last days of the church age of Laodicea. There are some movements today taking place in other countries, but for the most part, especially here in the United States, not much is happening in Spiritual revival. Yes, there are still people getting saved. Like I said, there is power in the Name of Jesus even if you falter on your doctrine. The lukewarm church does have a hot side to the lukewarmness. Sometimes that hot side will show through and do some good. But once it mixes with the cold and becomes lukewarm, God spews it out of His mouth. This church age is overlapping with God turning back to the Jews which I believe started happening on May 15. 1948. That is the day that Israel became a nation again. So, it would make sense that the last church age would signal the beginning of the turning back to Israel in kind of an overlapping of the last church age with the regathering of Israel when God will turn back to the Jewish people after the church is raptured. The Laodicean church age really manifested itself clearly in the 50s, 60s and 70s with the moral decline of music mixed with drugs, alcohol, sexuality, homosexuality and violence. This all manifested itself in the words of their songs with rock, disco, heavy metal, rap, country and whatever they call the poor excuse for music today. The sad thing is that a lot of these singers, musicians and bands are extremely gifted in their music, but they sell their God given gift to the world for fame and personal financial gain. People turned away from God and sort of went their own way with the free love and hippie movement that sparked a rebellious movement followed by a sharp moral decline in America followed by the government taking God out of our schools followed by the supreme court legalizing abortion followed by the legalizing and social acceptance of homosexuality and transgenderism followed by movements trying to erase our Christian heritage that this country was founded on and most recently followed by a redefinition of the God given definition of marriage. The type of church in this age is one that is turning away from God and don't even realize it. They think everything is fine and they think they are in God's will, but they don't realize that they are far from God. I believe the United States of America, that was founded on Christianity and freedom of religion without the state interfering with it; is now beginning to interfere with it with laws that took prayer out of our public schools, instituted abortion on demand with government funded abortion clinics and new laws designed to force Christians to recognize liberal/progressive agendas on marriage and homosexuality. In 2020, many state governments used a virus to extinguish our constitutional right of freedom of assembly in the church. They mandated that you couldn't go to church making it an illegal act. I do understand the need to avoid catching a deadly virus. The church should use extreme caution with their gathering together with common sense precautions, and the church should listen to suggestions of people that are acquainted with how the virus spreads. I just think it should be up to the church to do that, not the government violating their 1st amendment rights. Suddenly the state is now trying to control religion again just like what happened in the dark ages. Things went downhill fast form then until today when the common practice today seems to be to eliminate God and His Word from everything we do. There is a left-wing movement today that is gaining ground quickly and is under the excuse that, in their mind, this country was founded unfairly and recompence needs to be made by taking freedoms away from some and letting others slide. And taking money away from those who earned it and giving it to those who didn't in the name of that recompence. This type of person today is one that has grown Lazy in the good times and doesn't even realize that he and the church are slipping into apostasy and they are not even aware of their declining spirituality. They don't realize that they are in error. They think everything is fine and don't even realize they are wretched, miserable, poor, blind and naked, verse 17. I believe this will be a short church age. It is a coincidence that the first and the last church ages would be the shortest ages. And a good thing too in the case of the Laodicean church age because I believe this church age is even worse in turning away from God than Sardis was. I don't believe God will put up with this lukewarm decline in His church for long, verse 16. I think that even now, it is very close to the rapture of the church that will end this age. I believe we are most certainly currently in the last days of the Laodicean church age right now. The church today has compromised and merged with this world system. Yes, the church is very rich today, verse 17. We have multiple television networks dedicated to preaching the Gospel all over the world today. We have giant cathedrals and mega large stadium churches that hold multiple thousands of people. There has never before been more opportunity to reach so many people than today. But what are we doing with it? We don't even realize that we are destitute for the truth. The United States of America, that was founded on religious freedom during the church age of Philadelphia to provide a get away from the influence of the Roman/government church, has now adopted those same pagan celebrations that when this country was founded; people flocked to this new land of freedom to escape from theses pagan customs that, at that time, were forced on them to participate in. So, they came here to be able to have freedom of religion and escape the chokehold of the government's version of Christianity, only to find that those pagan festivals would follow them here in the next church age, but in a different way. We are not forced to take part in these festivals anymore; but we do it willingly because of the lack of knowledge of where these festivals came from. If you ask someone in America today where Christmas originated from; probably 99% of them would tell you at the birth of Jesus. That's the trouble with good times like in the Philadelphian church age; people get lazy and forget why they have it so good. They are lulled back into a lackadaisical time of wondering in the wilderness with no sense of purpose and direction until the end of the Laodicean age at the rapture of the church. This type of church is right now. Look around you and see it for yourself. We have willingly fallen back into that false religious system that the church age of Philadelphia brought us out of. But like I said, I believe this church age will be short and will end at the soon rapture of the church. But The false religious system will remain after the church is gone and follow the world into the tribulation through the false prophet. It will finally come to an end at the return of Jesus at the end of the tribulation at His second coming when we return with Jesus and He will set up His earthly kingdom where He will rule with a rod of iron in this world for a thousand years. There will be no more pagan festivals in that kingdom and the false religious system will finally be completely and utterly wiped out. In the description of the kingdom reign of Jesus in Revelation, you will not find any mention of any pagan like festival or any of its traditions. But you will see God put an end to it. The false Babylonian church will finally be abolished and destroyed forever. There will be no more Christmas, no more Easter and no more of the zodiac belief system seen after that day, praise The Name of Jesus, can you say amen?

**Revelation 18:1-2**
**1 And after these things I saw another angel come down from heaven, having great power; and the earth was lightened with his glory.**
**2 And he cried mightily with a strong voice, saying, Babylon the great is fallen, is fallen, and is become the habitation of devils, and the hold of every foul spirit, and a cage of every unclean and hateful bird.**

**Revelation 18:15-23**
**15 The merchants of these things, which were made rich by her, shall stand afar off for the fear of her torment, weeping and wailing,**
**16 And saying, Alas, alas, that great city, that was clothed in fine linen, and purple, and scarlet, and decked with gold, and precious stones, and pearls!**
**17 For in one hour so great riches is come to nought. And every shipmaster, and all the company in ships, and sailors, and as many as trade by sea, stood afar off,**

18 And cried when they saw the smoke of her burning, saying, What city is like unto this great city!

19 And they cast dust on their heads, and cried, weeping and wailing, saying, Alas, alas, that great city, wherein were made rich all that had ships in the sea by reason of her costliness! for in one hour is she made desolate.

20 Rejoice over her, thou heaven, and ye holy apostles and prophets; for God hath avenged you on her.

21 And a mighty angel took up a stone like a great millstone, and cast it into the sea, saying, Thus with violence shall that great city Babylon be thrown down, and shall be found no more at all.

22 And the voice of harpers, and musicians, and of pipers, and trumpeters, shall be heard no more at all in thee; and no craftsman, of whatsoever craft he be, shall be found any more in thee; and the sound of a millstone shall be heard no more at all in thee;

23 And the light of a candle shall shine no more at all in thee; and the voice of the bridegroom and of the bride shall be heard no more at all in thee: for thy merchants were the great men of the earth; for by thy sorceries were all nations deceived.

There is another characteristic of the Laodicean church age that crept in very subtilty and was dominant before anyone noticed. At the end of the Philadelphian church age, you began to see a wavering from the true message of the gospel of freedom in Christ. This pushed the church into the Laodicean church age by some pastors taking charge over their congregations with rules and requirements that began to burden the people and chase them off from the church, being turned off by all these new requirements. Some even taught a works salvation or taught that you could lose your salvation if you fall back into a sin. It resembles the Jewish priesthood where the scribes and pharisees made up their own rules and called them as being from God. It would seem the church is following the same pattern. I witnessed this myself in some churches in the eighties and nineties. In that day and age, it seemed like the pastor was kind of a boss and you were the lowly employee that better do what he says or you could be fired from that church, so to speak. These were strict rules on things like tithing, church attendance, knocking doors, dress codes in church and other dress codes for your daily life, some said men can't have a beard, others said men must have a beard. Men can't wear a short sleeve shirt. Women must wear a dress and it can't be red, and it must come down to their ankles. and they must wear their hair up in a bun in public. You can't wear jewelry, sometimes even a watch. Strict rules on watching TV and movies, some say you can't even have a TV in your house. Rules on what kind of music you can and cannot listen to; rules against dancing, dating, how long your hair is, what kind of job you can and cannot have, who you associate with. Rules against drinking anything with alcohol. There are those that say you can't have any modern conveniences. Some won't even have a car. They get around on horse and buggy. There are a lot of them out there that say you can't receive blood, even if it means saving your life, and they tell you if you do receive blood, you are condemned to hell. Many say you can't receive medical attention, that if God doesn't heal you, then it is just your turn to die. These are just a few of the things that people have rules about that are not in The Bible. This began to be a pharisaical type of ruling the church. They think they are high and mighty rulers of people and they cherish that position because of the power of it. In actuality, we are all equal but with different gifts. The gift of teaching doesn't give you power over another member to make your own rules. It just means that God has given you the assignment of teaching The Word of God in the church. In reality, you are no more important than a nursery worker or custodian or parking lot attendant or any other job God gives to someone in the church. The Bible does give an elder the power of organization and church discipline, but those are to be used in agreement with other elders and most importantly in agreement with The Word of God. Those elders that labor in The Word are to be counted worthy of double honor because they are the ones that seek out the truth of The Word, or at least they are supposed to. But that doesn't give them the right to lord over everyone. He is to teach with love and rule with love, not a hammer. When this mindset of rules and regulations began to take hold, in many cases, it got much worse. You had some radicals that took it to a new level and began to believe that they were superior in spirituality to others and that they had power to punish those that were not as spiritual as them. You began to see Hollywood mimic this by making TV shows and movies with what I call "the crazy Christian". They would portray a Christian as a crazy extremist that vexed his family with unreasonable rules that they could never keep and then punish them severely for not keeping those rules. Either that or they would think that it was their job to punish society for its sinfulness. They would be portrayed as isolating themselves from the rest of the world and wouldn't have anything to do with anyone but what they considered, the super righteous. Many of these TV show characters ended up murdering their family, or trying to, thinking that was the only way to extinguish the evil that possessed them. Or they would murder others that they thought God was telling them that they should kill. Yes, there really are some people out there that do extreme types of things like this. But these kinds of people are more like sociopaths, not Christians. I think these types of people are delusional and only think they are Christians. But in Hollywood, all they see is that delusional person making the news for doing these sorts of things, and because he claims to be a Christian, they portray that as a typical normal Christian. When Hollywood does have a levelheaded man of God in the script, it's usually of the Roman religion variety. They don't seem to know how to portray a real regular normal Christian. How could they? Someone that is not a Christian cannot know how a Christian should act. All they can do is go by what they see. And many times, they just see what they want to see. The world doesn't like Christians because they are convicted buy what we stand for, so they must exaggerate what they see and twist it into what they want you to think a Christian looks like, which to them is an unreasonable extremist. Then they portray that type of person as a typical Christian so they can show the world how unreasonable we are and how righteous they are for stopping an extremist like that. That way, they justify what they do by trying to discredit a true Christian for our stand against sin.

**1 Peter 5:1-3**
**1 The elders which are among you I exhort, who am also an elder, and a witness of the sufferings of Christ, and also a partaker of the glory that shall be revealed:**
**2 Feed the flock of God which is among you, taking the oversight thereof, not by constraint, but willingly; not for filthy lucre, but of a ready mind;**
**3 Neither as being lords over God's heritage, but being ensamples to the flock.**

**1 Timothy 5:17**
**17 Let the elders that rule well be counted worthy of double honour, especially they who labour in the word and doctrine.**

**Romans 12:3**
**3 For I say, through the grace given unto me, to every man that is among you, not to think of himself more highly than he ought to think; but to think soberly, according as God hath dealt to every man the measure of faith.**

**Matthew 23:22-24**
**22 And he that shall swear by heaven, sweareth by the throne of God, and by him that sitteth thereon.**
**23 Woe unto you, scribes and Pharisees, hypocrites! for ye pay tithe of mint and anise and cummin, and have omitted the weightier matters of the law, judgment, mercy, and faith: these ought ye to have done, and not to leave the other undone.**

**24 Ye blind guides, which strain at a gnat, and swallow a camel.**

**Matthew 23:26-28**
**26 Thou blind Pharisee, cleanse first that which is within the cup and platter, that the outside of them may be clean also.**
**27 Woe unto you, scribes and Pharisees, hypocrites! for ye are like unto whited sepulchres, which indeed appear beautiful outward, but are within full of dead men's bones, and of all uncleanness.**
**28 Even so ye also outwardly appear righteous unto men, but within ye are full of hypocrisy and iniquity.**

**Matthew 12:35**
**35 A good man out of the good treasure of the heart bringeth forth good things: and an evil man out of the evil treasure bringeth forth evil things.**

Rules are okay in the church, such as bylaws, leadership roles and discipline. You must have some rules to have order. But those rules need to be Biblical and follow guidelines set forth in The Bible. They need to be executed with love and compassion taking into consideration that not everyone is the same, therefore, everyone can't be dealt with the same. We need to leave out those rules that man wants to put in there that are not scriptural. All things are lawful to a Christian. Just not all things are expedient.

**1 Corinthians 6:12**
**12 All things are lawful unto me, but all things are not expedient: all things are lawful for me, but I will not be brought under the power of any.**

And we have The Holy Spirit to show us the difference.

1 John 2:20

20 But ye have an unction from the Holy One, and ye know all things.

1 John 2:27

27 But the anointing which ye have received of him abideth in you, and ye need not that any man teach you: but as the same anointing teacheth you of all things, and is truth, and is no lie, and even as it hath taught you, ye shall abide in him.

The type of church for this church age is one that doesn't put any kind of emphasis on holiness. They are happy with a watered-down gospel that is more feel good than is truth. As long as they hear an uplifting and inspiring message, they are okay with everything else. They reject a hell fire and brimstone message because that is frightening and not uplifting. They are also connected with the world so they reject a message that separates them from the world. They want instant gratification and support the idea of global warming and are a supporter of save the whales and wild life preservation. They are a great defender of animal rights yet they are okay with abortion. To them, everyone has good in them and it is unfair to say that Jesus is the only way to salvation. They think that, after all, these other religions worship God also, just in a different way. These types of people spend more time on social justice and special interest groups than they do on Biblical truths. In fact, they think The Bible is outdated and needs to be revised to more fit modern day thinking.

# CHAPTER 6
# I BRING NOT PEACE,
# BUT A SWARD

**Luke 2:13-14**
**13 And suddenly there was with the angel a multitude of the heavenly host praising God, and saying,**
**14 Glory to God in the highest, and on earth peace, good will toward men.**

Peace on earth, good will toward men is the central theme at Christmas time. There have been cease fires between waring nations at Christmas. People that don't like each other exchange greeting cards. But does this constitute peace on earth? People say that at least one day a year, there can be peace. Most think that when the angel said in Luke 2:14, "on earth peace, good will toward men," it meant world peace from wars. That is the kind of peace you hear Christmas being about. But all one has to do is look at the past two thousand years since that was said and see that peace from war was definitely not what the angel was talking about. If it was; then Matthew 10:34 would contradict it when Jesus said:

**Matthew 10:34**
**34 Think not that I am come to send peace on earth: I came not to send peace, but a sword.**

Jesus said in Luke that He doesn't bring peace, but He brings division.

**Luke 12:51-52**
**51 Suppose ye that I am come to give peace on earth? I tell you, Nay; but rather division:**
**52 For from henceforth there shall be five in one house divided, three against two, and two against three.**

The peace the angel was talking about is the inner peace that Jesus would bring through salvation, and the gift of The Holy Spirit.

**John 14:25-27**
**25 These things have I spoken unto you, being yet present with you.**
**26 But the Comforter, which is the Holy Ghost, whom the Father will send in my name, he shall teach you all things, and bring all things to your remembrance, whatsoever I have said unto you.**
**27 Peace I leave with you, my peace I give unto you: not as the world giveth, give I unto you. Let not your heart be troubled, neither let it be afraid.**

**Ephesians 2:12-17**
**12 That at that time ye were without Christ, being aliens from the commonwealth of Israel, and strangers from the covenants of promise, having no hope, and without God in the world:**
**13 But now in Christ Jesus ye who sometimes were far off are made nigh by the blood of Christ.**
**14 For he is our peace, who hath made both one, and hath broken down the middle wall of partition between us;**
**15 Having abolished in his flesh the enmity, even the law of commandments contained in ordinances; for to make in himself of twain one new man, so making peace;**

**16 And that he might reconcile both unto God in one body by the cross, having slain the enmity thereby:**
**17 And came and preached peace to you which were afar off, and to them that were nigh.**

To receive peace from God.

**Romans 1:7**
**7 To all that be in Rome, beloved of God, called to be saints: Grace to you and peace from God our Father, and the Lord Jesus Christ.**

And the peace of God.

**1 Corinthians 1:3**
**3 Grace be unto you, and peace, from God our Father, and from the Lord Jesus Christ.**

**Philippians 4:7**
**7 And the peace of God, which passeth all understanding, shall keep your hearts and minds through Christ Jesus.**

World peace from wars is not what it's talking about. There's only a false peace, then sudden destruction.

**1 Thessalonians 5:2-3**
**2 For yourselves know perfectly that the day of the Lord so cometh as a thief in the night.**
**3 For when they shall say, Peace and safety; then sudden destruction cometh upon them, as travail upon a woman with child; and they shall not escape.**

There is a thousand years of peace when Jesus shall rule and reign. But peace for today? No! Quite the opposite. In Matthew 24:7, Nation shall rise against nation. In verse 6, You shall hear of wars and rumors of wars. That doesn't sound like peace to me. Why would The Bible predict war if the angel meant that the birth of Jesus would bring peace from war? In Revelation 6:4, peace shall be taken from the earth.

**Revelation 6:4**
**4 And there went out another horse that was red: and power was given to him that sat thereon to take peace from the earth, and that they should kill one another: and there was given unto him a great sword.**

During the millennial reign of Jesus will there be peace, when we shall rule and reign with Jesus for a thousand years. But even after that, there will be one more war.

**Revelation 20:6-9**
**6 Blessed and holy is he that hath part in the first resurrection: on such the second death hath no power, but they shall be priests of God and of Christ, and shall reign with him a thousand years.**
**7 And when the thousand years are expired, Satan shall be loosed out of his prison,**
**8 And shall go out to deceive the nations which are in the four quarters of the earth, Gog and Magog, to gather them together to battle: the number of whom is as the sand of the sea.**
**9 And they went up on the breadth of the earth, and compassed the camp of the saints about, and the beloved city: and fire came down from God out of heaven, and devoured them.**

This is not going to be much of a battle. The fire of God will devout them, verse 9 above. In chapter 21 there will be lasting and final peace in the new heaven and new earth in the new Jerusalem.

**Revelation 21:1-2**
**1 And I saw a new heaven and a new earth: for the first heaven and the first earth were passed away; and there was no more sea.**
**2 And I John saw the holy city, new Jerusalem, coming down from God out of heaven, prepared as a bride adorned for her husband.**

But as for now; well, there is only inner peace through The Holy Spirit that is free to anyone who will receive Him. But for those who don't, no peace, only trouble, war and tribulation; Christmas or no Christmas. That's why today is the day of salvation. If God is calling you; accept Jesus as your Savior and be born again today if you haven't already. And receive real peace. The way you do that is to realize that you're a sinner in need of a Savior. Then confess with your mouth The Lord Jesus. Believe who He is; and believe in your heart that He died on the cross of Calvary for your sin, then after three days and three nights, The Spirit raised Him from the dead. Then receive Jesus in your life to save you and deliver you from the penalty of sin and direct your life through The Holy Spirit Who will live in you after salvation.

**Romans 3:23-28**
**23 For all have sinned, and come short of the glory of God;**
**24 Being justified freely by his grace through the redemption that is in Christ Jesus:**

**Romans 10:9-13**
**9 That if thou shalt confess with thy mouth the Lord Jesus, and shalt believe in thine heart that God hath raised him from the dead, thou shalt be saved.**
**10 For with the heart man believeth unto righteousness; and with the mouth confession is made unto salvation.**
**11 For the scripture saith, Whosoever believeth on him shall not be ashamed.**

12 For there is no difference between the Jew and the Greek: for the same Lord over all is rich unto all that call upon him.

13 For whosoever shall call upon the name of the Lord shall be saved.

1 Corinthians 12:13

13 For by one Spirit are we all baptized into one body, whether we be Jews or Gentiles, whether we be bond or free; and have been all made to drink into one Spirit.

Romans 6:1-14

1 What shall we say then? Shall we continue in sin, that grace may abound?

2 God forbid. How shall we, that are dead to sin, live any longer therein?

3 Know ye not, that so many of us as were baptized into Jesus Christ were baptized into his death?

4 Therefore we are buried with him by baptism into death: that like as Christ was raised up from the dead by the glory of the Father, even so we also should walk in newness of life.

5 For if we have been planted together in the likeness of his death, we shall be also in the likeness of his resurrection:

6 Knowing this, that our old man is crucified with him, that the body of sin might be destroyed, that henceforth we should not serve sin.

7 For he that is dead is freed from sin.

8 Now if we be dead with Christ, we believe that we shall also live with him:

9 Knowing that Christ being raised from the dead dieth no more; death hath no more dominion over him.

10 For in that he died, he died unto sin once: but in that he liveth, he liveth unto God.

11 Likewise reckon ye also yourselves to be dead indeed unto sin, but alive unto God through Jesus Christ our Lord.

12 Let not sin therefore reign in your mortal body, that ye should obey it in the lusts thereof.

13 Neither yield ye your members as instruments of unrighteousness unto sin: but yield yourselves unto God, as those that are alive from the dead, and your members as instruments of righteousness unto God.

14 For sin shall not have dominion over you: for ye are not under the law, but under grace.

1 John 5:11-13

11 And this is the record, that God hath given to us eternal life, and this life is in his Son.

12 He that hath the Son hath life; and he that hath not the Son of God hath not life.

13 These things have I written unto you that believe on the name of the Son of God; that ye may know that ye have eternal life, and that ye may believe on the name of the Son of God.

# CHAPTER 7
# GIFTS FOR PROFITS

In the festival of Purim, in the book of Esther, they exchanged food with each other. Kind of like a church fellowship dinner when everyone brings a dish for everyone to partake of.

**Esther 9:19**

**19 Therefore the Jews of the villages, that dwelt in the unwalled towns, made the fourteenth day of the month Adar a day of gladness and feasting, and a good day, and of sending portions one to another.**

**Esther 9:28**

**28 And that these days should be remembered and kept throughout every generation, every family, every province, and every city; and that these days of Purim should not fail from among the Jews, nor the memorial of them perish from their seed.**

But as far as exchanging gifts; it is not found in The Bible among God's people. The only instance in The Bible that people exchange gifts is, or rather, will be during the tribulation when the two witnesses preaching in the streets of Jerusalem are killed.

**Revelation 11:3-10**

**3 And I will give power unto my two witnesses, and they shall prophesy a thousand two hundred and threescore days, clothed in sackcloth.**

**4 These are the two olive trees, and the two candlesticks standing before the God of the earth.**

**5 And if any man will hurt them, fire proceedeth out of their mouth, and devoureth their enemies: and if any man will hurt them, he must in this manner be killed.**

**6 These have power to shut heaven, that it rain not in the days of their prophecy: and have power over waters to turn them to blood, and to smite the earth with all plagues, as often as they will.**

**7 And when they shall have finished their testimony, the beast that ascendeth out of the bottomless pit shall make war against them, and shall overcome them, and kill them.**

**8 And their dead bodies shall lie in the street of the great city, which spiritually is called Sodom and Egypt, where also our Lord was crucified.**

**9 And they of the people and kindreds and tongues and nations shall see their dead bodies three days and an half, and shall not suffer their dead bodies to be put in graves.**

**10 And they that dwell upon the earth shall rejoice over them, and make merry, and shall send gifts one to another; because these two prophets tormented them that dwelt on the earth.**

The people are so glad that these two witnesses of God are dead that they celebrate by exchanging gifts. Aside from the fact that nowhere in The Bible anywhere does it tell us to exchange gifts on Jesus's birthday, or any day for that matter. And aside from the fact that there is no example anywhere in The Bible of God's people exchanging gifts; there is considerable evidence that those that do exchange gifts at Christmas time are taking part in the support of this Babylonian religious system of idol worship. This scripture we just read in Revelation 11 shows that God knows about the practice of exchanging gifts. He also knows that it is not a Christian practice, but a worldly or pagan one. God never mentioned anything about His people, Jewish or Church, about exchanging gifts. It is not and never has been any kind of Biblical Christian tradition. However, it is well known to be a very common pagan tradition that has translated into a worldly tradition today attaching itself to Christmas. Now don't get me wrong, I'm not against giving gifts. But I have a problem with exchanging often useless, and many times ungodly or harmful gifts just because of tradition. Many times, it is the worlds marketing system that creates times to buy or exchange gifts such as Mother's Day, Father's Day, grandparents' day, birthdays, valentine's day, anniversaries, etc. Not that there is anything Biblically wrong with buying gifts on some of these days, but the world system pushes the buying of gifts on these and other days to advance their bottom-line profit.

**Revelation 18:3**
**3 For all nations have drunk of the wine of the wrath of her fornication, and the kings of the earth have committed fornication with her, and the merchants of the earth are waxed rich through the abundance of her delicacies.**

**Revelation 18:12-19**
**12 The merchandise of gold, and silver, and precious stones, and of pearls, and fine linen, and purple, and silk, and scarlet, and all thyine wood, and all manner vessels of ivory, and all manner vessels of most precious wood, and of brass, and iron, and marble,**
**13 And cinnamon, and odours, and ointments, and frankincense, and wine, and oil, and fine flour, and wheat, and beasts, and sheep, and horses, and chariots, and slaves, and souls of men.**

**14 And the fruits that thy soul lusted after are departed from thee, and all things which were dainty and goodly are departed from thee, and thou shalt find them no more at all.**
**15 The merchants of these things, which were made rich by her, shall stand afar off for the fear of her torment, weeping and wailing,**
**16 And saying, Alas, alas, that great city, that was clothed in fine linen, and purple, and scarlet, and decked with gold, and precious stones, and pearls!**
**17 For in one hour so great riches is come to nought. And every shipmaster, and all the company in ships, and sailors, and as many as trade by sea, stood afar off,**
**18 And cried when they saw the smoke of her burning, saying, What city is like unto this great city!**
**19 And they cast dust on their heads, and cried, weeping and wailing, saying, Alas, alas, that great city, wherein were made rich all that had ships in the sea by reason of her costliness! for in one hour is she made desolate.**

I think this correctly explains the market system of the world today getting you to waste your money on worldly goods with the senseless gift exchanging practice that has no scriptural basses at all. All of these gift buying occasions are designed to enrich these merchants. Her delicacies have made the merchants rich. Now, think; what time of year do merchants grow richest? If you said Christmas, you are right. What was Jesus angry about in these verses below?

**John 2:13-16**
**13 And the Jews' passover was at hand, and Jesus went up to Jerusalem,**
**14 And found in the temple those that sold oxen and sheep and doves, and the changers of money sitting:**
**15 And when he had made a scourge of small cords, he drove them all out of the temple, and the sheep, and the**

**oxen; and poured out the changers' money, and overthrew the tables;**

**16 And said unto them that sold doves, Take these things hence; make not my Father's house an house of merchandise.**

**Luke 19:45-46**
**45 And he went into the temple, and began to cast out them that sold therein, and them that bought;**
**46 Saying unto them, It is written, My house is the house of prayer: but ye have made it a den of thieves.**

As we read in Revelation 18:3, the merchants have become rich through her delicacies. Jesus was angry about those that were making a profit from people coming to worship at the temple. Do merchants today take advantage of the worship of Jesus? You know, if Christmas were abolished today, probably, a lot of merchants would fold up and go out of business. We can more than likely credit the success of Christmas to those merchants, and vice versa. They are all the time thinking of new ways to get you to turn loose of your hard-earned dollars by giving you an occasion to do so. It is also the end of the year, and merchants must pay tax on merchandise left in the store at the end of the year. So, Christmas is a way to clear out that merchandise. And it works. Give a merchant an occasion, pagan or not, and he will make it a reason for you to buy something. So, you ask; what's wrong with it? Because people spend money they don't have; that's what! Like our nation, people have borrowed beyond their limits. A lot of people that I know, and probably ones you know too, live from paycheck to paycheck because of paying back borrowed money at an inflated exorbitant interest rate. And then, what happens? Here comes another occasion, and there go the credit cards maxed out again. And Christmas is by far, the best friend of those merchants and credit card vendors that wish to separate you from your money. And that brings me to the connection between those two systems. Credit and merchants depend on each other. And Christmas keeps them both going. The merchants depend on credit cards so people that don't have the money can buy their Christmas goods anyway. And the credit card companies depend on merchants to advertise Christmas products to make them too attractive to turn down so you will use your credit cards after you have exhausted your bank accounts. Christmas can quickly exhaust bank accounts. Years ago, people would spend moderate amounts of money on Christmas presents. A doll or doll house or a hairbrush set for the girls, a baseball glove or a toy car for the boys. That's because people didn't have a lot of money back then and credit was not given without collateral to insure you pay it back. Back then, very few people had credit cards. Usually, only executives and important people. But today, just about everyone can get a credit card. Credit is big business today. Christmas gifts today are much much more elaborate. You have $300.00 or more game consoles, designer clothes and jewelry in the hundreds of dollars. One of the biggest advertisements at Christmas now is new $30,000.00 to $70,000.00 cars. There are not many inexpensive Christmas presents today. In fact, according to a poll I looked up on the internet, the average money spent per child at Christmas is well over $400.00. If you have two or three children, plus all your friends and other family members you buy for; that adds up real quick. And this is every year. An interesting fact is that most all major credit card companies are connected to one central location. This location is in Brussels Belgium, and the thing that connects them is a massive computer that takes up three stories of a building there. This computer is capable of transacting accounts from every major bank and every major credit card company in the world. Could this be the forerunner of the mark of the beast? I don't know, but the name of this computer is interestingly enough known as, "The Beast". The future apparently is here. Those scanners that your grocer slides your product over to find out the price of the product could fulfill verse 17 below. The information that you just read was from the 1$^{st}$ edition of this book researched in 1980. Today, a single smart phone is probably almost as powerful as that 3-story computer of 1980. But from what I understand, most credit card companies are still, to this day, all connected through that massive computer in Brussels Belgium.

> **Revelation 13:16-18**
> **16 And he causeth all, both small and great, rich and poor, free and bond, to receive a mark in their right hand, or in their foreheads:**
> **17 And that no man might buy or sell, save he that had the mark, or the name of the beast, or the number of his name.**
> **18 Here is wisdom. Let him that hath understanding count the number of the beast: for it is the number of a man; and his number is Six hundred threescore and six.**

I hear that there is experimentation with plans of using an implant to number everyone with a number to identify that person by a scanner like those used to scan groceries. This would enable Police, Armed Forces and Medical Personnel to identify a person without looking up records. This implant is unseen by the eye because it is just under the skin. You probably use this technology right now if you have one of those credit cards with a computer chip in it. These chips are small enough to slip under the skin of your hand or your forehead that could easily be scanned by one of those devices. It is a common practice to implant these chips in animals today. It could just as easily be implanted in humans. If you find yourself living in the tribulation; you would never want to take one of these chips in your hand or forehead because if it is the mark of the beast, you would be condemned to hell.

> **Revelation 14:9-11**
> **9 And the third angel followed them, saying with a loud voice, If any man worship the beast and his image, and receive his mark in his forehead, or in his hand,**
> **10 The same shall drink of the wine of the wrath of God, which is poured out without mixture into the cup of his**

indignation; and he shall be tormented with fire and
brimstone in the presence of the holy angels, and in the
presence of the Lamb:
11 And the smoke of their torment ascendeth up for ever
and ever: and they have no rest day nor night, who worship
the beast and his image, and whosoever receiveth the mark
of his name.

If it wasn't for that; it would seem, on the surface, to really make
a lot of sense once you think about it. No more credit card fraud.
No one can steel your card. It would eliminate the black market.
You couldn't avoid paying tax with a cash deal. No more cheating
on your income taxes. Your every transaction would be recorded
there for the government to see. No more robbing banks, purse
snatching, pick pockets, kidnapping for a ransom. There would
be no more cash, therefore no one would carry cash, so no one
could rob you of the cash you have on you because there will
be no cash. Even if someone robed you forcing you to use your
mark to transfer E-money into his account, the authorities would
immediately know who it was that robbed you because his name
would pop up on the transfer, so he would quickly be located by
tracking his chip and he would be arrested and forced to return the
E-money. Your doctor could access all your medical information
with a single scan. You wouldn't have to carry a driver's license
or identification or, like we said, money. No more losing a credit
card or money falling out of your pocket or locking your keys in
your car. No more filling out personal information forms such as
applications, questionnaires and those irritating medical papers
that take an hour to fill out. All your information would be in a
government data bank right there on that chip under your skin.
With key fobs today, you don't need a key for your car. The signal
from that key fob can automatically unlock your car door when
you get close to it and automatically turn on your ignition so that
all you have to do is push a button to start your car. It would
be simple to incorporate this same technology into that chip in

your hand or forehead. You could buy a car and the dealer could program your chip right there on the spot to work with your car. You would no longer need to carry a pocket full of keys. Your chip could be programed to unlock your car or your house or your place of business with no keys. Your chip could unlock all your locks. This technology is very much here today and is already being used. Right now, you can do all of that with your cellphone right now. It wouldn't take much to simply transfer that technology to a chip in your hand instead of a fob or cell phone. All of this technology is possible today, and being used today. During the tribulation, it will become mandatory. Even though it is very practical and would solve a lot of financial and social problems in todays society; it is still the mark of the beast; and must be avoided at all cost during the tribulation. The antichrist will be seen as an economic genus during the first part of the tribulation. This mark is probably how he will accomplish that title by doing just that; by solving a lot of the world's economic problems using this mark. Let me just remind you that the church will already be gone, raptured out of here when this mark is required. But if you miss the rapture, you will not want to take this mark at all cost or you would be condemned to the lake of fire, verses 9 and 10 above. With the technology of today, I think anyone can see that this is certainly possible. There was talk about people that had received a virus vaccine receiving a chip in their hand and it would be required to scan that chip before entering an aircraft or entering a large stadium event to prove that they wouldn't spread the virus. This idea was knocked down over concerns that this was too close to the mark of the beast. But credit is a universal language, breaking down barriers that governments never could. Revelation 18:3 says: "all nations have drunk of the wine of the wrath of her fornication", and in the same breath says: "and the kings of the earth have committed fornication with her, and the merchants of the earth are waxed rich through the abundance of her delicacies". It doesn't take a genius to see that most all nations celebrate Christmas, which is committing fornication with pagan customs. And the merchants of those nations get rich off of Christmas with the help of their good friend, credit. Come on, could it mean anything else? Of course, there are lots of other pagan customs involved here too. But we're talking about what I believe to be the biggest one; Christmas. The queen of Christmas lives. It's vain tradition that keeps her sitting on her throne just like we read in Revelation 18: 4-8. Can't you see. She's not a widow, because you keep her so called reincarnated husband/son alive with your tradition. So, she lives on as queen. You honor her throne at Christmas, because she is the one that sits on the throne of Christmas. You celebrate a false Christ and a deceived world honors him instead of Jesus.

> **Revelation 18:7**
> **7 How much she hath glorified herself, and lived deliciously, so much torment and sorrow give her: for she saith in her heart, I sit a queen, and am no widow, and shall see no sorrow.**

> **Jeremiah 51:17-18**
> **17 Every man is brutish by his knowledge; every founder is confounded by the graven image: for his molten image is falsehood, and there is no breath in them.**
> **18 They are vanity, the work of errors: in the time of their visitation they shall perish.**

You can't fool Jesus. He knows who He is, and He knows who the one being honored at Christmas time is. He's not stupid. He knows that it's not His birthday that you are celebrating. If you think you can pull the wool over the eyes of Jesus, then you are severely deceived. You had better check with Jesus before you celebrate this occasion any further. Pray about it and seek the guidance of The Holy Spirit. Read the scriptures to find out what The Bible says about this tradition, especially the hidden manna and examples that pertain to this celebration. That is, unless you just don't care what Jesus thinks about it because you're going to celebrate Christmas no matter what He or anyone else says. If that is your attitude, then why do you even have a Bible? You can just make up your own rules as you go. That is what a lot of people today do anyway. But if you are a true God-fearing Christian that is willing to search the scriptures to find the truth; then you will see, in the scriptures, the truth about what I am telling you. You have the choice to find it or ignore it. But if you have read this book up to this point, then you are responsible for what you have been told. Can you just ignore the solid proof I have given you? Can you rationalize it away and pretend it is alright to continue with this tradition? If so; at least I tried to warn you. That's all I can do. If you won't listen; then I shake the dust off my feet.

**Mark 6:11**
**11 And whosoever shall not receive you, nor hear you, when ye depart thence, shake off the dust under your feet for a testimony against them. Verily I say unto you, It shall be more tolerable for Sodom and Gomorrha in the day of judgment, than for that city.**

**Romans 1:18**
**18 For the wrath of God is revealed from heaven against all ungodliness and unrighteousness of men, who hold the truth in unrighteousness;**

# CHAPTER 8
# GOOD WILL TOWARD MEN?

**Luke 2:13-14**
**13 And suddenly there was with the angel a multitude of
the heavenly host praising God, and saying,**
**14 Glory to God in the highest, and on earth peace, good
will toward men.**

How many people do you know that practice good will toward men today? It looks more like, "look out for number one", to me. Have you driven on the freeway lately? People want to be in front of you on the freeway. They will move over in the fast lane and speed to get ahead of you on the freeway; then move back over in front of you and slow down to under the speed limit. This type of person is not really wanting to speed. In fact, they like going just under the speed limit. But they want to be ahead of you with no one in front of them. You wish to go the speed limit, so you move over to the fast lane to pass them. But when they see you move over to pass them; they speed up to the speed limit to keep you from passing them. Then if you think, okay, they are going to go the speed limit, so you move back over behind them again because you are not supposed to ride the fast lane on a freeway; it is only supposed to be used for passing. But when they see you move back over behind them; they slow down again. The only way you can get around this kind of slowpoke is to break the law and speed to get around them. But then they can't stand it because you are in front of them going the speed limit, so again, they speed to get around you and move back in front of you again, then slow down again to under the speed limit. Others fly by you at about 80 or 90 miles per hour weaving in and out of traffic. And that includes 18 wheelers. Between them and the guy trying to stay in front of you, it makes it hazardous to do the speed limit. People today are very aggressive on the road these days. You will be backed up in traffic in an exit lane with a long line of cars almost stopped. Then some selfish person will get in the next lane to pass everybody up, then cut someone off to get back in line at the last minute to get ahead of everyone else while you had to wait for all the cars in front of you. So, now you have to wait longer because of all the selfish drivers that cut in far ahead of you. These are just a couple of examples of many that you too have probably experienced driving among people with no good will at all. To have good will toward men one day out of the year on December 25$^{th}$; then the rest of the year step on whoever you can, seems a little hypocritical to me. People love the dollar today. The Bible says in Matthew 6:24 that you can't serve God and mammon. You will hate the one and love the other; or you will hold to the one and despise the other. Mammon is money, and most people today love money rather than Jesus. These days, if someone can figure out a way to beat you out of a dollar, he will jump on it no matter how poor you are or how much it hurts you. People call you on the phone to scam you out of your money. These people are just devils trying to steel from you with their well-planned deceit. I had one call me and tell me I wouldn't receive my social security check direct deposited in my bank anymore and that I needed to press 1 to connect with an agent to get details. I knew about this scam, that if you press 1, someone will take all of your financial information and use it to clean out your bank account. This scam works on a lot of people that receive a social security check. They think they have to press 1 or they will stop receiving their direct deposit check, so sadly, they fall for the scam. These are evil people that do these sorts of things all the time. Someone called me the other day and said my identity had been stolen and someone was using my Amazon account and that I needed to call a number they gave me and get it straightened out. It was a recording so I couldn't ask them questions like what is my name and account number which they probably couldn't answer if it wasn't really Amazon. So, I just hung up the phone and checked online to my Amazon account to see if something had been purchased on it that I didn't authorize, and there was nothing. There is very little good will toward men in today's society. People swamp your mailbox with ways to get money from you. If you get a letter in the mail that has "time sensitive, open immediately" stamped across the front of it, most of the time it's just junk mail or even a scam. Even the government, with their state lotteries, will take your last dollar. There is so much greed today that you don't know who to trust. It is very apparent that we are living in the last church age known as the Laodicean church age in Revelation 3:14-19 as we seen in Chapter 5 of this book. Today is a time of greed with people enriching themselves, taking from the poor. And a time of people having more trust in money than they trust in God. And then here comes Christmas; and for one day, you are going to have good will toward men? The good will toward men in Luke 2:14, refers to God showing good will to us by giving us His Son. Jesus shows good will toward us every day, and that's what we're supposed to do toward others. What do people do during a disaster? They wipe out the shelves in the stores of essentials that everyone needs. They stock up for themselves and leave none for others, so most people have to do without because of the greed of a few.

**John 13:34**
**34 A new commandment I give unto you, That ye love one another; as I have loved you, that ye also love one another.**

**Romans 15:1-3**
**1 We then that are strong ought to bear the infirmities of the weak, and**
**not to please ourselves.**

**2 Let every one of us please his neighbour for his good to edification.**
**3 For even Christ pleased not himself; but, as it is written, The reproaches of them that reproached thee fell on me.**

Now days, it's like every man for himself more than it is good will toward men. Most goodwill is done by Christians, and then only a few willing to give every day without needing a special occasion and then not expecting anything in return. Spreading good will toward others is supposed to be the lifestyle of Christians, not a token or a bribe or a way to get on someone's good side. Giving gives in return of itself, not in expectation of a return. But giving itself wants you to have more to give if you give to give, and not to receive, not one day a year, but every day.

**2 Corinthians 9:6-8**
**6 But this I say, He which soweth sparingly shall reap also sparingly; and he which soweth bountifully shall reap also bountifully.**
**7 Every man according as he purposeth in his heart, so let him give; not grudgingly, or of necessity: for God loveth a cheerful giver.**
**8 And God is able to make all grace abound toward you; that ye, always having all sufficiency in all things, may abound to every good work:**

The only time I hear good will toward men mentioned is at Christmas. It's funny; it takes a pagan celebration to ignite any good will with the world. And it only lasts a day. Satan will show just enough of the truth to get you hooked; then you're his. He will tell you: "you're a good Christian. You celebrate Christmas, don't you? You go to church that Sunday, don't you? You show good will toward men that day, don't you?" He would have you to believe that that is enough. It is a sad testimony to the church that most of us take part in this pagan ritual for any reason. But it is also a sign of the Laodicean church times that we are now in. Salvation is free. But that same salvation gives you a desire to do good things, not just one day a year, but every day. If you are a Christian, you shouldn't be able to scam someone. Your heart's desire should be to show good will toward others. It would be in your new nature to love your fellow man and want the best for him all the time.

> **John 13:33**
> **35 By this shall all men know that ye are my disciples, if ye have love one to another.**

> **2 Timothy 4:1-4:**
> **1 I charge thee therefore before God, and the Lord Jesus Christ, who shall judge the quick and the dead at his appearing and his kingdom;**
> **2 Preach the word; be instant in season, out of season; reprove, rebuke, exhort with all longsuffering and doctrine.**
> **3 For the time will come when they will not endure sound doctrine; but after their own lusts shall they heap to themselves teachers, having itching ears;**
> **4 And they shall turn away their ears from the truth, and shall be turned unto fables.**

Guess what? Verse 3 and 4 is here right now.

# CHAPTER 9
# IF ANY MAN BE IGNORANT

Are you going to celebrate Christmas this year? Can you just ignore all the evidence against celebrating it? Can you justify yourself in celebrating it? Can you look Jesus in the eye at the judgment seat and tell Him you did the right thing? If so, I would like to see your Biblical reasoning behind that. I can find no Biblical reasoning for Christmas. I only find paganism and the way of Balaam who caused Israel to forsake good reasoning. Are you going to tell Him "I didn't know"???? Are you going to tell Him that "I thought I was celebrating Your birthday"???? But in reality; you will be without excuse. The information is easily available to anyone who takes the time to look for it, not to mention, you have been given this information in this book to help you see the truth about Christmas. A pastor told me one time that I have it all wrong. He said "isn't it just like Jesus for Him to take a pagan celebration and turn it around to honor Him instead of the pagan god? I say, NO!! That is not just like Jesus at all. Everything I read in The Bible says that God doesn't want to be worshiped in the way the nations worship their gods. Why would Jesus want to be celebrated in a pagan way with pagan idols? Are you telling Jesus that you don't like the way The Bible tell us to worship Him so we want to use a pagan celebration to worship Him? That would be like a wife telling her husband that she doesn't like the cloths he picked out so she wants him to wear am outfit that she likes that used to belong to her ex-boyfriend. So, are you going to dress Jesus up in a pagan celebration to suit your desire to celebrate a pagan celebration?

**Deuteronomy 16:21-22**
21 Thou shalt not plant thee a grove of any trees near unto the altar of the LORD thy God, which thou shalt make thee.
22 Neither shalt thou set thee up any image; which the LORD thy God hateth.

**Deuteronomy 7:26:**
26 Neither shalt thou bring an abomination into thine house, lest thou be a cursed thing like it: but thou shalt utterly detest it, and thou shalt utterly abhor it; for it is a cursed thing.

**Deuteronomy 18:9**
9 When thou art come into the land which the LORD thy God giveth thee, thou shalt not learn to do after the abominations of those nations.

**Deuteronomy 18:14**
14 For these nations, which thou shalt possess, hearkened unto observers of times, and unto diviners: but as for thee, the Lord thy God hath not suffered thee so to do.

You may say to me; I disagree with your conclusion about Christmas. That's okay. Go ahead; slap Jesus in the face. Spit on His Name. You might as well if you will disgrace His Name by attaching It to a pagan god.

**2 Peter 2:9-16**
9 The Lord knoweth how to deliver the godly out of temptations, and to reserve the unjust unto the day of judgment to be punished:
10 But chiefly them that walk after the flesh in the lust of uncleanness, and despise government. Presumptuous are they, selfwilled, they are not afraid to speak evil of dignities.

11 Whereas angels, which are greater in power and might, bring not railing accusation against them before the Lord.
12 But these, as natural brute beasts, made to be taken and destroyed, speak evil of the things that they understand not; and shall utterly perish in their own corruption;
13 And shall receive the reward of unrighteousness, as they that count it pleasure to riot in the day time. Spots they are and blemishes, sporting themselves with their own deceivings while they feast with you;
14 Having eyes full of adultery, and that cannot cease from sin; beguiling unstable souls: an heart they have exercised with covetous practices; cursed children:
15 Which have forsaken the right way, and are gone astray, following the way of Balaam the son of Bosor, who loved the wages of unrighteousness;
16 But was rebuked for his iniquity: the dumb ass speaking with man's voice forbad the madness of the prophet.

I love the KJV wording in verse 16 above. Don't tell me God doesn't have a sense of humor. Even a dumb donkey knows more than this prophet. Is it going to take a dumb donkey to forbid you to take part in idol worship?

1 Corinthians 14:36-38
36 What? came the word of God out from you? or came it unto you only?
37 If any man think himself to be a prophet, or spiritual, let him acknowledge that the things that I write unto you are the commandments of the Lord.
38 But if any man be ignorant, let him be ignorant.

Can you ignore the evidence and remain ignorant about Christmas? I won't try to stop you. Be ignorant if you want. It's not my job to stop you from celebrating Christmas. My job is to inform you of the truth about it. What you do with that truth is out of my hands. "If any man be ignorant, let him be ignorant." By the way; that applies to women also. Is there anything that this world does worth setting Jesus aside even for one day? Who paid for your redemption? Who put aside all the pleasures of this world to save you from your sin? Who gave us a complete Word of God? Do you find in that Word that He gave us the Christmas celebration? Did He leave something out of His Word that should have been in there? No, God does not make mistakes at all. If it's not in there, then it wasn't meant to be. Nowhere in His Word does He tell us to celebrate anything that even resembles Christmas. Yet all through His Word, He tells us to abstain from the practice of pagan idol worship of which the Christmas celebration originated. There is no doubt that the Christmas celebration came from pagan forms of worship. Ask any pastor. They know the truth. Most of them keep it to themselves if they want to keep their jobs. Who is your Lord? Tammuz or Jesus? Who do you honor? Does Jesus want you to substitute Him for the birthday of Tammuz once a year? Does Jesus like you calling Tammuz "Jesus" so you can justify having your good time in The Name of Jesus even though it's not Him? It's time to take a stand against this false religion. Let's quit polluting the worship of our Lord. Let's quit bringing our vain traditions into the church. Tammuz is a false Christ who had no bodily resurrection and is worshipped as a sun god deity. Let's get serious church. Let's quit bringing our garbage dumps into the church. Let's quit putting Jesus, The real Christ, on a dunghill of idol worship once a year. Let's let Him put us where He wants us according to His Word, not some pagan tradition. Tammuz is a false Christ. A son of the sun god. Jesus is The Son of Almighty God. Which one do you want to serve?

**Exodus 20:1-7**
**1 And God spake all these words, saying,**
**2 I am the LORD thy God, which have brought thee out of the land of Egypt, out of the house of bondage.**
**3 Thou shalt have no other gods before me.**

**4 Thou shalt not make unto thee any graven image, or any likeness of any thing that is in heaven above, or that is in the earth beneath, or that is in the water under the earth:**
**5 Thou shalt not bow down thyself to them, nor serve them: for I the LORD thy God am a jealous God, visiting the iniquity of the fathers upon the children unto the third and fourth generation of them that hate me;**
**6 And shewing mercy unto thousands of them that love me, and keep my commandments.**
**7 Thou shalt not take the name of the LORD thy God in vain; for the LORD will not hold him guiltless that taketh his name in vain.**

Do you take His name in vain by attaching a false god to Him. The Bible says that the sun shall be darkened and eventually be completely destroyed and dissolved and melted with a fervent heat. What will happen to the sun god then?

**Mark 13:24-26**
**24 But in those days, after that tribulation, the sun shall be darkened, and the moon shall not give her light,**
**25 And the stars of heaven shall fall, and the powers that are in heaven shall be shaken.**
**26 And then shall they see the Son of man coming in the clouds with great power and glory.**

**2 Peter 3:12**
**12 Looking for and hasting unto the coming of the day of God, wherein the heavens being on fire shall be dissolved, and the elements shall melt with fervent heat?**

**Revelation 21:1**
**1 And I saw a new heaven and a new earth: for the first heaven and the first earth were passed away; and there was no more sea.**

The Spirit of God raised Jesus from the dead bodily as The Firstborn from the dead, and then ascended into heaven and is now seated at the right hand of the throne of God and will live forevermore. Tammuz is dead and gone. And even his legend will also end at the coming of Jesus when He will put an end to this sun worship. So, which one do you want to serve?

> **Colossians 1:18**
> **18 And he is the head of the body, the church: who is the beginning, the firstborn from the dead; that in all things he might have the preeminence.**

> **Hebrews 8:1**
> **1 Now of the things which we have spoken this is the sum: We have such an high priest, who is set on the right hand of the throne of the Majesty in the heavens;**

Jesus didn't start existing at His birth. He has always been.

> **John 8:56-58**
> **56 Your father Abraham rejoiced to see my day: and he saw it, and was glad.**
> **57 Then said the Jews unto him, Thou art not yet fifty years old, and hast thou seen Abraham?**
> **58 Jesus said unto them, Verily, verily, I say unto you, Before Abraham was, I am.**

He voluntarily lowered Himself to be born as an infant in this world. But He is no longer lowered and He is no longer an infant. He is now been raised to His former glory. Why would you want to lower Him again every year? Tammuz is worshipped even today as a child to the queen of heaven. That's because if he were allowed to grow up, that would take power away from the queen, so she has to keep him a child so she can retain her power. Therefore, he is celebrated every year as a child being born over and over again each and every year. Again, I know in some religions, Tammuz grows to a man. But this book is about the Roman religion that originated the Christmas (or winter solstice) celebration in which Tammuz remains a child.

**Hebrews 2:9-10**

**9 But we see Jesus, who was made a little lower than the angels for the suffering of death, crowned with glory and honour; that he by the grace of God should taste death for every man.**

**10 For it became him, for whom are all things, and by whom are all things, in bringing many sons unto glory, to make the captain of their salvation perfect through sufferings.**

**Philippians 2:5-9**

**5 Let this mind be in you, which was also in Christ Jesus:**

**6 Who, being in the form of God, thought it not robbery to be equal with God:**

**7 But made himself of no reputation, and took upon him the form of a servant, and was made in the likeness of men:**

**8 And being found in fashion as a man, he humbled himself, and became obedient unto death, even the death of the cross.**

**9 Wherefore God also hath highly exalted him, and given him a name which is above every name:**

As we read a couple of pages ago in Exodus 20:3, it said: "Have no other gods before me." Doesn't that also mean one's going by the same name as Jesus, but are not really Jesus?

**Galatians 4:8-11**

**8 Howbeit then, when ye knew not God, ye did service unto them which by nature are no gods.**

**9 But now, after that ye have known God, or rather are known of God, how turn ye again to the weak and beggarly elements, whereunto ye desire again to be in bondage?**
**10 Ye observe days, and months, and times, and years.**
**11 I am afraid of you, lest I have bestowed upon you labour in vain.**

**1 Corinthians 8:5-6**
**5 For though there be that are called gods, whether in heaven or in earth, (as there be gods many, and lords many,)**
**6 But to us there is but one God, the Father, of whom are all things, and we in him; and one Lord Jesus Christ, by whom are all things, and we by him.**

**Joshua 24:14-15**
**14 Now therefore fear the Lord, and serve him in sincerity and in truth: and put away the gods which your fathers served on the other side of the flood, and in Egypt; and serve ye the Lord.**
**15 And if it seem evil unto you to serve the Lord, choose you this day whom ye will serve; whether the gods which your fathers served that were on the other side of the flood, or the gods of the Amorites, in whose land ye dwell: but as for me and my house, we will serve the Lord.**

**Matthew 24:23-24**
**23 Then if any man shall say unto you, Lo, here is Christ, or there; believe it not.**
**24 For there shall arise false Christs, and false prophets, and shall shew great signs and wonders; insomuch that, if it were possible, they shall deceive the very elect.**

Do you serve God? Then don't mess around in idol worship. Do you serve idols? Then do the church a favor and get out from among true believers. It's all up to you. You can shrug it off and say, well, that's your interpretation. Okay then, prove me wrong. Let me see you tell me why we should celebrate Christmas. But I want to see scripture, not just your opinion. Investigate it for yourself. You'll find the truth if you look hard enough. You may well be cheating yourself out of reward in heaven if you ignore Gods Word. I did investigate it for 10 years while I wrote the first edition of this book. I did my homework. And I have continued to investigate it more than 30 years after that in these later editions. I wanted to make sure I knew what I was talking about before I came against something as popular as Christmas. I will give you 25 solid scriptural reasons why you shouldn't celebrate Christmas in Chapter 10 as a summary of this book. There are far more than 25 scriptural reasons, But I felt I would limit it to just 25. Give me even one good scriptural reason why you should celebrate it. I said scriptural reason, not your opinion. Find anywhere in The Bible even a hint that we should celebrate the birthday of Jesus every year or that we should celebrate anything that even resembles Christmas in any way. But I want to see scripture. I know the scripture says He was born and gives a few details about the events of His birth. But you know as well as I do that these details about His birth are only a small part of the Christmas celebration. The rest of it is pagan. And besides, The Bible doesn't tell us to celebrate those details with a special day. If so, The Bible would have told us when that day was. The Christmas celebration is mostly about the tree, exchanging gifts, Santa Claus, lights, decorations, parties, drinking (spiked eggnog and other alcoholic beverages), going to light displays and food. Jesus is usually stuck in there somewhere; but does He want to be? No, Jesus does not want to be mixed with idol worship. If you are saved, you will not lose your salvation for celebrating Christmas, or for any reason. But it's up to you whether you want to receive a full reward. Or if your satisfied to have burned up works and barely escape hell. We are not to keep company with idolaters. The works we do that are not scriptural will be burned up. You can still make it to heaven, but just barely yet so as by fire.

**Revelation 22:12**

**12 And, behold, I come quickly; and my reward is with me, to give every man according as his work shall be.**

**1 Corinthians 9:24-25**

**24 Know ye not that they which run in a race run all, but one receiveth the prize? So run, that ye may obtain.**
**25 And every man that striveth for the mastery is temperate in all things. Now they do it to obtain a corruptible crown; but we an incorruptible.**

**1 Corinthians 5:9-11**

**9 I wrote unto you in an epistle not to company with fornicators:**
**10 Yet not altogether with the fornicators of this world, or with the covetous, or extortioners, or with idolaters; for then must ye needs go out of the world.**
**11 But now I have written unto you not to keep company, if any man that is called a brother be a fornicator, or covetous, or an idolater, or a railer, or a drunkard, or an extortioner; with such an one no not to eat.**

Keep yourselves from idols. Are you going to invite an idol into your house this Christmas? Brethren, go after the higher calling. Seek a white stone, and find the hidden manna, which is the hidden Word of God. I personally believe that this white stone is limited just as the hidden manna is limited only to those that seek out the truth in God's Word. God doesn't reveal hidden manna to someone that doesn't search for it.

**1 John 5:21**

**21 Little children, keep yourselves from idols. Amen.**

**Revelation 2:17**

**17 He that hath an ear, let him hear what the Spirit saith unto the churches; To him that overcometh will I give to eat of the hidden manna, and will give him a white stone, and in the stone a new name written, which no man knoweth saving he that receiveth it.**

**1 Corinthians 2:7**

**7 But we speak the wisdom of God in a mystery, even the hidden wisdom, which God ordained before the world unto our glory:**

I believe that white stone is special. There are scholars that say everyone that gets saved will receive one of these stones. But in my opinion, in the context that it is in, talking about mixing idol worship with the worship of God as Balaam taught Israel; this could be saying that only those that overcome this practice by finding the hidden manna will receive one. And those that celebrate Christmas without checking it out with The Word of God will not receive one of those white stones because they ignored the hidden manna on Christmas. I don't say that lightly, because a whole lot of prominent well-known men of God celebrate Christmas. But in my interpretation of that verse, only those that overcome false religion and truly seek out the whole truth of the hidden manna will get one. I can't say this is a Bible fact. There is simply not enough information about the white stone to establish this as a Bible fact. But the white stone is only mentioned in the church at Pergamos where the introduction of pagan customs entered the church in the first place. So, it makes sense that it is talking about only those that find the hidden truth about the doctrine of Balaam and the mixing of paganism with God will receive one. When you receive one of these white stones, you will receive a new name that no one knows but you. What an honor that will be to receive a new name just like Jesus did.

**Revelation 19:12**

**12 His eyes were as a flame of fire, and on his head were many crowns; and he had a name written, that no man knew, but he himself.**

It could very well be that the white stone is exclusive for those that don't just blindly follow the crowd, but search out the truth in the hidden manna and the things of The Word of God that you have to work at to find. The deception of Christmas is not the only hidden manna found in The Bible. There are many more hidden truths in The Bible that are just waiting to be revealed to anyone that has a heart for the truth of God and will search for them. But you must set aside all your preconceived ideas and all your vain traditions and open your spiritual ears to the truth to find them. We serve a Lord that has been raised from the dead, not a baby in a manger. He's not in that manger anymore. Study Gods Word to prove what is the acceptable will of God. Don't close your spiritual ears to the truth. As God said to the church at Pergamos in Revelation 2:17, above, "He that has an ear, let him hear what the Spirit saith unto the churches". That means you listen to the hidden things that God has revealed only to those that will hear His Spirit and take the time to discover the truth. Any Christian is equipped to do this. But it takes willingness to allocate time to do it and open your spiritual ears despite a strong desire to participate in this unscriptural tradition. It says, "he that hath an ear to hear". This is not talking about natural ears. This is an ear that can hear Spiritual things. Not every Christian can hear Spiritual things. Only those that have their senses exercised. The way you exercise Spiritual senses is through God's Word. The more of God's Word you study, the stronger your Spiritual hearing is.

**Hebrews 5:13-14**

**13 For every one that useth milk is unskilful in the word of righteousness: for he is a babe.**

**14 But strong meat belongeth to them that are of full age,
even those who by reason of use have their senses exercised
to discern both good and evil.**

Don't take my word for anything. I am nothing. Look it up in God's
Word and let Him show you. Take time to read and meditate on the
verses of The Bible talked about in this book. I'm sure God will
reveal His Truth to you; but only if you seek the truth and accept
it no matter how it messes with your favorite pagan celebrations
and vain traditions.

# CHAPTER 10
# 25 BIBLICAL REASONS TO NOT CELEBRATE CHRISTMAS

S ome of the things in this list of 25 reasons, we have already mentioned in parts of this book. But they are repeated here with a little more information included with it because I wanted to include them in this list of 25 things. There were many more than 25 reasons, but I limited it to 25 of the main things that are easily explained and simple to understand.

1. You must get the story right and make full proof of your ministry.

You have to realize that at the time the Jews rejected Jesus and He turned to the Gentiles starting in about Acts chapter 10; these Gentiles had spent more that 2 thousand years celebrating the pagan celebration of the winter solstice later known as Saturnalia.

> **1 Corinthians 12:2-3**
> **2 Ye know that ye were Gentiles, carried away unto these dumb idols, even as ye were led.**
> **3 Wherefore I give you to understand, that no man speaking by the Spirit of God calleth Jesus accursed: and that no man can say that Jesus is the Lord, but by the Holy Ghost.**

It was a very popular celebration. At that time, it was basically Christmas with pagan names. Gentile Christians had to quit celebrating this pagan tradition because of its idol worship origins. And it was very hard for them to give up their favorite celebration, but the power of The Holy Spirit gave them the strength to do it. Then when Constantine came along and the pagan gods received Christian names, many Christians seen an opportunity to celebrate this fun time of year again because they reasoned within themselves that since it now had Christian names, it was okay. But many of them seen the flaw in that reasoning and refused to take part in this pagan tradition. This divided the church, and these true believers were labeled as heretics by the Roman/government church for rejecting these pagan celebrations. The time had come talked about in 2 Timothy, when sound doctrine was rejected, and people began to give in to the fables of paganism dressed up as Christian.

**2 Timothy 4:1-5.**
**1 I charge thee therefore before God, and the Lord Jesus Christ, who shall judge the quick and the dead at his appearing and his kingdom;**
**2 Preach the word; be instant in season, out of season; reprove, rebuke, exhort with all longsuffering and doctrine.**
**3 For the time will come when they will not endure sound doctrine; but after their own lusts shall they heap to themselves teachers, having itching ears;**
**4 And they shall turn away their ears from the truth, and shall be turned unto fables.**
**5 But watch thou in all things, endure afflictions, do the work of an evangelist, make full proof of thy ministry.**

"make full proof of thy ministry" verse 5. The question is; should you celebrate Christmas without first checking it out with scripture? Can you fully prove that Christmas is scriptural? Does The Bible back up what you are doing? The Bible does record the birth of Jesus; but does it say to celebrate it every year? Does The Bible say when it is? Does The Bible describe any of the ways it is celebrated? Is there enough information given to go ahead and celebrate this questionable celebration? I think not. There are misinterpretations and assumptions of what The Bible does say about it. Some things are not clear on what happened. People just assume Jesus was born in a lean-to animal stable with a slant straw roof held up with two sticks out in a field in the middle of nowhere, then was laid in a manger under that lean-to roof. I know we already went over this. But I wanted to include it as one of the 25 reasons in this chapter. I have added more information about it in this reason. He may or may not have been born in that stable. That word for inn here is "kataluma" or lodging place, which according to many scholars is better translated as the guestroom of a house. In fact, the exact same word is used to describe the upper room described as a guest chamber chosen by Jesus for the Passover meal.

> **Mark 14:14-15**
> **14 And wheresoever he shall go in, say ye to the goodman of the house, The Master saith, Where is the guestchamber, where I shall eat the passover with my disciples?**
> **15 And he will shew you a large upper room furnished and prepared: there make ready for us.**

It was more than likely a relative's house. They were in Joseph's hometown. They more than likely knew people or had relatives there. If it were a motel or inn like a place you would pay to stay overnight as we know today, the word "pandocheion" would have been used. This word was used for the word "inn" in the parable of the good Samaritan.

> **Luke 10:34-35**
> **34 And went to him, and bound up his wounds, pouring in oil and wine, and set him on his own beast, and brought him to an inn, and took care of him.**
> **35 And on the morrow when he departed, he took out two pence, and gave them to the host, and said unto him, Take**

**care of him; and whatsoever thou spendest more, when I come again, I will repay thee.**

Bethlehem was probably too small for an inn such as a motel or standard place to pay and stay. This inn was probably someone's house rented out for this time of censes so the owner of the house could make a little extra cash off of the crowded conditions. Even though they are both translated as "inn" in the KJV, look up these two words in your concordance dictionary, and then look up "upper room". In the case of where Mary with Jesus wanted to stay. It was more than likely a guest chamber with the same Greek word used as upper room in Mark 22:14-15, described as a "guest chamber" for the exact same word as kataluma used for inn in the case of Joseph and Mary and Jesus which would make sense to be a relative's house or a friend's house. All the guest rooms, or upper rooms, were taken. So, possibly, to accommodate them the best they could, they put them in the part of the house where the animals were brought in at night which was in the lower ground floor of the house that was usually open in the front to the outside to allow the animals to just walk in to escape cold or bad weather. Or it could have been possibly a separate shelter for the animals like a barn. Either way, a feeding trough, or manger, that Jesus was laid in, was usually kept there to feed the animals when they were brought in because of bad weather. But even at that, it doesn't actually say whether He was born there and laid in the manger; or if He was born somewhere else and then laid in the manger. In fact, the wording indicates that Jesus was already born when there was no room <u>for them,</u> (including Jesus), in the inn. It just says He was laid in the manger, which could have been some time after He was born that same day elsewhere. After all, they were there in Bethlehem days before Jesus was born.

**Luke 2:4-6**
**4 And Joseph also went up from Galilee, out of the city of Nazareth, into Judaea, unto the city of David, which is**

**called Bethlehem; (because he was of the house and lineage
of David:)**
**5 To be taxed with Mary his espoused wife, being great
with child.**
**6 And so it was, that, while they were there, the days were
accomplished that she should be delivered.**

They would have had time to secure a place for Mary to have the
child. We just don't know. Read the next verse in Luke 2:7 and ask
yourself, why was Jesus laid in a manger?

**Luke 2:7**
**7 And she brought forth her firstborn son, and wrapped
him in swaddling clothes, and laid him in a manger;
because there was no room for them in the inn.**

It says because there was no room for **them** in the inn. This could
indicate that Jesus was already born that day and with Mary when
there was no room for "them" that night in the inn. The word
"them" could include Jesus. The Bible always makes a defendant
distinction between day and night, and this is no exception. Most
people think Jesus was born at night at that manger scene and
immediately laid in the manger after His birth. The Bible tells us
different. Jesus was born during the day. This next verse tells us
why most people think it was night.

**Luke 2:8-10**
**8 And there were in the same country shepherds abiding
in the field, keeping watch over their flock by night.**
**9 And, lo, the angel of the Lord came upon them, and the
glory of the Lord shone round about them: and they were
sore afraid.**
**10 And the angel said unto them, Fear not: for, behold,
I bring you good tidings of great joy, which shall be to
all people.**

288

The shepherds were abiding in the same country keep watch over the flock by night when the angel told them about Jesus. But the angel did not tell them that Jesus was born this night. This next verse tells us that Jesus was born during the day in the city.

**Luke 2:11**
**11 For unto you is born this day in the city of David a Saviour, which is Christ the Lord.**

The angel only told them that they would find The Babe lying in a manger.

**Luke 2:12**
**12 And this shall be a sign unto you; Ye shall find the babe wrapped in swaddling clothes, lying in a manger.**

We just don't know for sure about these details. It's not clear. The better theory is, just what we said, that Joseph had relatives in that town, and he had a place to go that he knew the people or he was related to them. Jesus could very well have been born in the house of one of those relatives. Then after He was born, there were already people staying the night with those relatives in the upper, or guest, rooms because of the crowded conditions due to the census. So, because the house was already full in the guest rooms for that night, they had to use the lower room of the house that was part of the same house, but, like we said, was open to the outside and was used to bring the animals in if they had bad weather. Or also, like I said, it could have been a different barn type structure near the house. If it was present day, it would be like telling them, my rooms are full, but you can stay in the garage or in the shed out back. It could have been a room in the house by day but doubled as an animal shelter by night when they were not able to abide in the field by night. Then that could be where they stayed because the animals were in the fields by night because of the good weather. In that room was a feeding trough, or manger, that was used as a cradle for Jesus. The biggest reason for this would be that Greek word used for "inn" in verse 7, better fits this scenario of someone they knew. But again, we don't know these details for sure. Just one more thing. If we were supposed to celebrate this occasion, don't you think The Bible would have been clear on these details? But the information we do have can be better understood if you would just check your topical resources, commentaries, Bible dictionaries, historical references and concordances before you draw any conclusions about what tradition tells you. All this information is there and easily found. I'm nobody special. I'm not even considered by most people to be a real smart person except by my wife who might be a little biased. The point is; if I can find this information, you can too. It just takes a little effort. You'll be surprised at the things you will find that have been taught all these years as Bible that either The Bible doesn't say, or It says it different than has been taught throughout the years.

2. We are to shun unfruitful works of darkness.

> **Ephesians 5:11-17**
> **11 And have no fellowship with the unfruitful works of darkness, but rather reprove them.**
> **12 For it is a shame even to speak of those things which are done of them in secret.**
> **13 But all things that are reproved are made manifest by the light: for whatsoever doth make manifest is light.**
> **14 Wherefore he saith, Awake thou that sleepest, and arise from the dead, and Christ shall give thee light.**
> **15 See then that ye walk circumspectly, not as fools, but as wise,**
> **16 Redeeming the time, because the days are evil.**
> **17 Wherefore be ye not unwise, but understanding what the will of the Lord is.**

How do you understand what The Lord's will is? The answer is, of course; His Word. So, examining His Word; you won't find Christmas with all its tradition. You will, however, find the Christmas celebration in history as a pagan celebration; an unfruitful work of darkness known as Saturnalia, which was later changed to Christmas. We are to reprove such things, not celebrate them. Just get on any computer and search the word Saturnalia. It's all right there. Just for note reference; Saturnalia was not the original name either. The Romans gave it that name later. It was originally simply known as the winter solstice festival and called the birth of the new sun, and Tammuz was born on that same day.

3. You can lose reward for allowing yourself to be deceived when the truth is so clear.

Many tell me: "well, I'm not concerned with reward. I'm not working for Jesus for reward anyway. I don't expect anything in return from Him." That sounds real noble and unselfish of you. But really, it is a totally selfish statement. What you are really saying is: "I want to do what I want and not what The Bible says; so, I will justify that by acting unselfish about working for reward because I like celebrating Christmas and I am not going to listen to anything against it." You may think reward is not a big deal right now; and that as long as you are honoring Jesus with this celebration; you think that will be taken into consideration and you will not lose reward. Am I right? The thing is; Jesus is not like the liberal left that says all the kids get a trophy just for participating in the game. With Jesus, the reward is for those that actually do the work. Those that don't, will be left out. Rewards must be earned. These rewards that you must earn have nothing to do with your salvation. These rewards are eternal and are a huge deal in your position in the kingdom of God. What you do in the here and now is what determines your position in His kingdom later.

**1 Corinthians 3:7-8**

7 So then neither is he that planteth any thing, neither he that watereth; but God that giveth the increase.

8 Now he that planteth and he that watereth are one: and every man shall receive his own reward according to his own labour.

**1 Corinthians 3:13-14**

13 Every man's work shall be made manifest: for the day shall declare it, because it shall be revealed by fire; and the fire shall try every man's work of what sort it is.

14 If any man's work abide which he hath built thereupon, he shall receive a reward.

**Colossians 2:18**

18 Let no man beguile you of your reward in a voluntary humility and worshipping of angels, intruding into those things which he hath not seen, vainly puffed up by his fleshly mind,

**Colossians 3:23-25**

23 And whatsoever ye do, do it heartily, as to the Lord, and not unto men;

24 Knowing that of the Lord ye shall receive the reward of the inheritance: for ye serve the Lord Christ.

25 But he that doeth wrong shall receive for the wrong which he hath done: and there is no respect of persons.

**Hebrews 11:25-26**

25 Choosing rather to suffer affliction with the people of God, than to enjoy the pleasures of sin for a season;

26 Esteeming the reproach of Christ greater riches than the treasures in Egypt: for he had respect unto the recompence of the reward.

**2 John 8**

**8 Look to yourselves, that we lose not those things which we have wrought, but that we receive a full reward.**

**Revelation 22:12**

**12 And, behold, I come quickly; and my reward is with me, to give every man according as his work shall be.**

Your reward is not really how much you do, but rather the quality of what you do with what God gives you to work with.

**Mark 10:29-31**

**29 And Jesus answered and said, Verily I say unto you, There is no man that hath left house, or brethren, or sisters, or father, or mother, or wife, or children, or lands, for my sake, and the gospel's,**

**30 But he shall receive an hundredfold now in this time, houses, and brethren, and sisters, and mothers, and children, and lands, with persecutions; and in the world to come eternal life.**

**31 But many that are first shall be last; and the last first.**

Are you giving yourself to a false god that can never reward you for it?

**1 Kings 18:27-28**

**27 And it came to pass at noon, that Elijah mocked them, and said, Cry aloud: for he is a god; either he is talking, or he is pursuing, or he is in a journey, or peradventure he sleepeth, and must be awaked.**

**28 And they cried aloud, and cut themselves after their manner with knives and lancets, till the blood gushed out upon them.**

In verse 28, they thought they were serving their god by cutting themselves. But their god cannot reward them for that, as is pointed out in this scripture below. Their god did nothing to help them against Elijah.

> **1 Kings 18:29**
> **29 And it came to pass, when midday was past, and they prophesied until the time of the offering of the evening sacrifice, that there was neither voice, nor any to answer, nor any that regarded.**

Idol worship leads to all kinds of destruction. So, you say, well, I don't cut myself. There are other ways to harm yourself. Do you sacrifice your finances, putting yourself in a financial bind? Do you sacrifice your credibility with your kids by lying to them about what Christmas really is? No matter what you tell anyone about Christmas, it is still only a form of idol worship, and you are giving your time and money to honor an idol that can never reward you for it. However, The true God can burn up your vain works, or give you reward for exposing such hidden idol worship, 1 Corinthians 3:13-15. There are consequences for taking part in idol worship and the worlds activities even if you do it ignorantly. You are supposed to prove what is the good and acceptable and perfect will of God.

> **Romans 12:1-2**
> **1 I beseech you therefore, brethren, by the mercies of God, that ye present your bodies a living sacrifice, holy, acceptable unto God, which is your reasonable service.**
> **2 And be not conformed to this world: but be ye transformed by the renewing of your mind, that ye may prove what is that good, and acceptable, and perfect, will of God.**

4. Submit yourselves to God. Not the world.

**1 Peter 4:1-6**
**1 Forasmuch then as Christ hath suffered for us in the flesh, arm yourselves likewise with the same mind: for he that hath suffered in the flesh hath ceased from sin;**
**2 That he no longer should live the rest of his time in the flesh to the lusts of men, but to the will of God.**
**3 For the time past of our life may suffice us to have wrought the will of the Gentiles, when we walked in lasciviousness, lusts, excess of wine, revellings, banquetings, and abominable idolatries:**
**4 Wherein they think it strange that ye run not with them to the same excess of riot, speaking evil of you:**
**5 Who shall give account to him that is ready to judge the quick and the dead.**
**6 For for this cause was the gospel preached also to them that are dead, that they might be judged according to men in the flesh, but live according to God in the spirit.**

The will of the unsaved Gentile world is to celebrate Christmas, simply because most all of them do. And they would think it strange for Christians not to, verse 4 above. They think it's a Christian celebration because Christians make such a big deal about it. That's how they can justify themselves doing what they do at Christmas. So, for a Christian to continue celebrating Christmas only continues to make the lost world keep feeling justified in the farce they make of Jesus at that time. And some that only think they are saved, but are not; feel comfortable about salvation and serving Jesus because they attend church on these special pagan celebrations.

5. We are supposed to renounce the hidden things of dishonesty.

**2 Corinthians 4:1-2**
**1 Therefore seeing we have this ministry, as we have received mercy, we faint not;**

**2 But have renounced the hidden things of dishonesty, not walking in craftiness, nor handling the word of God deceitfully; but by manifestation of the truth commending ourselves to every man's conscience in the sight of God.**

Are you blinded to the truth about Christmas? Open your eyes and let The Word of God guide you, and give you light.

**2 Corinthians 4:3-4**
**3 But if our gospel be hid, it is hid to them that are lost:**
**4 In whom the god of this world hath blinded the minds of them which believe not, lest the light of the glorious gospel of Christ, who is the image of God, should shine unto them.**

Don't handle The Word of God deceitfully, but renounce the hidden things of dishonesty. You know, there are groups of people out there that go under the name of Christian, but when you take a closer look at their lives and their doctrine, you find that they aren't Christian at all. That's deceit. And that's what Christmas does; deceives you into thinking it is Christian, but when you examine it closely; you find that it only resembles Christianity enough to make you believe it is, but veers off from Christianity into idol worship without you knowing it, unless you are on your toes to see it. False religion can be very convincing. Many people are easily deceived into believing a deception of the devil. That will happen during the tribulation.

**2 Thessalonians 2:7-11**
**7 For the mystery of iniquity doth already work: only he who now letteth will let, until he be taken out of the way.**
**8 And then shall that Wicked be revealed, whom the Lord shall consume with the spirit of his mouth, and shall destroy with the brightness of his coming:**
**9 Even him, whose coming is after the working of Satan with all power and signs and lying wonders,**

10 And with all deceivableness of unrighteousness in them that perish; because they received not the love of the truth, that they might be saved.

11 And for this cause God shall send them strong delusion, that they should believe a lie:

Revelation 16:13-15

13 And I saw three unclean spirits like frogs come out of the mouth of the dragon, and out of the mouth of the beast, and out of the mouth of the false prophet.

14 For they are the spirits of devils, working miracles, which go forth unto the kings of the earth and of the whole world, to gather them to the battle of that great day of God Almighty.

15 Behold, I come as a thief. Blessed is he that watcheth, and keepeth his garments, lest he walk naked, and they see his shame.

Revelation 19:20

20 And the beast was taken, and with him the false prophet that wrought miracles before him, with which he deceived them that had received the mark of the beast, and them that worshipped his image. These both were cast alive into a lake of fire burning with brimstone.

2 John 7

7 For many deceivers are entered into the world, who confess not that Jesus Christ is come in the flesh. This is a deceiver and an antichrist.

Matthew 24:24

24 For there shall arise false Christs, and false prophets, and shall shew great signs and wonders; insomuch that, if it were possible, they shall deceive the very elect.

Christmas is like the tares sown among the wheat. The tares resemble the wheat, but when it is grown, it is a weed. It's not the real thing. Both wheat and tares exist together in this world until Jesus comes to separate them. Christmas is a tare. Like the false Christians; it only resembles the wheat until it is grown and shows its true colors. One day, Christmas will manifest itself for what it is; nothing but a pagan celebration masquerading as Christian. Like a tare masquerading as wheat. It seems as though the whole church is welcoming this tare in the church as if it were wheat. But this tare doesn't deceive all of us!

**Matthew 13:24-30**
**24 Another parable put he forth unto them, saying, The kingdom of heaven is likened unto a man which sowed good seed in his field:**
**25 But while men slept, his enemy came and sowed tares among the wheat, and went his way.**
**26 But when the blade was sprung up, and brought forth fruit, then appeared the tares also.**
**27 So the servants of the householder came and said unto him, Sir, didst not thou sow good seed in thy field? from whence then hath it tares?**
**28 He said unto them, An enemy hath done this. The servants said unto him, Wilt thou then that we go and gather them up?**
**29 But he said, Nay; lest while ye gather up the tares, ye root up also the wheat with them.**
**30 Let both grow together until the harvest: and in the time of harvest I will say to the reapers, Gather ye together first the tares, and bind them in bundles to burn them: but gather the wheat into my barn.**

**Ephesians 4:14**
**14 That we henceforth be no more children, tossed to and fro, and carried about with every wind of doctrine, by the**

**sleight of men, and cunning craftiness, whereby they lie
in wait to deceive;**

I think to say Christmas is okay to celebrate would be handling
The Word of God deceitfully, and in error as we seen a couple of
verses ago in 2nd Corinthians 4:1-2. We are supposed to seek out the
truth and expose deceitful lies, not just accept any non-scriptural
lie that comes along masquerading as Christian that can lead to our
destruction or cause us to fall form our own steadfastness.

> **2 Peter 3:16-17**
> **16 As also in all his epistles, speaking in them of these
> things; in which are some things hard to be understood,
> which they that are unlearned and unstable wrest, as they
> do also the other scriptures, unto their own destruction.
> 17 Ye therefore, beloved, seeing ye know these things
> before, beware lest ye also, being led away with the error
> of the wicked, fall from your own stedfastness.**

6. We are supposed to be more noble and search the scriptures to
verify whether the things we do are of God or not. And don't do
them if they are not.

> **Acts 17:11**
> **11 These were more noble than those in Thessalonica, in
> that they received the word with all readiness of mind, and
> searched the scriptures daily, whether those things were so.**

Be more noble. Learn The Word and receive The Word. There is
reward for going deeper into the things of God. Don't be suckered
in by something that only seems to be of God on the surface.
Seek God's Word. Find out if Christmas really is of God or not.
There are many deceivers and imitators out there. Don't settle
for anything but the genuine article. Don't mistake the tare for
the wheat like we seen in reason 5. Don't mistake Christmas for

Jesus. That's not Him. It's only a tare. It looks like Jesus, but it will eventually manifest itself into what it is, a weed of Idol worship. But if you search The scriptures, you will recognize the tare now before it matures into a full-blown weed. That way you can avoid the embarrassment of finding out later that you have been deceived by this weed all these years like many people will find out at the Judgement Seat of Christ.

7. A warning to ministers to keep your congregation from the wolves of deception. Expose a falsehood to them. If it is not Biblical; you shouldn't act like it is.

Think about it. For over a month out of the year, people celebrate a pagan celebration which is the birthday of a false Christ named Tammuz, calling him Jesus. I know you think you are celebrating the birth of Jesus, and you think that as long as you are putting The Name of Christ in Christmas, that it is really His birthday you are celebrating. But the celebration of Saturnalia wasn't changed. It still has all the elements of Saturnalia, including the tree. The only change is the name of Tammuz has been changed to Jesus and the events of Bethlehem have been sown into the equation. I have already been over all of the elements of this celebration and have shown you the history behind them. All of those elements are pagan. If you are a minister of Jesus, are you going to tell me that it is okay to do that? To take a pagan celebration and call it Christian? Really?? Think about what you are saying. With this kind of reasoning, you could set up any statue of an idol in the church and use all of the ways that religion worships that idol as long as you call the idol Jesus and say you are worshipping Jesus. Right?? Tell me if that is any different!! Would you allow a little fat guy with his legs crossed with his hands on his knees with his index finger and thumb forming a circle to be set on the altar of the church as long as you called him Jesus? You could say that this little fat guy was born in Bethlehem on a cold winter night. You could celebrate him in all the ways of the eastern religion he came from as long as you add a little Bible in the story and call him Jesus. Right? No!! that's not right!! Wouldn't you agree??? Then neither is it right to celebrate Tammuz even if you add a few Bible details of the birth of Jesus in the story, even calling Tammuz by The Name of Jesus!!!!

**Acts 20:27-31**

**27 For I have not shunned to declare unto you all the counsel of God.**

**28 Take heed therefore unto yourselves, and to all the flock, over the which the Holy Ghost hath made you overseers, to feed the church of God, which he hath purchased with his own blood.**

**29 For I know this, that after my departing shall grievous wolves enter in among you, not sparing the flock.**

**30 Also of your own selves shall men arise, speaking perverse things, to draw away disciples after them.**

**31 Therefore watch, and remember, that by the space of three years I ceased not to warn every one night and day with tears.**

**Titus 1:7-14**

**7 For a bishop must be blameless, as the steward of God; not selfwilled, not soon angry, not given to wine, no striker, not given to filthy lucre;**

**8 But a lover of hospitality, a lover of good men, sober, just, holy, temperate;**

**9 Holding fast the faithful word as he hath been taught, that he may be able by sound doctrine both to exhort and to convince the gainsayers.**

**10 For there are many unruly and vain talkers and deceivers, specially they of the circumcision:**

**11 Whose mouths must be stopped, who subvert whole houses, teaching things which they ought not, for filthy lucre's sake.**

**12 One of themselves, even a prophet of their own, said,
The Cretians are alway liars, evil beasts, slow bellies.
13 This witness is true. Wherefore rebuke them sharply,
that they may be sound in the faith;
14 Not giving heed to Jewish fables, and commandments
of men, that turn from the truth.**

Stay away from fables. Follow only Gods Word. Don't mix It with anything. The Word is sufficient enough without adding anything. You must add quite a lot to justify Christmas. You would also have to unequally yoke yourself together with the world because the world celebrates Christmas. We are not to be conformed to the things of this world.

**2 Corinthians 6:14-15
14 Be ye not unequally yoked together with unbelievers: for
what fellowship hath righteousness with unrighteousness?
and what communion hath light with darkness?
15 And what concord hath Christ with Belial? or what part
hath he that believeth with an infidel?**

**James 4:4
4 Ye adulterers and adulteresses, know ye not that the
friendship of the world is enmity with God? whosoever
therefore will be a friend of the world is the enemy of God.**

We will go over this in greater detail in reason 8 but a friend of the world is enmity against God. It's easy to see that Christmas is a friend of the world. To go against the flow is hard, and very unpopular. But it's a narrow path, and few there be that find it.

**Matthew 7:13-14
13 Enter ye in at the strait gate: for wide is the gate, and
broad is the way, that leadeth to destruction, and many
there be which go in thereat:**

**14 Because strait is the gate, and narrow is the way, which leadeth unto life, and few there be that find it.**

Doesn't it even seem irrational to assume that the world would celebrate the birth of someone it hates? Or that Jesus would accept a celebration of the world involving a form of idol worship as a celebration for Him? It's all too easy to see for you not to get it. There is nothing wrong with celebrating Jesus. But when you celebrate something and involve Jesus in that celebration; you must have some scripture to show that what you are doing will honor Him, not dishonor Him. It is sufficient for us to remember that through His birth; He became flesh and lived among us, then endured the cross for our sin and died on that cross and was raised from the dead three days later as the firstborn from the dead. Many believe that He came into being when He was born into this world. NO, NO and again NO. He came into this world as a child that grew to be a man for the first time. But He already existed before He was born and He has always existed as The second Person of The Trinity, and He is still The second Person of The Trinity and The Son of God and He always will be. He is proclaimed in John to be The Word who created all things in the beginning. So, He is The eternal second Person of The Trinity, The Word, and Jesus, The Son of God. But just as verse 1 below says, He has always been with God and He is God.

**John 1:1-14**
**1 In the beginning was the Word, and the Word was with God, and the Word was God.**
**2 The same was in the beginning with God.**
**3 All things were made by him; and without him was not any thing made that was made.**
**4 In him was life; and the life was the light of men.**
**5 And the light shineth in darkness; and the darkness comprehended it not.**
**6 There was a man sent from God, whose name was John.**

7 The same came for a witness, to bear witness of the Light, that all men through him might believe.

8 He was not that Light, but was sent to bear witness of that Light.

9 That was the true Light, which lighteth every man that cometh into the world.

10 He was in the world, and the world was made by him, and the world knew him not.

11 He came unto his own, and his own received him not.

12 But as many as received him, to them gave he power to become the sons of God, even to them that believe on his name:

13 Which were born, not of blood, nor of the will of the flesh, nor of the will of man, but of God.

14 And the Word was made flesh, and dwelt among us, (and we beheld his glory, the glory as of the only begotten of the Father,) full of grace and truth.

John 8:57-58

57 Then said the Jews unto him, Thou art not yet fifty years old, and hast thou seen Abraham?

58 Jesus said unto them, Verily, verily, I say unto you, Before Abraham was, I am.

Acts 14:15-16

15 And saying, Sirs, why do ye these things? We also are men of like

passions with you, and preach unto you that ye should turn from these vanities unto the living God, which made heaven, and earth, and the sea, and all things that are therein:

16 Who in times past suffered all nations to walk in their own ways.

Contrary to popular belief; Jesus is not the reason for the season. We will see in reason 25 that even a lot of the secular world knows

Christmas is not a Christian celebration, but a lie made to look like it is Christian!

We are not to take the worship of our Lord lightly. Let's show the upmost caution when we tack The Holy Name of Jesus on anything.

> **Colossians 2:18**
> **18 Let no man beguile you of your reward in a voluntary humility and worshipping of angels, intruding into those things which he hath not seen, vainly puffed up by his fleshly mind,**

The Name of Jesus shouldn't be attached to a lie. Especially form a minister of the truth. You must recognize and shun useless and erroneous ways of worshiping our Lord. His Name is too precious and too Holy to be used on a pagan god. You stain The Name of Jesus when you mix It with an idol. Far be it from me to attach Jesus to the filthiness of an idol. Why would Jesus want to be attached to the abomination of a false Christ? That would be like adding a scoop of dirt to your soap in the washing machine, and then expect the cloths to come out clean. In like manor, to add a scoop of the dirt of idol worship to the worship of Jesus will pollute your whole worship. We are supposed to be holy for He is Holy. And that means don't mess around with idol worship.

> **Philippians 2:10-11**
> **10 That at the name of Jesus every knee should bow, of things in heaven, and things in earth, and things under the earth;**
> **11 And that every tongue should confess that Jesus Christ is Lord, to the glory of God the Father.**
>
> **1 Peter 1:15-16**
> **15 But as he which hath called you is holy, so be ye holy in all manner of conversation;**

**16 Because it is written, Be ye holy; for I am holy.**

**2 Timothy 1:9**

**9 Who hath saved us, and called us with an holy calling, not according to our works, but according to his own purpose and grace, which was given us in Christ Jesus before the world began,**

The devil wanted the body of Moses, I believe to make it an idol. But Moses was buried in a secrete place; and I believe it was for that very reason.

**Jude 8-13**

**8 Likewise also these filthy dreamers defile the flesh, despise dominion, and speak evil of dignities.**

**9 Yet Michael the archangel, when contending with the devil he disputed about the body of Moses, durst not bring against him a railing accusation, but said, The Lord rebuke thee.**

**10 But these speak evil of those things which they know not: but what they know naturally, as brute beasts, in those things they corrupt themselves.**

**11 Woe unto them! for they have gone in the way of Cain, and ran greedily after the error of Balaam for reward, and perished in the gainsaying of Core.**

**12 These are spots in your feasts of charity, when they feast with you, feeding themselves without fear: clouds they are without water, carried about of winds; trees whose fruit withereth, without fruit, twice dead, plucked up by the roots;**

**13 Raging waves of the sea, foaming out their own shame; wandering stars, to whom is reserved the blackness of darkness for ever.**

**Deuteronomy 34:5-6**
**5 So Moses the servant of the Lord died there in the land**
**of Moab, according to the word of the Lord.**
**6 And he buried him in a valley in the land of Moab, over**
**against Beth-peor: but no man knoweth of his sepulchre**
**unto this day.**

I think Satan wanted them to worship the body of Moses to distract them from worshiping The One greater than Moses. The way of Cain is like that; worshiping God in a wrong way with the wrong kind of sacrifice. The devil loves to mix something in with the worship of God to water it down and make it ineffective and even harmful to the believer, like the doctrine of Balaam, who mixed idol worship in the camp of Israel, just like Christmas does to the church. These verses above, in Jude, describe the plight of those that blatantly teach false doctrine. Don't let yourself be called out at the judgment seat of Christ by listening to these teachers of false doctrine. Let's stick with what The Word of God says. In this age of grace, God shows mercy toward us who are truly saved and will not send a Christian to hell for celebrating Christmas. If you truly got saved, you were sealed by The Holy Spirit until the day of redemption. But like we already discussed in 1st Corinthians 3:13-15, you can have reward taken away that would have been yours, not to mention, affect your position in the kingdom by listening to these false teachers instead of checking it out in The Word.

**Ephesians 1:11-14**
**11 In whom also we have obtained an inheritance, being**
**predestinated according to the purpose of him who**
**worketh all things after the counsel of his own will:**
**12 That we should be to the praise of his glory, who first**
**trusted in Christ.**
**13 In whom ye also trusted, after that ye heard the word of**
**truth, the gospel of your salvation: in whom also after that**
**ye believed, ye were sealed with that holy Spirit of promise,**

**14 Which is the earnest of our inheritance until the
redemption of the purchased possession, unto the praise
of his glory.**

Whether you celebrate Christmas or not is up to you. You have
been given the facts. What you do with these facts is your decision.
Even though a Christian will escape hell, there are other things to
consider. Like whether Jesus is pleased with us or not. Will He be
pleased with us celebrating a pagan ritual and tacking His Holy
Name to it? Think about it. Can you celebrate Christmas knowing
all of this? I know I can't. Have you been suckered into teaching
a blatant lie that can easily be proven to be a lie, that December
25th is the birthday of Jesus? If so, you're not much of a minister
of the truth, are you?

**James 1:5-8
5 If any of you lack wisdom, let him ask of God, that giveth
to all men liberally, and upbraideth not; and it shall be
given him.
6 But let him ask in faith, nothing wavering. For he that
wavereth is like a wave of the sea driven with the wind
and tossed.
7 For let not that man think that he shall receive any thing
of the Lord.
8 A double minded man is unstable in all his ways.**

**2 Peter 3:17
17 Ye therefore, beloved, seeing ye know these things
before, beware lest ye also, being led away with the error
of the wicked, fall from your own stedfastness.**

**1 John 4:4-6
4 Ye are of God, little children, and have overcome them:
because greater is he that is in you, than he that is in
the world.**

**5 They are of the world: therefore speak they of the world, and the world heareth them.**

**6 We are of God: he that knoweth God heareth us; he that is not of God heareth not us. Hereby know we the spirit of truth, and the spirit of error.**

8. The world loves Christmas. God hates what the world loves. So, how can you make God love what the world loves and make The Bible conform to Christmas? You can't!! I know we have mentioned this a couple of times already in this book, but I wanted to include this as one of the 25 reasons.

**1 John 2:15-17**

**15 Love not the world, neither the things that are in the world. If any man love the world, the love of the Father is not in him.**

**16 For all that is in the world, the lust of the flesh, and the lust of the eyes, and the pride of life, is not of the Father, but is of the world.**

**17 And the world passeth away, and the lust thereof: but he that doeth the will of God abideth for ever.**

**Luke 21:17**

**17 And ye shall be hated of all men for my name's sake.**

**Luke 6:22**

**22 Blessed are ye, when men shall hate you, and when they shall separate you from their company, and shall reproach you, and cast out your name as evil, for the Son of man's sake.**

**John 3:20**

**20 For every one that doeth evil hateth the light, neither cometh to the light, lest his deeds should be reproved.**

**1 John 3:13**
**13 Marvel not, my brethren, if the world hate you.**

These scriptures all reveal that what the world loves, God hates. And we are commanded to love not the things of the world. If Christmas was of God, then the world would hate it. Even unbelievers love Christmas. Why? Because it is a worldly celebration. If it were a Biblical celebration, you wouldn't see the world making a big thing out of it. It's just a fact that the world would hate it. Conduct your own experiment. Ask any person if they are a Christian. If they say no; then ask them if they celebrate Christmas. I suspect 10 out of 10 times they will say yes, they celebrate Christmas. I've known lots of unbelievers; every single one of them celebrates Christmas. Why do you think that is?

9. We are not to serve other gods or copy the ways of the nations in how they served their gods.

> **Deuteronomy 12:30-31**
> **30 Take heed to thyself that thou be not snared by following them, after that they be destroyed from before thee; and that thou inquire not after their gods, saying, How did these nations serve their gods? even so will I do likewise.**
> **31 Thou shalt not do so unto the Lord thy God: for every abomination to the Lord, which he hateth, have they done unto their gods; for even their sons and their daughters they have burnt in the fire to their gods.**

Saturnalia is a pagan celebration with its name changed to Christmas. A small amount of Biblical information was added into it to make it seem legitimately Christian. But this above scripture tells us not to copy from those pagan celebrations in the worship of our God. Because some of the details of the Christmas celebration are Biblical does not make it okay to celebrate. It is the mixing of paganism to Christianity that makes it unacceptable. That mixing is what makes it the doctrine of Balaam and unacceptable to a Christian.

**2 Kings 16:1-4**

**1 In the seventeenth year of Pekah the son of Remaliah Ahaz the son of Jotham king of Judah began to reign.**

**2 Twenty years old was Ahaz when he began to reign, and reigned sixteen years in Jerusalem, and did not that which was right in the sight of the LORD his God, like David his father.**

**3 But he walked in the way of the kings of Israel, yea, and made his son to pass through the fire, according to the abominations of the heathen, whom the LORD cast out from before the children of Israel.**

**4 And he sacrificed and burnt incense in the high places, and on the hills, and under every green tree.**

King Ahaz walked in the way of the kings of Israel and made his son to pass through the fire according to the abominations of the heathen whom The Lord cast out from before the children of Israel. Notice that he copied the ways of the nations, which by the way, included green trees, verse 4. But the important fact is that the ways of the nations now is to celebrate Christmas, which also copies the ways of idol worship and also involves green trees.

**Jeremiah 10:2-4**

**2 Thus saith the Lord, Learn not the way of the heathen, and be not dismayed at the signs of heaven; for the heathen are dismayed at them.**

**3 For the customs of the people are vain: for one cutteth a tree out of the forest, the work of the hands of the workman, with the axe.**

**4 They deck it with silver and with gold; they fasten it with nails and with hammers, that it move not.**

I have given you several examples in The Bible of this mixing of God's people with paganism. And there are many more that I haven't given. It would make this book too long to include all of them. Just remember, God is against this practice.

> **Revelation 2:14**
> **14 But I have a few things against thee, because thou hast there them that hold the doctrine of Balaam, who taught Balac to cast a stumblingblock before the children of Israel, to eat things sacrificed unto idols, and to commit fornication.**

10. We are not to compromise with the world no matter how much influence we are under to do so.

Note: You can include this next scripture in reason 9 as well.

> **2 Kings 17:29-41**
> **29 Howbeit every nation made gods of their own, and put them in the houses of the high places which the Samaritans had made, every nation in their cities wherein they dwelt.**
> **30 And the men of Babylon made Succothbenoth, and the men of Cuth made Nergal, and the men of Hamath made Ashima,**
> **31 And the Avites made Nibhaz and Tartak, and the Sepharvites burnt their children in fire to Adrammelech and Anammelech, the gods of Sepharvaim.**
> **32 So they feared the LORD, and made unto themselves of the lowest of them priests of the high places, which sacrificed for them in the houses of the high places.**
> **33 They feared the LORD, and served their own gods, after the manner of the nations whom they carried away from thence.**
> **34 Unto this day they do after the former manners: they fear not the LORD, neither do they after their statutes, or**

**after their ordinances, or after the law and commandment which the LORD commanded the children of Jacob, whom he named Israel;**

**35 With whom the LORD had made a covenant, and charged them, saying, Ye shall not fear other gods, nor bow yourselves to them, nor serve them, nor sacrifice to them:**

**36 But the LORD, who brought you up out of the land of Egypt with great power and a stretched out arm, him shall ye fear, and him shall ye worship, and to him shall ye do sacrifice.**

**37 And the statutes, and the ordinances, and the law, and the commandment, which he wrote for you, ye shall observe to do for evermore; and ye shall not fear other gods.**

**38 And the covenant that I have made with you ye shall not forget; neither shall ye fear other gods.**

**39 But the LORD your God ye shall fear; and he shall deliver you out of the hand of all your enemies.**

**40 Howbeit they did not hearken, but they did after their former manner.**

**41 So these nations feared the LORD, and served their graven images, both their children, and their children's children: as did their fathers, so do they unto this day.**

This is a story of compromise. Verse 33 says that they feared The Lord, and at the same time served their own gods after the manner of the nations whom they carried away from thence. It is a sad picture here. The Lord wants them to serve only Him, but they would not give up their false gods. Oh yes, they will fear The Lord, but other gods also. It's a compromise that still exist today with Christmas when you say, yes, I'll serve Jesus, but I want to do it my way, not the way The Bible says. Do you remember the popular song where the singer proudly sings: "I did it my way"? Well, you can tell that to Jesus at the Judgment seat of Christ; but somehow, I don't think that He'll be amused that you were so bold to do it your way.

11. Is The Lord now talking about you when He told Ezekiel: "Son of man, seest thou what they do?"

**Ezekiel 8:1-18**

**1 And it came to pass in the sixth year, in the sixth month, in the fifth day of the month, as I sat in mine house, and the elders of Judah sat before me, that the hand of the Lord GOD fell there upon me.**

**2 Then I beheld, and lo a likeness as the appearance of fire: from the appearance of his loins even downward, fire; and from his loins even upward, as the appearance of brightness, as the colour of amber.**

**3 And he put forth the form of an hand, and took me by a lock of mine head; and the spirit lifted me up between the earth and the heaven, and brought me in the visions of God to Jerusalem, to the door of the inner gate that looketh toward the north; where was the seat of the image of jealousy, which provoketh to jealousy.**

**4 And, behold, the glory of the God of Israel was there, according to the vision that I saw in the plain.**

**5 Then said he unto me, Son of man, lift up thine eyes now the way toward the north. So I lifted up mine eyes the way toward the north, and behold northward at the gate of the altar this image of jealousy in the entry.**

**6 He said furthermore unto me, Son of man, seest thou what they do? even the great abominations that the house of Israel committeth here, that I should go far off from my sanctuary? but turn thee yet again, and thou shalt see greater abominations.**

**7 And he brought me to the door of the court; and when I looked, behold a hole in the wall.**

**8 Then said he unto me, Son of man, dig now in the wall: and when I had digged in the wall, behold a door.**

**9 And he said unto me, Go in, and behold the wicked abominations that they do here.**

10 So I went in and saw; and behold every form of creeping things, and abominable beasts, and all the idols of the house of Israel, pourtrayed upon the wall round about.

11 And there stood before them seventy men of the ancients of the house of Israel, and in the midst of them stood Jaazaniah the son of Shaphan, with every man his censer in his hand; and a thick cloud of incense went up.

12 Then said he unto me, Son of man, hast thou seen what the ancients of the house of Israel do in the dark, every man in the chambers of his imagery? for they say, The LORD seeth us not; the LORD hath forsaken the earth.

13 He said also unto me, Turn thee yet again, and thou shalt see greater abominations that they do.

14 Then he brought me to the door of the gate of the LORD's house

which was toward the north; and, behold, there sat women weeping for Tammuz.

15 Then said he unto me, Hast thou seen this, O son of man? turn thee yet again, and thou shalt see greater abominations than these.

16 And he brought me into the inner court of the LORD's house, and, behold, at the door of the temple of the LORD, between the porch and the altar, were about five and twenty men, with their backs toward the temple of the LORD, and their faces toward the east; and they worshipped the sun toward the east.

17 Then he said unto me, Hast thou seen this, O son of man? Is it a light thing to the house of Judah that they commit the abominations which they commit here? for they have filled the land with violence, and have returned to provoke me to anger: and, lo, they put the branch to their nose.

18 Therefore will I also deal in fury: mine eye shall not spare, neither will I have pity: and though they cry in mine ears with a loud voice, yet will I not hear them.

This is the sad story of abomination in the temple. Notice in verse 14. the direct reference to Tammuz. God must have wanted us to know that there was a Tammuz, so He gave enough reference to him to provoke us to find out who he was. I believe that God didn't want to waste scripture on explaining who Tammuz was in The Bible, and why should He? In the scheme of things, Tammuz is nothing. He is not worthy of an explanation of him in The Holy Word of God. Tammuz is only a speck; a blemish, in the realm of God. He is not worthy of anything more than the mention of his name only to confirm him in history. God gave us a brain to find out who he is for ourselves and He made sure there was enough historical information on him to tell us. Then comparing that history to scripture; we can see that it is verified through scripture. One final note on these verses; notice verses 5 & 6. Ezekiel is told to lift up his eyes toward the north, and behold, northward at the gate of the altar, this image of jealous in the entry. Then in this very sad verse, verse 6, He said: "Son of man, seest thou what they do?" It's like a father with a rebellious son, and the father is grieving over the son's disobedience. Can you feel the grief of God in this verse? Is God saying, "Son of man, seest thou what they do?" about you celebrating Christmas? Christmas is even associated with the northern gate. Do you think it is an accident that Santa Claus made his home at the North Pole? Look at Psalms 48:1-2. The sides of the north is where the city of the great King is. The city of the great King is not at the north pole. I believe this is talking about the northern hemisphere. But the association with the north is, I believe, no accident. The north is considered the top of the world. This is not something I can prove to be Biblically true. But it does seem like there is evidence of the north being important in the things of God.

**Leviticus 1:11**
**11 And he shall kill it on the side of the altar northward before the Lord: and the priests, Aaron's sons, shall sprinkle his blood round about upon the altar.**

**Psalms 75:6-7**
**6 For promotion cometh neither from the east, nor from the west, nor from the south.**
**7 But God is the judge: he putteth down one, and setteth up another.**

**Job 26:7**
**7 He stretcheth out the north over the empty place, and hangeth the earth upon nothing.**

Lucifer was desirous to exalt his throne above the stars of God; and to sit upon the mount of the congregation, on the sides of the north.

**Isaiah 14:12-14**
**12 How art thou fallen from heaven, O Lucifer, son of the morning! how**
**art thou cut down to the ground, which didst weaken the nations!**
**13 For thou hast said in thine heart, I will ascend into heaven, I will exalt my throne above the stars of God: I will sit also upon the mount of the congregation, in the sides of the north:**
**14 I will ascend above the heights of the clouds; I will be like the most High.**

Do you turn to paganism and idol worship once a year because it's fun? We will all find out in the end if the things that I have told you are true or not. I have given you scripture to support my position on the subject of Christmas. Can you do the same? Can you prove that Christmas is not a pagan celebration modified to fit Christianity? Let's make full proof of our ministry. The proofs that I stand on in this book are first and foremost the scriptures given, and then the historical facts. There are countless resources like encyclopedias, topical Bibles, commentaries, Bible dictionaries, concordances, historical books and references, the internet, not to mention countless sermons on any subject that you want on YouTube. I didn't quote any of their references in this book. I left that for you to look up for yourself. But I have studied this subject with all these resources and much more and they all agree that Christmas is a pagan celebration with the names changed to Christian names. But they also all rationalize it away with flawed unbiblical reasoning and find an excuse to celebrate these pagan celebrations anyway to appease the people. It seems like the favorite excuse in the church is to say that it gives pastors a chance to preach to those that only come on Christmas. That sounds really logical and noble on the surface but where is the scripture to back it up? Really, it is still only an excuse, not Bible fact. Let me ask you this; is it okay to lie to someone to get them in church so you can preach the truth to them? You are telling them that December 25th is the birthday of Jesus to get them in church. You, as a pastor, know that this is false. If you don't, then you are not much of a pastor. December 25th is not and cannot be the day of the birth of Jesus and you know it, pastor. So, you are willingly using a blatant lie to deceive people into thinking it is the day of the birth of Jesus just to draw them into the church simply so you can preach to them? Then when you get them in the church, you continue the lie and preach on the bases of that lie. In reason 25 in this book. Even a lot of the world knows that you are preaching a lie. If you, as a pastor actually do believe that Jesus was born on December 25th, you need to do some research on the subject. Do you have a mind? Use it to reason things out no matter how it appears. Looks can be deceiving, so don't fall into this Christmas deception. Don't be caught in this deception when He who comes to judge our works as a Christian shall come.

12. Jesus healed a leper. Then He told the leper not to tell anyone, but to go to the priest and offer for his cleansing those things which Moses commanded for a testimony unto them. Because of his disobedience, the work of Jesus was hindered. Are you going to hinder the work of Jesus with your disobedience of taking part

in an idol worship celebration because it seems, in your mind, to glorify The Name of Jesus?

> **Mark 1:40-44**
> **40 And there came a leper to him, beseeching him, and kneeling down to him, and saying unto him, If thou wilt, thou canst make me clean.**
> **41 And Jesus, moved with compassion, put forth his hand, and touched him, and saith unto him, I will; be thou clean.**
> **42 And as soon as he had spoken, immediately the leprosy departed from him, and he was cleansed.**
> **43 And he straitly charged him, and forthwith sent him away;**
> **44 And saith unto him, See thou say nothing to any man: but go thy way, shew thyself to the priest, and offer for thy cleansing those things which Moses commanded, for a testimony unto them.**

In verse 45 below, he didn't do what he was told. Instead, he began to publish it much and spread it around insomuch that Jesus could no more openly enter into the city, but was out in desert places; and they came to him from every quarter.

> **Mark 1:45**
> **45 But he went out, and began to publish it much, and to blaze abroad the matter, insomuch that Jesus could no more openly enter into the city, but was without in desert places: and they came to him from every quarter.**

Do we hinder the work that Jesus wants us to do by disobeying Him, even if it seems to glorify Him like this guy did by telling the people of his healing, seemingly honoring Him, but really disobeying Him? Christmas seems to publish The Name of Jesus well, only to get bogged down in greed like when the leper published his healing and people came, not to worship Jesus, but to get something from Him. People celebrate Christmas for the flesh.

To receive Christmas presents, and see lights and decorations, not from the heart, but to get something for themselves. Do we then just go about doing our own thing? The Christmas celebration is our own thing, not of God. Or do we glorify Him by obeying His Word? Isn't obedience better than sacrifice? Which, by the way, in this next passage, describes how Saul was seemingly, in his own mind, doing a service to God, verse 13. But it was really an act of disobedience, verse 14 & 18-19. Just like Christmas.

> **1 Samuel 15:12-26**
>
> **12 And when Samuel rose early to meet Saul in the morning, it was told Samuel, saying, Saul came to Carmel, and, behold, he set him up a place, and is gone about, and passed on, and gone down to Gilgal.**
>
> **13 And Samuel came to Saul: and Saul said unto him, Blessed be thou of the Lord: I have performed the commandment of the Lord.**
>
> **14 And Samuel said, What meaneth then this bleating of the sheep in mine ears, and the lowing of the oxen which I hear?**
>
> **15 And Saul said, They have brought them from the Amalekites: for the people spared the best of the sheep and of the oxen, to sacrifice unto the Lord thy God; and the rest we have utterly destroyed.**
>
> **16 Then Samuel said unto Saul, Stay, and I will tell thee what the Lord hath said to me this night. And he said unto him, Say on.**
>
> **17 And Samuel said, When thou wast little in thine own sight, wast thou not made the head of the tribes of Israel, and the Lord anointed thee king over Israel?**
>
> **18 And the Lord sent thee on a journey, and said, Go and utterly destroy the sinners the Amalekites, and fight against them until they be consumed.**

**19 Wherefore then didst thou not obey the voice of the Lord, but didst fly upon the spoil, and didst evil in the sight of the Lord?**

**20 And Saul said unto Samuel, Yea, I have obeyed the voice of the Lord, and have gone the way which the Lord sent me, and have brought Agag the king of Amalek, and have utterly destroyed the Amalekites.**

**21 But the people took of the spoil, sheep and oxen, the chief of the things which should have been utterly destroyed, to sacrifice unto the Lord thy God in Gilgal.**

**22 And Samuel said, Hath the Lord as great delight in burnt offerings and sacrifices, as in obeying the voice of the Lord? Behold, to obey is better than sacrifice, and to hearken than the fat of rams.**

**23 For rebellion is as the sin of witchcraft, and stubbornness is as iniquity and idolatry. Because thou hast rejected the word of the Lord, he hath also rejected thee from being king.**

**24 And Saul said unto Samuel, I have sinned: for I have transgressed the commandment of the Lord, and thy words: because I feared the people, and obeyed their voice.**

**25 Now therefore, I pray thee, pardon my sin, and turn again with me, that I may worship the Lord.**

**26 And Samuel said unto Saul, I will not return with thee: for thou hast rejected the word of the Lord, and the Lord hath rejected thee from being king over Israel.**

To obey is better than sacrifice, verse 22 above. Christmas is a vain sacrifice. It is better to obey God and His Word than to look to the pagans to copy their sacrifice for their gods. Notice in verse 24, Saul blamed the people for his sin. This sounds real similar to when Adam blamed Eve for his sin and Eve blamed the serpent.

**Genesis 3:12-13**
**12 And the man said, The woman whom thou gavest to be with me, she gave me of the tree, and I did eat.**

**13 And the Lord God said unto the woman, What is this that thou hast done? And the woman said, The serpent beguiled me, and I did eat.**

One of mankind's earliest sins is to blame someone else for his own mistakes. In reality, if you can be talked into doing something you know is wrong, or if you can be deceived into doing something that is not Biblical because you are too lazy to check it out for yourself; then there is no one to blame but yourself. Will you tell God at the judgement seat that you only celebrated this pagan celebration because everyone else was doing it? I don't think that excuse will fly then just as it didn't fly with Adam and Eve. Notice verse 15, When Saul said: **"and the rest we have utterly destroyed";** he makes it sound like a good thing, like: "we kept the best sheep to present as a sacrifice to The Lord, and the best oxen to use. And then we did exactly as you said and utterly destroyed the rest". Only, that is not what he was commanded to do. He was commanded to utterly destroy all of them. Him doing it as a sacrifice to The Lord is supposed to make it alright; just like you making Jesus the reason for the season is supposed to make it alright. Only, it doesn't.

13. Are you offering strange fire before The Lord?

> **Leviticus 9:23-10:2**
> **23 And Moses and Aaron went into the tabernacle of the congregation, and came out, and blessed the people: and the glory of the Lord appeared unto all the people.**
> **24 And there came a fire out from before the Lord, and consumed upon the altar the burnt offering and the fat: which when all the people saw, they shouted, and fell on their faces.**
> **Ch 10:1 And Nadab and Abihu, the sons of Aaron, took either of them his censer, and put fire therein, and put**

**incense thereon, and offered strange fire before the Lord, which he commanded them not.**
**2 And there went out fire from the Lord, and devoured them, and they died before the Lord.**

Nadab and Abihu offered strange fire before The Lord in the wilderness of Sinai and as a result, died. Shouldn't we be careful what kind of worldly thing we attach The Name of Jesus to, like Christmas. Could The Lord be wondering why we, as Christians, separated from the world, are taking part in this worldly celebration? Could this be strange fire? God didn't let Nadab and Abihu get away with it. If you celebrate the birthday of Tammuz and call him Jesus; to me, that amounts to strange fire.

Beware of bringing the wrong kind of sacrifice to God.

**Genesis 4:3-5**
**3 And in process of time it came to pass, that Cain brought of the fruit of the ground an offering unto the Lord.**
**4 And Abel, he also brought of the firstlings of his flock and of the fat thereof. And the Lord had respect unto Abel and to his offering:**
**5 But unto Cain and to his offering he had not respect. And Cain was very wroth, and his countenance fell.**

Cain didn't bring a blood sacrifice and God didn't accept it, but God did accept Abel's blood sacrifice. Because of Cain's jealously of God accepting Abel's sacrifice and not his; he murdered his brother Abel.

**Genesis 4:8**
**8 And Cain talked with Abel his brother: and it came to pass, when they were in the field, that Cain rose up against Abel his brother, and slew him.**

Again, God takes things seriously. He doesn't accept the wrong kind of sacrifice. If you are sacrificing a lot of time and money into Christmas, then it could all be in vain. Would God accept a pagan celebration to honor Him? Just like Cain; people get mad when I tell them the truth about Christmas. That is the same kind of pride that motivated Cain to kill his brother, Abel, because of the jealously stirred up in him that God didn't accept his sacrifice the way he wanted to bring it. People think they are serving God and honoring Jesus in celebrating Christmas. Most people don't even know the truth about it, just like Cain didn't know the truth about his sacrifice until it was rejected by God. That is exactly why I am writing this book. To inform those that are ignorant to the truth about Christmas. Now that you know the truth, are you going to accept it? Or are you going to stand against this truth? I would hope that you wouldn't rebel to the point of murder like Cain did, but there are consequences from God for not receiving His truth.

**Romans 1:18-22**
**18 For the wrath of God is revealed from heaven against all ungodliness and unrighteousness of men, who hold the truth in unrighteousness;**
**19 Because that which may be known of God is manifest in them; for God hath shewed it unto them.**
**20 For the invisible things of him from the creation of the world are clearly seen, being understood by the things that are made, even his eternal power and Godhead; so that they are without excuse:**
**21 Because that, when they knew God, they glorified him not as God, neither were thankful; but became vain in their imaginations, and their foolish heart was darkened.**
**22 Professing themselves to be wise, they became fools,**

**John 4:24**
**24 God is a Spirit: and they that worship him must worship him in spirit and in truth.**

**Ephesians 4:24-25**

**24 And that ye put on the new man, which after God is created in righteousness and true holiness.**

**25 Wherefore putting away lying, speak every man truth with his neighbour: for we are members one of another.**

**2 Timothy 4:2-4**

**2 Preach the word; be instant in season, out of season; reprove, rebuke, exhort with all longsuffering and doctrine.**

**3 For the time will come when they will not endure sound doctrine; but after their own lusts shall they heap to themselves teachers, having itching ears;**

**4 And they shall turn away their ears from the truth, and shall be turned unto fables.**

**2 Peter 2:1-3**

**1 But there were false prophets also among the people, even as there shall be false teachers among you, who privily shall bring in damnable heresies, even denying the Lord that bought them, and bring upon themselves swift destruction.**

**2 And many shall follow their pernicious ways; by reason of whom the way of truth shall be evil spoken of.**

**3 And through covetousness shall they with feigned words make merchandise of you: whose judgment now of a long time lingereth not, and their damnation slumbereth not.**

**1 John 4:5-6**

**5 They are of the world: therefore speak they of the world, and the world heareth them.**

**6 We are of God: he that knoweth God heareth us; he that is not of God heareth not us. Hereby know we the spirit of truth, and the spirit of error.**

**3 John 4**
**4 I have no greater joy than to hear that my children walk in truth.**

How much truth is there in Christmas? Not much! December 25th is not the birthday of Jesus. The Christmas tree does not Biblically pertain to Jesus in any way, but it does Biblically pertain to idol worship. There is no mention in The Bible of God's people exchanging gifts. There is no Biblical example of Santa Claus or flying reindeer, and the list goes on.

14. As we talked a little bit about before: It is part of the Christmas tradition that three kings from the east seen a star and followed it to Bethlehem where they came upon baby Jesus in the manger where they gave Him gifts. Let me straighten you out on this story.

First; it doesn't say kings at all. Notice in Matthew 2:1-2, it says that they were wise men, not kings.

**Matthew 2:1**
**1 Now when Jesus was born in Bethlehem of Judaea in the days of Herod the king, behold, there came wise men from the east to Jerusalem,**

Second; I can safely say that despite hearing it all my life, Jesus was not born in a manger. A manger is only a feeding trough and Mary couldn't have fit in a feeding trough to have Jesus. The Bible says that they laid Jesus in that manger. But even at that, the manger they laid Him in is not the location that the wise men came to see Him. When the wise men came, He was in a house. We will see this in just a little bit, but first:

Thirdly: it doesn't say how many wise men. It is only assumed there was three wise men because there were three gifts, but it could have been any number of wise men. Wise men of those days were thought to be astronomers from the east who studied the stars. An unbiblical guess of mine is perhaps they were descendants from the wise men in Daniel's time. These wise men of Daniel's time couldn't interpret the king's dream, so the king ordered them killed. But Daniel interpreted the dream and saved their lives. After that happened, they all believed in the God of Daniel and, again, a guess of mine, that perhaps they studied the prophecies of the coming of Christ which is why they knew of his birth. I won't put all of that story in here. You can look it up in Daniel chapter 2 if you want to read it. But can you see the problem here? These wise men could clearly see that this star meant the coming of The Messiah. Why didn't the priest of Israel know this from their writings? They were the ones that were supposed to know and reveal this to the people. These astronomers also studied the arrangement of the stars to conclude that the birth of The Messiah would be in the sign of Virgo concluding Jesus would be born of a virgin. By the way, Virgo could put the birth of Jesus sometime in the September timeframe which would agree with a lot of scholars of when Jesus was born. We will talk more about this September timeframe in reason 18, but there is a theory that the lining up of the stars talked about in Revelation 12:1-2 is what these astronomers might have seen, and that is how they could penpoint when Jesus was to be born. I can't be sure if that theory is true or not, but it does fit the narrative of them studying the stars. These were seasoned astronomers and they had studied the stars all their lives. So, it makes sense that they figured this out or perhaps God revealed it to them through the wonders of the heavens.

**Revelation 12:1-2**
**1 And there appeared a great wonder in heaven; a woman clothed with the sun, and the moon under her feet, and upon her head a crown of twelve stars:**
**2 And she being with child cried, travailing in birth, and pained to be delivered.**

**Joel 2:30**
**30 And I will shew wonders in the heavens and in the earth,**
**blood, and fire, and pillars of smoke.**

No, I am not giving credibility to the zodiac with these scriptures. I am just saying that God can use signs in the heavens to tell us things if He wants to. It is man that corrupts what God has given us turning it into idol worship. God did say He can use signs in the sun and the moon and the stars. God put the constellations in the heavens. And He perhaps set them in the heavens as signs for us to see. So perhaps God set these signs of the stars in the heavens to give us a glimpse into prophecy through patterns of the stars in the night sky. But, as magnificent as they are, these star patterns were never meant to be worshiped. The queen of heaven has used these star patterns to create a false system of the worship of the stars, today called the zodiac.

**Luke 21:25**
**25 And there shall be signs in the sun, and in the moon, and in the stars; and upon the earth distress of nations, with perplexity; the sea and the waves roaring;**

**Daniel 2:24**
**24 Therefore Daniel went in unto Arioch, whom the king had ordained to destroy the wise men of Babylon: he went and said thus unto him; Destroy not the wise men of Babylon: bring me in before the king, and I will shew unto the king the interpretation.**

Fourthly; these wise men said that they had seen a star in the east, and yet they were from the east. So how could they be from the east and follow an eastern star to the west of where they were? They didn't. I guess you could interpret this as they seen a star in the east means that they were in the east when they seen the star. But if that was the case, why didn't the star they seen in the first place led them to Jesus? It didn't, because they were asking Herod where Jesus was, verse 2. It is only after they left from talking to Herod that the star appeared again and showed them where Jesus was, verse 9. In any case, the Hollywood version has them following a star all the way from the east to the manger scene which did not happen, verse 9 below.

And finally, fifthly; notice in verse 11, below, Jesus was not a baby, but a young child, probably at least a year old and possibly approaching two years old, because when Herod made the decree that every child two and under should be killed, he must have known that Jesus could be near two years old by asking the wise men when they had first seen the star.

**Matthew 2:2-11**

**2 Saying, Where is he that is born King of the Jews? for we have seen his star in the east, and are come to worship him.**

**3 When Herod the king had heard these things, he was troubled, and all Jerusalem with him.**

**4 And when he had gathered all the chief priests and scribes of the people together, he demanded of them where Christ should be born.**

**5 And they said unto him, In Bethlehem of Judaea: for thus it is written by the prophet,**

**6 And thou Bethlehem, in the land of Juda, art not the least among the princes of Juda: for out of thee shall come a Governor, that shall rule my people Israel.**

**7 Then Herod, when he had privily called the wise men, inquired of them diligently what time the star appeared.**

**8 And he sent them to Bethlehem, and said, Go and search diligently for the young child; and when ye have found him, bring me word again, that I may come and worship him also.**

> **9 When they had heard the king, they departed; and, lo,
> the star, which they saw in the east, went before them, till
> it came and stood over where the young child was.**
> **10 When they saw the star, they rejoiced with exceeding
> great joy.**
> **11 And when they were come into the house, they saw the
> young child with Mary his mother, and fell down, and
> worshipped him: and when they had opened their treasures,
> they presented unto him gifts; gold, and frankincense,
> and myrrh.**

An angel warned the wise men about Herod. Isn't it great how God will send something to warn us of impending danger? There have been many times in my life that I was warned by something of impending danger to avoid.

> **Matthew 2:12**
> **12 And being warned of God in a dream that they should
> not return to Herod, they departed into their own country
> another way.**

When Herod realized that they had left without telling him where Jesus was, he was furious and committed an atrocity against the Jews.

> **Matthew 2:16**
> **16 Then Herod, when he saw that he was mocked of the
> wise men, was exceeding wroth, and sent forth, and slew all
> the children that were in Bethlehem, and in all the coasts
> thereof, from two years old and under, according to the
> time which he had diligently inquired of the wise men.**

15. Beware of the leaven of the Pharisees. Only one small false doctrine can corrupt your entire worship.

**Matthew 16:6-12**

**6 Then Jesus said unto them, Take heed and beware of the leaven of the Pharisees and of the Sadducees.**

**7 And they reasoned among themselves, saying, It is because we have taken no bread.**

**8 Which when Jesus perceived, he said unto them, O ye of little faith, why reason ye among yourselves, because ye have brought no bread?**

**9 Do ye not yet understand, neither remember the five loaves of the five thousand, and how many baskets ye took up?**

**10 Neither the seven loaves of the four thousand, and how many baskets ye took up?**

**11 How is it that ye do not understand that I spake it not to you concerning bread, that ye should beware of the leaven of the Pharisees and of the Sadducees?**

**12 Then understood they how that he bade them not beware of the leaven of bread, but of the doctrine of the Pharisees and of the Sadducees.**

In verse 12, it tells us that the leaven is the doctrine of the Pharisees. They were to beware because of the doctrine that was mostly good but had a little false doctrine mixed in. Just as most of the bread is dough with only a little leaven mixed in. But that little bit of leaven changes all together the look and texture of the bread. Even as the little bit of false doctrine changes the meaning of the of true doctrine. So, if you accept Christmas, which is a false Christian tradition with a false Christ; and you accept that false Christ as Jesus; that can open the door to accept anyone going by the name of Jesus just because they say they are Him. Then that also opens the door for false doctrines to enter in. For instance, it would not be right to accept Tammuz as The Christ at Christmas time and then deny that other false gods are Christ also. There is a movement today that says Christ manifested Himself in many religious

331

leaders of many other religions; and that they are all the same Christ. This is known as universalism, or a one world religion. It's a new age philosophy. Of course, it is a false religion. But if you celebrate Christmas, you are taking part in that universal religion that says you can call anyone you like by the name of Jesus. The christ of Christmas is not The Christ of The Bible. It is Tammuz, a false Christ. Tammuz is the leaven of Christmas that the devil tries to mix in with The Word of God in an attempt to corrupt The whole Word.

16. A stern warning about seeking to please men instead of God.

A question for pastors; do you know this truth about Christmas but celebrate it anyway to please men instead of God?

> **Galatians 1:10**
> **10 For do I now persuade men, or God? or do I seek to please men? for if I yet pleased men, I should not be the servant of Christ.**

Or, even if you are not a pastor and you know the truth about Christmas; do you celebrate Christmas to please your family? Do you say: I do it for the kids? What does The Bible say about that?

> **Luke 14:26**
> **26 If any man come to me, and hate not his father, and mother, and wife, and children, and brethren, and sisters, yea, and his own life also, he cannot be my disciple.**

This isn't saying to hate your family. It is saying do not put your family before God. Your family is not an excuse to take part in idol worship practices. Jesus and paganism do not mix. You must then choose God or family. And in the same way, pastors, don't put your job, your income or church membership before the truth. Christmas is not the truth about Jesus. Is your job as pastor more important than the truth of The Bible??? If so, that sounds like a sell out to me. Sounds like you are selling Jesus to the Christmas season to keep your job.

17. There are stiff penalties for spreading or condoning false doctrine. And Christmas is a falsehood, being nothing of what it appears to be, but is really a deceptive teaching, bending and changing what really happened at the birth of Jesus described in The Word of God where the truth is found. Now which do you want; The real truth? Or a corrupted truth that is mixed with a lie?

> **2 Corinthians 11:3-4**
> **3 But I fear, lest by any means, as the serpent beguiled Eve through his subtilty, so your minds should be corrupted from the simplicity that is in Christ.**
> **4 For if he that cometh preacheth another Jesus, whom we have not preached, or if ye receive another spirit, which ye have not received, or another gospel, which ye have not accepted, ye might well bear with him.**

> **2 Corinthians 11:13-14**
> **13 For such are false apostles, deceitful workers, transforming themselves into the apostles of Christ.**
> **14 And no marvel; for Satan himself is transformed into an angel of light.**

> **2 Peter 2:3.**
> **3 And through covetousness shall they with feigned words make merchandise of you: whose judgment now of a long time lingereth not, and their damnation slumbereth not.**

Christmas is a false Christian tradition designed to make merchandise of Jesus. You are simply the pawn that the devil uses to make that happen. Without you, he couldn't pull it off. He needs you to mix Tammuz with Christ for it to work. Without you to keep it going, it would just die out. Without Christians making a big deal out of Christmas, the world couldn't get their spiritual fix and feel like they have fulfilled their spiritual duty for the year. So, instead of using a false Christian holiday to make them feel spiritual, perhaps they would turn to Jesus instead and see true Christianity and get saved.

18. No one knows the day Jesus was born.

The Bible doesn't say when that day was. That's a pretty important fact to leave out of The Bible if we are supposed to celebrate His birth. We already talked about reasons why it couldn't have been December in chapter 2 of this book. But there is another reason we didn't mention in that chapter. When the angel told Zacharias that his wife would bear a child who would be John the Baptist; it was while he was serving as priest in the temple in the division of Abijah.

> **Luke 1:5-31**
> **5 There was in the days of Herod, the king of Judaea, a certain priest named Zacharias, of the course of Abia: and his wife was of the daughters of Aaron, and her name was Elisabeth.**
> **6 And they were both righteous before God, walking in all the commandments and ordinances of the Lord blameless.**
> **7 And they had no child, because that Elisabeth was barren, and they both were now well stricken in years.**
> **8 And it came to pass, that while he executed the priest's office before God in the order of his course,**
> **9 According to the custom of the priest's office, his lot was to burn incense when he went into the temple of the Lord.**
> **10 And the whole multitude of the people were praying without at the time of incense.**
> **11 And there appeared unto him an angel of the Lord standing on the right side of the altar of incense.**

12 And when Zacharias saw him, he was troubled, and fear fell upon him.

13 But the angel said unto him, Fear not, Zacharias: for thy prayer is heard; and thy wife Elisabeth shall bear thee a son, and thou shalt call his name John.

14 And thou shalt have joy and gladness; and many shall rejoice at his birth.

15 For he shall be great in the sight of the Lord, and shall drink neither wine nor strong drink; and he shall be filled with the Holy Ghost, even from his mother's womb.

16 And many of the children of Israel shall he turn to the Lord their God.

17 And he shall go before him in the spirit and power of Elias, to turn the hearts of the fathers to the children, and the disobedient to the wisdom of the just; to make ready a people prepared for the Lord.

18 And Zacharias said unto the angel, Whereby shall I know this? for I am an old man, and my wife well stricken in years.

19 And the angel answering said unto him, I am Gabriel, that stand in the presence of God; and am sent to speak unto thee, and to shew thee these glad tidings.

20 And, behold, thou shalt be dumb, and not able to speak, until the day that these things shall be performed, because thou believest not my words, which shall be fulfilled in their season.

21 And the people waited for Zacharias, and marvelled that he tarried so long in the temple.

22 And when he came out, he could not speak unto them: and they perceived that he had seen a vision in the temple: for he beckoned unto them, and remained speechless.

23 And it came to pass, that, as soon as the days of his ministration were accomplished, he departed to his own house.

**24 And after those days his wife Elisabeth conceived, and hid herself five months, saying,**

**25 Thus hath the Lord dealt with me in the days wherein he looked on me, to take away my reproach among men.**

**26 And in the sixth month the angel Gabriel was sent from God unto a city of Galilee, named Nazareth,**

**27 To a virgin espoused to a man whose name was Joseph, of the house of David; and the virgin's name was Mary.**

**28 And the angel came in unto her, and said, Hail, thou that art highly favoured, the Lord is with thee: blessed art thou among women.**

**29 And when she saw him, she was troubled at his saying, and cast in her mind what manner of salutation this should be.**

**30 And the angel said unto her, Fear not, Mary: for thou hast found favour with God.**

**31 And, behold, thou shalt conceive in thy womb, and bring forth a son, and shalt call his name JESUS.**

Luke 1:35-38

**35 And the angel answered and said unto her, The Holy Ghost shall come upon thee, and the power of the Highest shall overshadow thee: therefore also that holy thing which shall be born of thee shall be called the Son of God.**

**36 And, behold, thy cousin Elisabeth, she hath also conceived a son in her old age: and this is the sixth month with her, who was called barren.**

**37 For with God nothing shall be impossible.**

**38 And Mary said, Behold the handmaid of the Lord; be it unto me according to thy word. And the angel departed from her.**

Starting the first month of the Jewish religious calendar, the month of Nisan, each division of priest served two weeks a year in the order of the 24 priests in the temple one week at a time every 6 months from sabbath to sabbath of each of those weeks. Abijah was the eighth out of 24 in that order. And there were times when all the priest served during the feast days that were not part of their regular course, so those times need to be calculated in to the timeline of the birth of Jesus because these special feast days would add days to some of the normal 6 months between each one serving in their regular course.

> **1 Chronicles 24:7-10**
> **7 Now the first lot came forth to Jehoiarib, the second**
> **to Jedaiah,**
> **8 The third to Harim, the fourth to Seorim,**
> **9 The fifth to Malchijah, the sixth to Mijamin,**
> **10 The seventh to Hakkoz, the eighth to Abijah,**

The dating of this is not an exact science, but it is logical. So, Zacharias served in the course of Abijah which was 8th out of the order of 24 priests. These courses started with the Jewish new year on Nisan on the religious calendar, on our calendar, that would be the March/April timeframe. Because of the feast days involved in that part of the year, that would add two weeks to the year for the course of Abijah. So, the 1st course of Abijah would actually start on the 10th week of the year in the month of Sivan which would put Zacharias's 1st course in early June on our calendar. Then for his 2nd course, you would have to account for the fall feast days which would put Zacharias's 2nd course in the month of Kislev which was in the November/December timeframe, but again, the feast days of Israel would probably push his 2nd course into December. Then at the end of the year, you had days to make up the full year because the Jewish religious calendar year wasn't a full 365 days because the months were counted by the lunar cycle which always left days to make up at the end of the year to make a full year, and they also had to adjust for leap year. But I'm thinking that they found a way to make up those days so that the courses would always begin on their new year at the 1st of Nisan.

Perhaps they rotated the priest every year to make up those days; each year changing which priest or priests, would make up those days that year. That is just a guess, but I can't see them changing whose course it starts out with in the month of Nisan. It only makes sense that the first course for the new year would always be the priest with the 1st course. Luke 1:8 indicates that this was one of Zacharias's regular courses, not one of the special events during the feast or make up days: and the logic of timing tells us that it was more than likely his June course, not his December course that he was told that Elizabeth would bear him a son that would be John the Baptist. His December course would put Jesus being born in about March which doesn't fit any criteria of why He would be born in early spring close to Passover. Passover does not hold any significance to the birth of Jesus. Passover is more a type of His death and resurrection. So, we know that it was more than likely his first course in June. It says in verse 24 that Elizabeth hid herself for five months; then in her sixth month, verse 26, Jesus was conceived, verse 36. So, simple math should give us a good estimation of about when Jesus was born. To estimate this; take the early to middle part of June; allow the week of his course, and after that, however long it took for Elizabeth to get pregnant, which was probably not long because the angel had given him this prophecy as if it would be right after his course. So, that would put us into late June to start Elizabeth's pregnancy. then six months after that, verse 36, Jesus was conceived probably in December which would coincide with the festival of lights, or Hanukkah, since Jesus is the light of the world; it would only make since if He was conceived on the festival of lights. Jesus would have been born nine months after that or 15 months after Elizabeth became pregnant. This would put Jesus being born sometime in September around the feast of tabernacles which would agree with the theme of that feast of Jesus dwelling, or tabernacling, among us.

**John 1:14**
**14 And the Word was made flesh, and dwelt among us,**
**(and we beheld his glory, the glory as of the only begotten**
**of the Father,) full of grace and truth.**

The days of the Jewish months don't coincide with our months, so a Jewish month might start in the middle of our month and last until the middle of our next month. So, even with this calculation, we still can't know the exact day. My personal opinion is that Jesus didn't want us to know the day of His birth because that was not to be our focus. I don't think Jesus wanted us to put as much emphasis on His birth as on His death and resurrection. We are not told in The Bible to remember Him as a child with any kind of event or ceremony. But we are told to remember Him as our Savior that died on the cross of Calvary in which He gave us the exact day that that happened, which was the 1st day of Passover on the 14th day of Nisan, which was the day of preparation before the high sabbath which started at sundown.

**Leviticus 23:4**
**5 In the fourteenth day of the first month at even is the**
**Lord's passover.**

Then after three days and three nights, He was risen from the dead and He conquered death as the first fruits from the dead. He didn't have a problem giving us the exact day of His death because He wanted us to remember that day. So, if He also wanted us to remember His birth; why didn't He give us that day also?

**John 19:31**
**31 The Jews therefore, because it was the preparation, that**
**the bodies should not remain upon the cross on the sabbath**
**day, (for that sabbath day was an high day,) besought**
**Pilate that their legs might be broken, and that they might**
**be taken away.**

**1 Corinthians 11:24-26**

**24 And when he had given thanks, he brake it, and said, Take, eat: this is my body, which is broken for you: this do in remembrance of me.**

**25 After the same manner also he took the cup, when he had supped, saying, This cup is the new testament in my blood: this do ye, as oft as ye drink it, in remembrance of me.**

**26 For as often as ye eat this bread, and drink this cup, ye do shew the Lord's death till he come.**

He will not come again as a child. He will come again as The Son of man with power and great glory.

**Matthew 24:30**

**30 And then shall appear the sign of the Son of man in heaven: and then shall all the tribes of the earth mourn, and they shall see the Son of man coming in the clouds of heaven with power and great glory.**

Do you think Jesus wants us to focus on His life before His ministry started at the age of 30? He began to be about 30 years old when He was baptized by John which is when He started His ministry. This was the required age to serve as a priest.

**Numbers 4:1-4**

**1 And the Lord spake unto Moses and unto Aaron, saying,**

**2 Take the sum of the sons of Kohath from among the sons of Levi, after their families, by the house of their fathers,**

**3 From thirty years old and upward even until fifty years old, all that enter into the host, to do the work in the tabernacle of the congregation.**

**4 This shall be the service of the sons of Kohath in the tabernacle of the congregation, about the most holy things:**

**Luke 3:22-23**

**22 And the Holy Ghost descended in a bodily shape like a dove upon him, and a voice came from heaven, which said, Thou art my beloved Son; in thee I am well pleased.**

**23 And Jesus himself began to be about thirty years of age, being (as was supposed) the son of Joseph, which was the son of Heli,**

It would have been simple for The Bible to put the day Jesus was born right here where it says He began to be about 30. But it didn't mention what day it was. It doesn't even tell us what time of year it was. My guess is that it was one of the fall feast days to commemorate the start of His earthly ministry which also agrees with a September birthday that we established a little earlier. Obviously, Luke knew when His birthday was because he says right here that Jesus began to be about 30, but the date is not mentioned. Why? It's because that was not what Jesus wanted us to focus on. What do we know about Jesus before the age of 30? Not much. We know a few details about His birth. Then wise men came to see Him as a young child, probably at about the age of 1½, after which Herod tried to have Him killed by killing every child two and under. We see Him preaching in the temple at the age of twelve years old. We also know that He was a carpenter. Besides that, we hear nothing about Him until age 30 except that He grew in wisdom.

**Mark 6:3**

**3 Is not this the carpenter, the son of Mary, the brother of James, and Joses, and of Juda, and Simon? and are not his sisters here with us? And they were offended at him.**

**Luke 2:40**

**40 And the child grew, and waxed strong in spirit, filled with wisdom: and the grace of God was upon him.**

Jesus didn't come the first time to receive the glory of ruling this world. For 30 years, He never called attention to Himself as a ruler or someone important in this present world. He later told Pilate that His kingdom was not of this world.

> **John 18:33-36**
> **33 Then Pilate entered into the judgment hall again, and called Jesus, and said unto him, Art thou the King of the Jews?**
> **34 Jesus answered him, Sayest thou this thing of thyself, or did others tell it thee of me?**
> **35 Pilate answered, Am I a Jew? Thine own nation and the chief priests have delivered thee unto me: what hast thou done?**
> **36 Jesus answered, My kingdom is not of this world: if my kingdom were of this world, then would my servants fight, that I should not be delivered to the Jews: but now is my kingdom not from hence.**

Even those in His home town knew nothing about who He really was at that time, even though they watched Him grow up. In other words, He didn't announce to the people in His home town, that He grew up in, that He was the Messiah, verse 22 below.

> **Luke 4:16-24**
> **16 And he came to Nazareth, where he had been brought up: and, as his custom was, he went into the synagogue on the sabbath day, and stood up for to read.**
> **17 And there was delivered unto him the book of the prophet Esaias. And when he had opened the book, he found the place where it was written,**
> **18 The Spirit of the Lord is upon me, because he hath anointed me to preach the gospel to the poor; he hath sent me to heal the brokenhearted, to preach deliverance to**

the captives, and recovering of sight to the blind, to set at
liberty them that are bruised,

19 To preach the acceptable year of the Lord.

20 And he closed the book, and he gave it again to the
minister, and sat down. And the eyes of all them that were
in the synagogue were fastened on him.

21 And he began to say unto them, This day is this scripture
fulfilled in your ears.

22 And all bare him witness, and wondered at the gracious
words which proceeded out of his mouth. And they said, Is
not this Joseph's son?

23 And he said unto them, Ye will surely say unto me this
proverb, Physician, heal thyself: whatsoever we have heard
done in Capernaum, do also here in thy country.

24 And he said, Verily I say unto you, No prophet is
accepted in his own country.

However, there will come a time when He will be ruler over
this world.

**Revelation 19:11-15**

11 And I saw heaven opened, and behold a white horse;
and he that sat upon him was called Faithful and True, and
in righteousness he doth judge and make war.

12 His eyes were as a flame of fire, and on his head were
many crowns; and he had a name written, that no man
knew, but he himself.

13 And he was clothed with a vesture dipped in blood: and
his name is called The Word of God.

14 And the armies which were in heaven followed him
upon white horses, clothed in fine linen, white and clean.

15 And out of his mouth goeth a sharp sword, that with it
he should smite the nations: and he shall rule them with a
rod of iron: and he treadeth the winepress of the fierceness
and wrath of Almighty God.

**Revelation 20:4**

**4 And I saw thrones, and they sat upon them, and judgment was given unto them: and I saw the souls of them that were beheaded for the witness of Jesus, and for the word of God, and which had not worshipped the beast, neither his image, neither had received his mark upon their foreheads, or in their hands; and they lived and reigned with Christ a thousand years.**

I don't think Jesus wanted us to focus a lot on His life before His baptism by John. That seems to be when He wanted us to start paying attention. He didn't seem to be much concerned with us knowing a lot about Him before that time other than what we already mentioned from information in The Bible. Jesus didn't bring much attention to Himself before He started His ministry. Only after His baptism did He say most of the things that He wanted us to pay attention to. Like we said, even in His home town where He grew up and people seen Him every day; and not even they realized who He really was and is. They thought of Him as just another kid on the block. They said in verse 22 above, is this not Joseph's son, as if He were just a normal kid, like everyone else.

19. People always try to attach a natural object to the worship of God. A statue, a tree, a cross, a picture of Jesus, rosary beads, even a candle. Do not kneel before one of these things thinking you are kneeling to Jesus? You do not need any of those things to worship Jesus. We have all seen those movies and TV shows where some religious person has a room or a closet with a table full of religious symbols, and they kneel before these objects to pray. This is not scriptural, and it actually borders on idol worship. You should kneel before God Himself, not some object that is supposed to represent Him.

**Exodus 20:4-5**

**4 Thou shalt not make unto thee any graven image, or any likeness of any thing that is in heaven above, or that is in the earth beneath, or that is in the water under the earth: 5 Thou shalt not bow down thyself to them, nor serve them: for I the Lord thy God am a jealous God, visiting the iniquity of the fathers upon the children unto the third and fourth generation of them that hate me;**

**Amos 5:25-26**

**25 Have ye offered unto me sacrifices and offerings in the wilderness forty years, O house of Israel? 26 But ye have borne the tabernacle of your Moloch and Chiun your images, the star of your god, which ye made to yourselves.**

Christmas is nothing more than an assortment of objects to distract us from the worship of our Lord that was raised from the grave and now lives forever, as we, who are saved, will also. And like in Amos 5:26, that we just read; a star is used many times on the tree. The shape of the tree with lights and a star on top is said to symbolize the universe with the Christmas lights being all the stars of the universe and the star on top or end of it representing God at the end of the universe in the third heaven. The tree is widest at the bottom and narrows going toward the top displaying the universe as if you were looking down an endless desert road that starts out wide where you are standing and narrows down as you look miles ahead till you see it narrow to a point that you can't see it anymore. This is said to represent Jesus as an evergreen tree, never dying out in the winter and never losing its green leaves or green needles. And the shape of the tree is said to represent the endlessness of the universe and the endlessness of Jesus; narrowing down to the top of the tree with the star of God at the top which would be the end of the universe. I was told this by a pastor. He couldn't give any scriptural reference for this comparison. Which means, it sounds real good; but this story doesn't line up with The Bible. We should be careful making comparisons like this that borders on making an idol out of an object. Once you start assigning unbiblical material objects in conjunction with the worship of God, you are headed down a dangerous road.

> **Leviticus 26:1**
> **1 Ye shall make you no idols nor graven image, neither rear you up a standing image, neither shall ye set up any image of stone in your land, to bow down unto it: for I am the Lord your God.**

This visual Babylonian system of worship, which includes Christmas, will be brought down. Never attach any object to the worship of The Lord other than what The Bible attaches. There are those natural objects used such as bread and wine in communion and there were the objects used in temple worship connected with the feast of Israel which some are outdated now that Jesus has come and fulfilled those prophecies. There are still three of those that are unfulfilled. The next one in line is Rash Hashanah, or the feast of trumpets which, I Believe, marks the rapture of the church, but that is another subject. In the celebration of these feast and in the communion, those objects are not worshipped, they are simply symbols of the prophecies that they represent. And the communion is a remembrance of Jesus and a promise of His soon return. No one should bow before these objects. They are used to remind us of what He did.

> **Luke 22:19-20**
> **19 And he took bread, and gave thanks, and brake it, and gave unto them, saying, This is my body which is given for you: this do in remembrance of me.**
> **20 Likewise also the cup after supper, saying, This cup is the new testament in my blood, which is shed for you.**

**1 Corinthians 10:16-22**

**16 The cup of blessing which we bless, is it not the communion of the blood of Christ? The bread which we break, is it not the communion of the body of Christ?**

**17 For we being many are one bread, and one body: for we are all partakers of that one bread.**

**18 Behold Israel after the flesh: are not they which eat of the sacrifices partakers of the altar?**

**19 What say I then? that the idol is any thing, or that which is offered in sacrifice to idols is any thing?**

**20 But I say, that the things which the Gentiles sacrifice, they sacrifice to devils, and not to God: and I would not that ye should have fellowship with devils.**

**21 Ye cannot drink the cup of the Lord, and the cup of devils: ye cannot be partakers of the Lord's table, and of the table of devils.**

**22 Do we provoke the Lord to jealousy? are we stronger than he?**

Nothing should be used to represent, or replace God in worship. The worship of our Lord is a serious thing that should be done right. We don't need any material thing to represent God other than what He told us to use to represent Him in communion. He lives in us. We have Him alive and well living inside of every Christian, so why would we need something to represent Him when He's right here in you? I should note here that the bread and the wine in communion do not turn into the actual body and blood of Jesus like some religions today believe. They are only symbols of His body and His blood. A picture of what He did for us.

**Romans 8:9-11**

**9 But ye are not in the flesh, but in the Spirit, if so be that the Spirit of God dwell in you. Now if any man have not the Spirit of Christ, he is none of his.**

**10 And if Christ be in you, the body is dead because of sin; but the Spirit is life because of righteousness.**
**11 But if the Spirit of him that raised up Jesus from the dead dwell in you, he that raised up Christ from the dead shall also quicken your mortal bodies by his Spirit that dwelleth in you.**

**Micah 5:3-6**
**3 Therefore will he give them up, until the time that she which travaileth hath brought forth: then the remnant of his brethren shall return unto the children of Israel.**
**4 And he shall stand and feed in the strength of the LORD, in the majesty of the name of the LORD his God; and they shall abide: for now shall he be great unto the ends of the earth.**
**5 And this man shall be the peace, when the Assyrian shall come into our land: and when he shall tread in our palaces, then shall we raise against him seven shepherds, and eight principal men.**
**6 And they shall waste the land of Assyria with the sword, and the land of Nimrod in the entrances thereof: thus shall he deliver us from the Assyrian, when he cometh into our land, and when he treadeth within our borders.**

This passage in Micah, above, Describes the end of God dealing with the Gentile nations and turning again to Israel. Then in verse 6, above, they will waste the land of Assyria and the land of Nimrod of where Christmas started as the winter solstice celebration. Then finally verse 13-15 below, ties it right in with sun worship, and the groves used in sun worship,

**Micah 5:13-15**
**13 Thy graven images also will I cut off, and thy standing images out of the midst of thee; and thou shalt no more worship the work of thine hands.**

**14 And I will pluck up thy groves out of the midst of thee:
so will I destroy thy cities.
15 And I will execute vengeance in anger and fury upon
the heathen, such as they have not heard.**

**2 Kings 18:4
4 He removed the high places, and brake the images, and
cut down the groves, and brake in pieces the brasen serpent
that Moses had made: for unto those days the children of
Israel did burn incense to it: and he called it Nehushtan.**

They even made an idol out of the brasen serpent that Moses made in
the wilderness to cure their snake bites. They were burning incense
to it. Moses was told by God Himself to build that brasen serpent.
It was of God. But they mixed the practice of burning incense to
their idols with the brasen serpent, which was mixing idol worship
with the worship of God; just like Christmas. Incense was used in
the temple in the worship of God, but it was not burnt in an idol. As
you can see, just as Saturnalia was changed to Christmas, they also
changed the name of the brasen serpent. Except, this was changed
from a name God gave it to a name they chose. It is not known
for sure what Nehushtan, verse 4 above, means, but some have
speculated it to mean, "Divine serpent", kind of making it a god.

**Luke 1:9-11
9 According to the custom of the priest's office, his lot was
to burn incense when he went into the temple of the Lord.
10 And the whole multitude of the people were praying
without at the time of incense.
11 And there appeared unto him an angel of the Lord
standing on the right side of the altar of incense.**

Like I said; incense was used in temple worship, but incense is
also used in idol worship and it is usually attached to an inanimate
object like we just read in 2 Kings18:4. Even today, there are

statues of a fat guy worshiped in an eastern religion that has holes to put incense in to burn. The brasen serpent is a perfect example of using an instrument of God to worship God the wrong way, turning the worship of God into idol worship. It would seem that man wants to worship something tangible that he can see with his eyes and touch with his hands. They reject an invisible God that you must have faith that He is real. Gideon thought it would be a good idea to make a golden Ephod for God, but that also turned out to be just another mistake of worshiping God in a wrong way. Good intentions, but a bad idea.

**Judges 8:24-28**
**24 And Gideon said unto them, I would desire a request of you, that ye would give me every man the earrings of his prey. (For they had golden earrings, because they were Ishmaelites.)**
**25 And they answered, We will willingly give them. And they spread a garment, and did cast therein every man the earrings of his prey.**
**26 And the weight of the golden earrings that he requested was a thousand and seven hundred shekels of gold; beside ornaments, and collars, and purple raiment that was on the kings of Midian, and beside the chains that were about their camels' necks.**
**27 And Gideon made an ephod thereof, and put it in his city, even in Ophrah: and all Israel went thither a whoring after it: which thing became a snare unto Gideon, and to his house.**
**28 Thus was Midian subdued before the children of Israel, so that they lifted up their heads no more. And the country was in quietness forty years in the days of Gideon.**

The Christmas celebration is mostly visual. The colors, decorations and lights are all designed to please the eye. It is a feel-good visual display of a false narrative that seems right in your eyes but falls short of being right. The worship of God is not a natural or a visual experience. It is spiritual.

**John 4:24**
**24 God is a Spirit: and they that worship him must worship him in spirit and in truth.**

Part of spiritual worship is truth. You can't mix truth with a lie and call it spiritual. You can call Christmas a spiritual holiday all you want, but truth is not in it, and therefore it is not spiritual, but a work of darkness. If it were spiritual, it could be backed up in The Bible. Yes, the birth of Jesus is recorded in The Bible, but December 25th is not it, and The Bible doesn't set any celebration to it. There would be nothing wrong with celebrating the birth of Jesus as long as you didn't substitute Jesus for the birthday of an idol and call the idol by The Name of Jesus on a day that couldn't possibly be the birthday of Jesus but is the birthday of that false Christ we have been talking about. Can't you see, it's the act of that substitution that mixes Jesus with Tammuz that makes it idol worship. Calling it Christian, makes Christmas a lie and not scriptural. Besides, Jesus was probably born in September. And that is easily researched and found to be a solid theory backed up in The Bible as we have seen in this book and will see again in reason 24. So, if it is the birth of Jesus you want to celebrate, do it in September. But leave all of the pagan symbols out of it.

**1 John 1:6**
**6 If we say that we have fellowship with him, and walk in darkness, we lie, and do not the truth:**

**John 3:21**
**21 But he that doeth truth cometh to the light, that his deeds may be made manifest, that they are wrought in God.**

**Romans 1:24-25**

**24 Wherefore God also gave them up to uncleanness through the lusts of their own hearts, to dishonour their own bodies between themselves:**

**25 Who changed the truth of God into a lie, and worshipped and served the creature more than the Creator, who is blessed for ever. Amen.**

Christmas is a natural worldly celebration and is a lie. You cannot make it the truth because you want it to be. Truth is backed up by truth. The Bible is truth. And The Bible tells us that a tree cut down and made to stand upright and decked with silver and gold is connected to idol worship, something we should not do.

**Jeremiah 10:2-4**

**2 Thus saith the Lord, Learn not the way of the heathen, and be not dismayed at the signs of heaven; for the heathen are dismayed at them.**

**3 For the customs of the people are vain: for one cutteth a tree out of the forest, the work of the hands of the workman, with the axe.**

**4 They deck it with silver and with gold; they fasten it with nails and with hammers, that it move not.**

20. There is a standard in The Bible that says you can't make something holy by touching it with a holy thing. But if you touch something with a defiled thing, it will always defile the thing you touched.

**Haggai 2:11-14**

**11 Thus saith the Lord of hosts; Ask now the priests concerning the law, saying,**

**12 If one bear holy flesh in the skirt of his garment, and with his skirt do touch bread, or pottage, or wine, or oil,**

**or any meat, shall it be holy? And the priests answered**
**and said, No.**
**13 Then said Haggai, If one that is unclean by a dead body**
**touch any of these, shall it be unclean? And the priests**
**answered and said, It shall be unclean.**
**14 Then answered Haggai, and said, So is this people,**
**and so is this nation before me, saith the Lord; and so is**
**every work of their hands; and that which they offer there**
**is unclean.**

Now, this is not the same thing as Jesus making us holy when we get saved. Jesus does not purify our old man by leaving us like we are and touching us, purifying the sin that is in us, therefore making us holy. He purifies us by giving us a completely new man and new life in The Holy Spirit freeing us totally form that unholy sin. We die to sin and are buried with Christ in baptism, then raised in newness of life. being born again means the old man is dead. That means we die to our former life and walk in a new life. We are not talking about people in this touching to make it holy concept. The miracle of salvation only works on people, not objects or idol worship celebrations. A better example of this passage in Haggai would be, if you drop a cube of frozen pure clean water into a glass of sewer water, the pure water in that cube of ice will not purify the sewer water in that glass. But if you drop a cube of frozen sewer water into a glass of clean fresh water, it will always pollute the clean fresh water every time. So, you can't make Christmas holy by mixing or touching it with the Holy Name of Jesus. But you will corrupt your worship of Jesus by touching it with the defilement of the idol worship involved in Christmas. In other words, you can't make Christmas about Jesus because Christmas is a pagan celebration and could never be holy for that reason, just as sin can never become holy. On the other hand, you can corrupt your worship of Jesus by mixing it with a corrupted idol worship celebration like Christmas. Many people use this concept that doesn't work. They try to mix the sin that they are doing with the worship of Jesus just as Aaron, the priest, tried to mix the golden calf with the worship of God in Moses's day by saying "tomorrow is a feast to the Lord". Aaron saying that didn't make it a feast to The Lord. It was still just idol worship.

> **Acts 7:41-43**
> **41 And they made a calf in those days, and offered sacrifice unto the idol, and rejoiced in the works of their own hands.**
> **42 Then God turned, and gave them up to worship the host of heaven; as it is written in the book of the prophets, O ye house of Israel, have ye offered to me slain beasts and sacrifices by the space of forty years in the wilderness?**
> **43 Yea, ye took up the tabernacle of Moloch, and the star of your god Remphan, figures which ye made to worship them: and I will carry you away beyond Babylon.**

People today try to do the same thing by mixing homosexuality, abortion, polygamy, a new definition of marriage and many more sinful things in with the church to make it okay. Making these things acceptable in the church will never make them acceptable with God.

> **Exodus 32:4-5**
> **4 And he received them at their hand, and fashioned it with a graving tool, after he had made it a molten calf: and they said, These be thy gods, O Israel, which brought thee up out of the land of Egypt.**
> **5 And when Aaron saw it, he built an altar before it; and Aaron made proclamation, and said, To morrow is a feast to the Lord.**

It didn't work then, and it will not work now. You cannot mix idol worship with the worship of Jesus and make it work. It will never work.

21. Because everyone is doing it. We went over this in chapter 2 of this book, but I wanted to include it in this list of 25 reasons. To do something simply because everyone else is doing it is an indication that you cannot think for yourself. Don't be one of those that blindly follow something simply because everyone is doing it.

> **Romans 14:12-13**
> **12 So then every one of us shall give account of himself to God.**
> **13 Let us not therefore judge one another any more: but judge this rather, that no man put a stumblingblock or an occasion to fall in his brother's way.**

> **2 Peter 3:16-17**
> **16 As also in all his epistles, speaking in them of these things; in which are some things hard to be understood, which they that are unlearned and unstable wrest, as they do also the other scriptures, unto their own destruction.**
> **17 Ye therefore, beloved, seeing ye know these things before, beware lest ye also, being led away with the error of the wicked, fall from your own stedfastness.**

> **Luke 6:39**
> **39 And he spake a parable unto them, Can the blind lead the blind? shall they not both fall into the ditch?**

Are you blinded to the truth about Christmas? Would you rather stay deceived than to learn the truth and not be able to participate in your favorite tradition? Most people I show this truth to still celebrate Christmas. They just don't care what it represents. They don't care that it's pagan. They don't care what The Bible says about it. They simply ignore all of that and celebrate it anyway because everyone else they know is doing it, even though they offer no scriptural reason why.

22. Take heed to this severe warning to believers about making the same mistakes as Israel did in the wilderness when they served other gods and took The Lord God lightly. Don't lust after the things that they lusted after. I'm not here to enforce this rule. If you want to celebrate Christmas, go for it. It's your life and I can't dictate what you do with it. I am just here to warn you that you are headed down a destructive path just as the Israelites did and ended up in judgement for it. So, no, I am not the Christian police waiting to arrest you for participating in pagan practices. I'm just a lowly preacher of the truth trying to dispel this fallacy that has deceived millions upon millions of people throughout many ages. If you choose to be ignorant to this truth; that is your choice.

**1 Corinthians 10:1-22**

**1 Moreover, brethren, I would not that ye should be ignorant, how that all our fathers were under the cloud, and all passed through the sea;**

**2 And were all baptized unto Moses in the cloud and in the sea;**

**3 And did all eat the same spiritual meat;**

**4 And did all drink the same spiritual drink: for they drank of that spiritual Rock that followed them: and that Rock was Christ.**

**5 But with many of them God was not well pleased: for they were overthrown in the wilderness.**

**6 Now these things were our examples, to the intent we should not lust after evil things, as they also lusted.**

**7 Neither be ye idolaters, as were some of them; as it is written, The people sat down to eat and drink, and rose up to play.**

**8 Neither let us commit fornication, as some of them committed, and fell in one day three and twenty thousand.**

**9 Neither let us tempt Christ, as some of them also tempted, and were destroyed of serpents.**

**10** Neither murmur ye, as some of them also murmured, and were destroyed of the destroyer.

**11** Now all these things happened unto them for ensamples: and they are written for our admonition, upon whom the ends of the world are come.

**12** Wherefore let him that thinketh he standeth take heed lest he fall.

**13** There hath no temptation taken you but such as is common to man: but God is faithful, who will not suffer you to be tempted above that ye are able; but will with the temptation also make a way to escape, that ye may be able to bear it.

**14** Wherefore, my dearly beloved, flee from idolatry.

**15** I speak as to wise men; judge ye what I say.

**16** The cup of blessing which we bless, is it not the communion of the blood of Christ? The bread which we break, is it not the communion of the body of Christ?

**17** For we being many are one bread, and one body: for we are all partakers of that one bread.

**18** Behold Israel after the flesh: are not they which eat of the sacrifices partakers of the altar?

**19** What say I then? that the idol is any thing, or that which is offered in sacrifice to idols is any thing?

**20** But I say, that the things which the Gentiles sacrifice, they sacrifice to devils, and not to God: and I would not that ye should have fellowship with devils.

**21** Ye cannot drink the cup of the Lord, and the cup of devils: ye cannot be partakers of the Lord's table, and of the table of devils.

**22** Do we provoke the Lord to jealousy? are we stronger than he?

Do we provoke The Lord to jealousy by celebrating Christmas? Do you believe you are greater than God, so you can just make your own rules? No, absolutely not! You are not greater than God!!!

357

We are to follow God's rules. We are not qualified to make rules apart from God. Nether is any false god qualified to change God's Word to say that Jesus was born on December 25th. We are not to drink of the cup or eat of the bread of a false Christ. Do not blur the line between Christ and Tammuz. Tammuz is not Christ. He never has been, and he never will be. He is only a Christ wannabe. Don't accommodate him at Christmas time making him Christ for a day. The birthday of Tammuz is December 25th. Not Jesus! The devil loves taking the focus away from Jesus, even if it's only one day a year. You may think Christmas focuses on Jesus, but it is a false Christ that only masquerades as Jesus that is the focus. Even if you think you are focusing on the real Jesus, you're not, because it is not His birthday. You might as well try to say Halloween is His birthday. If you could pick a day to celebrate the birth of Jesus, would you pick Halloween, a high holy day of cult worship? No, it would be a contradiction to connect a cult worship day of Halloween to Jesus. So why would you pick the day a false Christ was born to celebrate the birth of Jesus??? That doesn't even make sense. December 25th is the birthday of a pagan false Christ. Tammuz calling himself Jesus on that day may fool you, but not me.

23. Remember, the devil is after your kids because if he can get a hold on them; then he knows he has a foothold on the next generation. And he has many weapons at his disposal that he uses to trap your kids. Like drugs, alcohol, sensuality, materialism, internet, games, movies, television, music, parties, sports, false religion and rebellion only to name a few. Some kids spend the whole day in front of a computer screen which is not healthy. But those are obvious, and he has to use those discretely in the shadows and back alleys. Other powerful weapons he has at his disposal are the subtle ones. And those are, in my opinion, the most dangerous. One way he does this is to steal The Word from those that hear it. One way he does that is by mixing it with a lie. This started even in the beginning with Eve.

**Genesis 3:4-5**
**4 And the serpent said unto the woman, Ye shall not surely die:**
**5 For God doth know that in the day ye eat thereof, then your eyes shall be opened, and ye shall be as gods, knowing good and evil.**

He took the truth of God and mixed it with a lie to deceive Eve, above, and he steels The Word of God from the hearts of the lost lest they should get saved, below.

**Luke 8:12**
**12 Those by the way side are they that hear; then cometh the devil, and taketh away the word out of their hearts, lest they should believe and be saved.**

In doing this, they change the truth of God into a lie., verse 25 below.

**Romans 1:22-25**
**22 Professing themselves to be wise, they became fools,**
**23 And changed the glory of the uncorruptible God into an image made like to corruptible man, and to birds, and fourfooted beasts, and creeping things.**
**24 Wherefore God also gave them up to uncleanness through the lusts of their own hearts, to dishonour their own bodies between themselves:**
**25 Who changed the truth of God into a lie, and worshipped and served the creature more than the Creator, who is blessed for ever. Amen.**

And one of those subtle weapons at his disposal is Christmas. I was watching one of those Christmas cartoons a while back and didn't think much about it until one day I was thinking about a passage in The Bible, and suddenly I connected it with that cartoon. In John chapter 11, You remember, Lazarus of Bethany had died while waiting on Jesus to come heal him because Mary, the sister of Lazarus, had sent for Jesus to come heal him. Jesus abode two more days where he was, then made the journey to Judaea where Lazarus was. But when He arrived, Mary told Him basically that He was too late, then Martha said that Lazarus had already been dead four days.

> **John 11:32**
> **32 Then when Mary was come where Jesus was, and saw him, she fell down at his feet, saying unto him, Lord, if thou hadst been here, my brother had not died.**

> **John 11:39**
> **39 Jesus said, Take ye away the stone. Martha, the sister of him that was dead, saith unto him, Lord, by this time he stinketh: for he hath been dead four days.**

But they soon found out that Jesus is never late because He raised Lazarus from the dead that day and turned their sorrow into joy. The cartoon I am talking about is one of the Frosty the snowman TV specials. I believe it was Frosty Returns. At the end of the cartoon, Frosty and a small girl get locked in a hot house for plants and couldn't find a way out, and Frosty melted because of the warmth of the hot house and no one showed up in time to unlock the door and save him from melting. The little girl that was with him was very sad and full of sorrow. But then, Santa Claus showed up, but it was too late because Frosty had already been melted a long time. But the little girl's sorrow was turned into joy when Santa raised Frosty from that puddle of melted snow to being a snow man again. Even if it was only a snow man; the wrong message is getting across very subtlety here. The cartoon didn't mention Jesus or God in raising frosty back to life. You can take that cartoon and multiply it many times over with other ones that do things that only Jesus can do which I believe gives our children the wrong message. The devil is a liar and a deceiver, and he wouldn't hesitate to come against your child as he has done to others. How do you expect your kids to believe you are telling them the truth about Jesus if you have lied to them about who's birthday December 25ᵗʰ is, and about when Jesus was born?

**John 10:10**
**10 The thief cometh not, but for to steal, and to kill, and to destroy: I am come that they might have life, and that they might have it more abundantly.**

24. The few parts of Christmas that are in The Bible are usually not even told accurately by the world during Christmas, and sometimes, the Biblical aspect is purposely left out. Again, we mentioned this before, but not in this scenario. Like we discussed in chapter 2 and in reason 18. The shepherds were abiding in the fields by night. The custom of the shepherds at that time was to coral the flocks by night in wintertime for the rainy season. December 25ᵗʰ on the Jewish calendar would be in the tenth month of Tevet. This tenth month is the Jewish religious calendar. The Jewish civil calendar new year starts in the fall while the Jewish religious calendar new year starts in the spring. This month of Tevet is from the religious calendar, and would be the Jewish month for the Christmas celebration. We already read in Ezra 10:9 that at that time of year, in the month of Kislev, which is the month right before Tevet, would be a time of much rain and apparently cold because they were trembling. And the weather would just get worse in Tevet. Christmas is about half way through the month of Tevet. Shepherds would not be abiding in the fields by night in these kinds of conditions. I know you might say that there could be some good days at that time of year that possible they were grazing the sheep. But this is unlikely because it was the custom for them to be corralled. And even though the winters in Israel are not severe, it still affects the grass growing to graze on. So, overall, because of all of the negative variables in the weather and that time of year being described in Ezra 10:13 as cold and rainy: in my opinion, December is a bad guess on the

time of Jesus birth. But no matter what time of year it was; we are to celebrate His death, burial and resurrection. Not His birth. Yes, we praise God that Jesus was born into this world as an infant and grew into a man and became our savior. But nowhere in The Bible does it tell us to set aside a day to recognize His birth. If The Bible doesn't tell us to do that, why should we? Especially on the same day as the birth of a false Christ.

> **1 Corinthians 11:25-26**
> **25 After the same manner also he took the cup, when he had supped, saying, This cup is the new testament in my blood: this do ye, as oft as ye drink it, in remembrance of me.**
> **26 For as often as ye eat this bread, and drink this cup, ye do shew the Lord's death till he come.**

> **Luke 3:21-23**
> **21 Now when all the people were baptized, it came to pass, that Jesus also being baptized, and praying, the heaven was opened,**
> **22 And the Holy Ghost descended in a bodily shape like a dove upon him, and a voice came from heaven, which said, Thou art my beloved Son; in thee I am well pleased.**
> **23 And Jesus himself began to be about thirty years of age, being (as was supposed) the son of Joseph, which was the son of Heli,**

Here, it was close to His birthday because it says that He began to be about 30. Do you think this scene of Him being baptized in the Jordan would take place in late December? Not likely. This is when He started His ministry after His baptism by John the Baptist. Jesus's ministry is thought to have been 3 ½ years long. So, if He was 30 years old when He was baptized and started His ministry; that would make Him 33 ½ years old at His crucifixion. And we know that His crucifixion took place in the evening of Passover which was the 14th day of the 1st month on the Jewish religious calendar, which is Nisan. On our calendar, it would be a different day each year, but is always either late March or early April depending on which day the 14th day of Nisan falls on our calendar each year.

> **Leviticus 23:5**
> **5 In the fourteenth day of the first month at even is the Lord's passover.**

I agree with that timeframe of 3 ½ years. It seems to fit all the limited information we have on the length of His ministry. But it is argued by some to be 3 years. In either case; if He was born December 25th, and if his birthday was when he was baptized as it says in verse 23, and we know His death was at Passover. You can't count back from Passover and get 3 or 3 ½ years out of that and make it end up in December. Passover takes place in late March or early April. Three years after December 25th would put us right back at December 25th at His crucifixion. We already know that it wasn't winter. He was crucified in the spring at Passover. In fact, there is no scenario of a December birth that fits 3 years. Then 3 ½ years from December 25th would put us into June, well after Passover. So, neither one of those scenarios fit a December 25th birth. But if He was born when most scholars agree; in September, probably close to the time of the Feast of Tabernacles; 3 ½ years would fit, putting us right at spring time and at Passover when we know that He was crucified. Counting 3½ Years back from Passover would put you in the September timeframe. But no matter when His birth was; nowhere in The Bible are we instructed to remember His birth with any kind of celebration. And again, we are not given any information in The Bible on what day of the year He was born. So again, you have to ask yourself, why would The Bible not give us that information if God wanted us to celebrate His birth every year?

25. If you are a pastor, it is your responsibility to figure out the mysteries of God and teach the people. The complete truth is only available to those that take the time to search it out in The Word of God. Not everyone does this. But it is up to you to make sure it gets done. You will be rewarded for doing so.

> **1 Timothy 5:17-18**
> **17 Let the elders that rule well be counted worthy of double honour, especially they who labour in the word and doctrine.**
> **18 For the scripture saith, Thou shalt not muzzle the ox that treadeth out the corn. And, The labourer is worthy of his reward.**

If you, as a pastor, withhold this truth about Christmas from your congregation; you will be held accountable with a greater judgement than the ones you kept this information from. This is not a judgement of hell. The judgement you will suffer for not preaching the truth will be loss of reward at The Judgement Seat of Christ.

> **James 3:1**
> **1 My brethren, be not many masters, knowing that we shall receive the greater condemnation.**

> **1 Corinthians 4:1-2**
> **1 Let a man so account of us, as of the ministers of Christ, and stewards of the mysteries of God.**
> **2 Moreover it is required in stewards, that a man be found faithful.**

What are the mysteries of God? Do you know any mysteries of God? If not, then how can you be a steward of them? Some things just don't jump out in front of your face and say: "here I am". Sometimes you have to look for it. Sometimes you have to look really hard. Pastor, you are required to look, verse 2. What are you going to do when you stand before Jesus and have to give an answer to Him for your silence about things that you should have been abstaining from and things you should have been teaching against? Things that even some of the secular world knows about. One day while I was in my work truck going to pick up some supplies for my job, I was flipping through the channels on the radio, (this was sometime in the 80's), I happened across a very popular secular rock station that I heard The Name of Jesus spoken, so I listened to it to find out what they were saying. There were two DJs, a man and a woman, talking about Christmas. The man said something good about Christmas, and the woman said to him that Christmas was a time when Christians celebrate the birth of Jesus and use pagan symbols to do it. She went on to tell him that we can blame Constantine for that, and how it was him that mixed this pagan celebration with Christianity and it isn't even really the birthday of Jesus, but really a pagan tradition converted to Christianity. How would she know that? It's there to find, that's how! She found it; why can't you? As far as I know; she was not even a Christian. I guess she could have been, but after all, it was a secular rock station. Yet she knew full well with great detail where Christmas came from as she went on to explain with surprising accuracy. So, if this rock DJ knows all of this; shouldn't you? Pastor????? You're the one that's supposed to know it. Pastor, you're the one that is trusted to find the truth and tell it to the congregation. Not have to hear it over a secular rock station that doesn't even regard God with any kind of honor. Are you like the Pharisees that couldn't recognize the birth of their Messiah, yet Gentile wise men come to town looking for the savior that they knew was already born? Just like you as a Christian can't see Christmas for what it is, yet a DJ on a secular rock station knows full well the fallacy of Christmas and accurately publicly rebukes us Christians right there on the radio for being so stupid to not know this and for being deceived into celebrating this false birthday of Jesus. Another time I was watching a television show called Millennium, and one of the characters said to the character called Frank: "December has always been a religious month with the Druids, Hanukkah and winter solstice. The Romans changed Saturnalia into Christmas and it's not even the day of Christ birth." What a shame that a DJ on a secular rock radio station and a TV show in Hollywood preaches more truth than most pastors do about this pagan celebration. Hollywood certainly does not regard God. They usually stand against anything Christian except Christmas which Hollywood loves. I was surprised to hear them speak against their favorite holiday. But they could have been doing it to make Christians look like a bunch of deceived idiots. That would fit their narrative of hating Christianity. Every year, most all of your TV shows have their Christmas episodes with all the pagan symbols included. That's why I was surprised to hear this show tell the truth about their favorite holiday and put Christmas in a bad light. The point is that Christians are being made fun of for their ignorance of Christmas origins. Even some of the world, that most likely aren't even Christians, know that this Celebration has nothing to do with Jesus. Church, do you have the courage to make a very unpopular stand that will turn the world and most of the church against you? Since I have taken a stand against Christmas, I have been the target of persecution from both the world and the church; and you will be too if you come against this most popular pagan celebration. Are you willing to suffer for Jesus and for the truth? Ministers, you could empty your congregation with this truth because most Christians do not accept this information about Christmas. You could be fired and lose your income as pastor with this teaching. You could be hated and scorned and ridiculed by people that you thought were good Christian people if you speak against their favorite day of the year. The good thing is, you are in good company if you are being treated this way, because Jesus was treated that way for telling truth that the world and His own people, the religious hierarchy, didn't like.

**Matthew 5:10-12**

**10 Blessed are they which are persecuted for righteousness' sake: for theirs is the kingdom of heaven.**

**11 Blessed are ye, when men shall revile you, and persecute you, and shall say all manner of evil against you falsely, for my sake.**

**12 Rejoice, and be exceeding glad: for great is your reward in heaven: for so persecuted they the prophets which were before you.**

**John 15:19-21**

**19 If ye were of the world, the world would love his own: but because ye are not of the world, but I have chosen you out of the world, therefore the world hateth you.**

**20 Remember the word that I said unto you, The servant is not greater than his lord. If they have persecuted me, they will also persecute you; if they have kept my saying, they will keep yours also.**

**21 But all these things will they do unto you for my name's sake, because they know not him that sent me.**

Are you willing to stand with Jesus while everyone else walks away? It gets lonely sometimes when it seems like you are the only one around taking such an unpopular stand for Jesus; but just remember who you are standing with!!!! JESUS!!!!! Really, He is all you need to make a majority; just you and Jesus.

**2 Timothy 4:14-18**

**14 Alexander the coppersmith did me much evil: the Lord reward him according to his works:**

**15 Of whom be thou ware also; for he hath greatly withstood our words.**

**16 At my first answer no man stood with me, but all men forsook me: I pray God that it may not be laid to their charge.**

**17 Notwithstanding the Lord stood with me, and strengthened me; that by me the preaching might be fully known, and that all the Gentiles might hear: and I was delivered out of the mouth of the lion.**

**18 And the Lord shall deliver me from every evil work, and will preserve me unto his heavenly kingdom: to whom be glory for ever and ever. Amen.**

Elijah felt that same way when he went to Horeb, the mountain of God also known as Mount Sinai where he listened for the voice of God when he thought he was all alone. But God told him that He has 7000 others that hadn't bowed to Baal. If feeling like standing alone is good enough for Elijah, it's good enough for me too. And I've got to believe that, just like Elijah, there are thousands of others out there that know this truth and are out there seemingly, to them, also standing alone for the truth.

**1 Kings 19:14**

**14 And he said, I have been very jealous for the Lord God of hosts: because the children of Israel have forsaken thy covenant, thrown down thine altars, and slain thy prophets with the sword; and I, even I only, am left; and they seek my life, to take it away.**

**1 Kings 19:18**

**18 Yet I have left me seven thousand in Israel, all the knees which have not bowed unto Baal, and every mouth which hath not kissed him.**

By the way, verse 18 shows us that God takes note of those that stand for His truth. Even though no names were mentioned in that 7000, God still honored them and recognized each one of that 7000 in His Word for not giving in to idol worship. I'm sure they will get recognized, each one by name, in His Kingdom. Get in on the ground floor now. Be counted among the 7000, so to speak, or however many people God has that haven't bowed to the Christmas celebration. Let Him take notice of you, that you refuse to follow the crowd down the path of idol worship. Let Him know that you stand with Him and for the truth. Please listen to me. Make no mistake, there will be a day of reckoning when this ungodly practice will be exposed. Don't be one of the ones with egg on your face when it happens. Don't be the pastor that deceived the congregation. Don't be the church member that kept silent when you see a brother or even your pastor in error and you do nothing to reveal the truth to them. No, it's not your responsibility to stop anyone from doing these things; that's God's job. But it is your responsibility to tell them if they are in error. It's up to them if they listen to the truth and believe your evidence of this error. If you give them solid evidence of what you are saying; or even if you give them a copy of this book; they must weigh that evidence and make a Biblical decision on it. They should be able to give you a solid Biblical answer if they believe you are wrong on what you are telling them or what this book is saying. Forget their opinions or personal feelings about it. Tell them you want hard scriptural evidence to back up what they are doing. It's easy to just keep silent and not get involved in exposing a false teaching. Be diligent to check into it and find the truth for yourself. Study to show yourself approved. Don't be taken in by the popularity of this fun day and allow yourself to be drawn into this Christmas deception.

# IN CONCLUSION:

Just because something is desirable, looks right and seems right in your mind doesn't mean it is right. Satan can accommodate those things to deceive you. You must also have solid proof from The Word of God of what you're doing to give an answer to those who would question you about it. The DJ on the secular radio station and the TV show I seen didn't falsely accuse Christians of practicing idol worship. They were right. They rightfully questioned Christians on why we celebrate a clearly pagan celebration and call it Christian. It is a disgrace that they know more than most Christians do. This pagan celebration can appear as a good Christian holiday, but is really an illusion.

> **2 Corinthians 11:14**
> **14 And no marvel; for Satan himself is transformed into an angel of light.**

> **1 Peter 3:14-17**
> **14 But and if ye suffer for righteousness' sake, happy are ye: and be not afraid of their terror, neither be troubled;**
> **15 But sanctify the Lord God in your hearts: and be ready always to give an answer to every man that asketh you a reason of the hope that is in you with meekness and fear:**
> **16 Having a good conscience; that, whereas they speak evil of you, as of evildoers, they may be ashamed that falsely accuse your good conversation in Christ.**

**17 For it is better, if the will of God be so, that ye suffer for well doing, than for evil doing.**

Sometimes a person must stand alone on a principal that you believe to be true and is backed up by The Bible. That is exactly what I am doing. If I believed God was okay with Christmas even a little bit, I would be right there with you celebrating it. I was 28 years old when I first found out that Christmas was not the birth of Jesus. Before that time, I too would always look forward to Christmas time every year because it was always a time of family get togethers and just all-around good sights and sounds that bring up fond memories of better times. So, I understand your reasoning for wanting to take part in this festive occasion. The only problem is that it is not scriptural. And that is a serious problem. It is clear to see that it is indeed just a pagan celebration painted up and disguised to look like it is Christian. Before this was revealed to me, I had no idea that Christmas had anything to do with paganism. Up to that point, I thought December 25th was the actual birthday of Jesus. No pastor or evangelist or any person even in my church ever told me any different up to that point in my life. As a matter of fact, all I heard from any pastor is that it was the birthday of Jesus. I was shocked when I found out the truth. I didn't believe it at first because it sounded so blasphemous. I couldn't believe someone was saying anything against Christmas. But it didn't take but a small amount of investigation to find that it was true. Something that I have been taught all my life by people that I trusted to teach the truth of The Bible were deceiving me either out of ignorance or on purpose because they wanted to celebrate it. It took 28 years before I learned the truth. Where are the Bible teachers? I suspect there are millions upon millions of people out there in the same boat as I was. They simply don't know. I could have stayed deceived my whole life if not for that one person that had enough backbone to expose this lie to me. That is why I am writing this book. I don't want you to be one of those deceived people that simply haven't heard the truth. If you are a pastor and neglect to tell the truth about Christmas; shame on you!! It is a disgrace that you keep this information from your congregation. You should re-evaluate if you are fit to be a pastor or not. You can't just pick and choose what you want to be true and what you want to be false. You must go by what The Bible says. There is a price to pay for withholding the truth from the people that count on you to tell them the truth. Especially a preacher that knows this and withholds this information from his congregation and goes along with the lie like it really is the birthday of Jesus, even though he knows it's not.

**Romans 1:18-25**

**18 For the wrath of God is revealed from heaven against all ungodliness and unrighteousness of men, who hold the truth in unrighteousness;**

**19 Because that which may be known of God is manifest in them; for God hath shewed it unto them.**

**20 For the invisible things of him from the creation of the world are clearly seen, being understood by the things that are made, even his eternal power and Godhead; so that they are without excuse:**

**21 Because that, when they knew God, they glorified him not as God, neither were thankful; but became vain in their imaginations, and their foolish heart was darkened.**

**22 Professing themselves to be wise, they became fools,**

**23 And changed the glory of the uncorruptible God into an image made like to corruptible man, and to birds, and fourfooted beasts, and creeping things.**

**24 Wherefore God also gave them up to uncleanness through the lusts of their own hearts, to dishonour their own bodies between themselves:**

**25 Who changed the truth of God into a lie, and worshipped and served the creature more than the Creator, who is blessed for ever. Amen.**

**Ephesians 4:14-15**

14 That we henceforth be no more children, tossed to and fro, and carried about with every wind of doctrine, by the sleight of men, and cunning craftiness, whereby they lie in wait to deceive;

15 But speaking the truth in love, may grow up into him in all things, which is the head, even Christ:

**2 Timothy 2:16-18**

16 But shun profane and vain babblings: for they will increase unto more ungodliness.

17 And their word will eat as doth a canker: of whom is Hymenaeus and Philetus;

18 Who concerning the truth have erred, saying that the resurrection is past already; and overthrow the faith of some.

**2 Timothy 4:1-4**

1 I charge thee therefore before God, and the Lord Jesus Christ, who shall judge the quick and the dead at his appearing and his kingdom;

2 Preach the word; be instant in season, out of season; reprove, rebuke, exhort with all longsuffering and doctrine.

3 For the time will come when they will not endure sound doctrine; but after their own lusts shall they heap to themselves teachers, having itching ears;

4 And they shall turn away their ears from the truth, and shall be turned unto fables.

**1 Timothy 1:4-7**

4 Neither give heed to fables and endless genealogies, which minister questions, rather than godly edifying which is in faith: so do.

5 Now the end of the commandment is charity out of a pure heart, and of a good conscience, and of faith unfeigned:

**6 From which some having swerved have turned aside unto vain jangling;**
**7 Desiring to be teachers of the law; understanding neither what they say, nor whereof they affirm.**

# A FINAL CHALLENGE TO YOU

I want to apologize in advance to pastors that are reading this portion of this book. I am rather harsh on you in this section. Please don't take it personally. I am just speaking generally and not to anyone individually. In saying that; I do not apologize for telling you the truth if it applies to you. I say these things with love in an effort to motivate you to be bold when it comes to wrong things that are going on in the church today. So, here it is. Prove me wrong. It's not enough for you to just say so. That's how false religious systems that includes Christmas get started in the first place. If you are a Christian, aren't you interested in what God really wants from you and not so much what you want to do? Myself, I don't think I stand much of a chance of getting this message across to very many people simply because the tradition of Christmas is so strong, and it is very hard to stand against this strong tradition. I have been trying for more than 30 years back when I finished writing the 1st edition of this book with not much success. I spent 10 years putting that 1st edition together. If I was writing this book to make a lot of money from it, I picked the wrong subject. I had trouble giving away copies of the first and second editions of this book. Most people tell me: "I don't want to know about this because I don't want to be responsible for knowing the truth about it". I really don't know why this third edition would be any different. But what we as men think can't be done, God can accomplish that and more. The point is, to get with the program now and don't wait until you're on the opposite side of what God is on. God will judge all false religions and they will come short of His Glory and God will use the saints to judge the earth. Are you informed enough in The Word of God to judge the earth at that time, or will you need to go through a refresher course at the university of heaven judging school to be able to discern what God's will is? If you are truly a Christian, and especially if you are a pastor, I shouldn't have to lecture you on the fallacies of these pagan celebrations. Every Christian, and for sure, every pastor should check these things out for themselves to make sure that what you are doing lines up with The Bible. It's a simple task to see for yourself. So, why do so many Christians and pastors ignore the truth or simply don't search for the truth about Christmas? I have no idea. It seems so easy to me to see the truth about it. Can you explain to me how you can ignore it? Please explain it to me because I want to know how you can be allowed to judge the world while you took part in the things that you are judging. For that matter, how are you allowed to be a pastor when you are taking part in Satan's work of deception and lies and spreading that deception and lies to your own congregation? I'm not interested in your lame opinion. Explain it to me with The Bible. Show me scripturally.

> **1 Corinthians 6:2-3**
> **2 Do ye not know that the saints shall judge the world? and if the world shall be judged by you, are ye unworthy to judge the smallest matters?**
> **3 Know ye not that we shall judge angels? how much more things that pertain to this life?**

## IF YOU CAN'T DETERMINE WHAT GOD WILL JUDGE NOW; THEN HOW DO YOU EXPECT TO BE A JUDGE FOR HIM LATER IN HIS KINGDOM?

I can remember hearing only one radio minister tell the truth about Christmas boldly right there on the radio for everyone to hear. It was Charles Halff on the radio program, "The Christian Jew

Hour". He was a Messianic Jewish teacher that was extremely knowledgeable of The Word of God. He probably sacrificed world recognition with his stand against Christmas. Most Jewish Christians know the truth about Christmas. Jews are usually raised on the Old Testament and when they become an adult; they already know it very well, and the Old Testament is full of descriptions of idol worship that fit the Christmas celebration. So, if a Jew gets saved, he puts his knowledge of the Old Testament together with the New Testament and immediately recognizes an Old Testament idol worship when he sees one. For that reason, most Jews immediately see Christmas for the idol worship that it is. Unfortunately, today, he no longer teaches on the radio. There are numerous other radio and TV ministers that I listen to now that I admire for their knowledge. But none of them, no, not even one of them, preaches the truth about Christmas. These other ministers I listen to are extremely knowledgeable in The Bible, yet at Christmas time, every single one of them seems to set aside their knowledge and give in to the masses. Even Bible scholars leave their knowledge at the doorstep of the church and participate in this most powerful pagan tradition that is found nowhere in The Bible to be a Christian celebration. Why? There is no way that these Bible scholars, preachers and ministers, many with multiple doctorate degrees in theology don't know about Christmas and where it came from and what it stands for. Yet me; a lowly nothing, that wasn't even very good in high school, with a bad case of dyslexia, that stumbles to even read anything can easily see the truth about this pagan ritual with absolute clarification, proof and verification that it is easily researched and found that, without question, is a pagan celebration that originated at the tower of Babel. When I hear one these preachers on TV and the radio, and even from the pulpit of a church speak of Christmas and Easter as if it were a scriptural day, I just want to stand up and shout at the TV, or pound the radio, or get up out of the pew at church and ask the preacher where he is getting his information. The only thing I can think of as an answer for this is that just as Rome was proclaimed a Christian Empire by the emperor, but soon found out that that decision could very well end his reign as emperor because of the uprising of the pagan population when he told them that they could no longer celebrate their pagan rituals. So, he compromised with them and allowed them to give Christian names to the pagan gods so they could keep their celebrations as long as they had Christian names. In the same sense; when a minister is confronted with this popular celebration; and he finds out that it is nothing but a pagan celebration, and then when he tries to tell the truth about it, he is instantly in danger of losing his job as minister. So, he compromises with the populace of the church and sets aside the truth about it for the Christmas season and allows the congregation to be deceived into thinking December 25$^{th}$ is the birthday of Jesus. Either that or he acknowledges the pagan aspect of Christmas, and will even preach the truth about it from the pulpit, but at the end of his sermon, he tells his congregation that even though it is of pagan origin, it is okay to celebrate it now because it has been changed to a Christian celebration. Therefore, he compromises the truth of this pagan idol worship celebration and it's false Christ named Tammuz and allows this false Christ to walk in the front door of the church and sit on his throne of Christmas proclaiming himself to be Jesus for a day, with the red carpet rolled out by the pastor of that church telling him; come on in and make yourself at home. As long as we can call you Jesus, you are welcome here. Therefore, it continues. Too bad these scared ministers don't grow a spine and take a stand against this farce that is made of Jesus during this celebration. Like I said at the beginning of this book: I have no expectations that I can change the minds of these gutless preachers that have joined themselves with paganism to satisfy men rather than God. Still, I must try. It would be nice if ministers wouldn't worry so much about their job and concentrate on preaching the truth no matter how much it hurts their image. They should know that God will take care of them. If all ministers would do this; the truth would be exposed for all to see. I felt a calling to enter the ministry when I was in my 30s. That was quickly extinguished when anyone found out my stand on Christmas, Easter and other pagan celebrations. They knew that if I was pastor, that would put an end to their pagan celebrations in their church. I do still preach in whatever settings I can. This book is one of those settings. No, I'm not perfect. I make plenty of mistakes. I have had plenty of sin in my life, but I don't stay in those mistakes or those sins, I turn to Jesus to get victory over those mistakes and those sins. I have always studied God's Word with an open mind to let me be wrong and let God be right no matter how much I didn't like it. Anyone can misinterpret something The Bible is saying. But if you are diligent in that study; God will show you the truth and correct your misinterpretation. And when that happens to me, I immediately correct my mistake and go on from there. Don't forget, the truth will make you free.

> **John 8:31-32**
> **31 Then said Jesus to those Jews which believed on him, If ye continue in my word, then are ye my disciples indeed;**
> **32 And ye shall know the truth, and the truth shall make you free.**

When God reveals something to me that I have wrong, I call on Him to show me the truth and help me to overcome that error in my life whether it is an error in doctrine or an error of sin in my life. Why would I want to stay in an error? You can't be prideful about these things and try to defend an error even though you know it's wrong just to save face and not look ignorant. Ignorance is staying in that error out of pride. You must just ignore those that would scoff at you for changing your mind on something. They are the ignorant ones. If they are truly Christians, they should rejoice that you have seen the truth. Every Christian, if he is truthful, has experienced this kind of correction from something he has believed wrong. But on the subject of Christmas, I have spent a lot of time, actually decades, getting this right. I am very confident that this book is exactly right. God will be my Judge on this. We will all see in the end who is right. Wouldn't it be worth a little investigation on your part to make sure you end up on the right side of this issue? Isn't Jesus worth getting our worship of Him right? When I was first told about this truth, believe me, I looked for even a slither of evidence in The Bible that would allow me to continue celebrating Christmas. Not only did I not find even one iota of scripture supporting Christmas other than He was born and a few details about His birth; I found that The Bible from Genesis to Revelation condemns this practice of mixing God with idol worship and emphatically rejects it. You would have to be really deceived not to see the clear evidence in The Bible on this. It is not hard to find at all. A child could see this truth. I wouldn't take such a bold stand on this if I wasn't absolutely sure of my facts. But still, don't believe me on my word alone. You must check it out for yourself and examine the scriptures to find the truth. That is all I ask. I am confident that you will find the same thing I found. It's all too easy to see; that is unless you just don't want to see it like many Christians today. Like I already said; I'm not trying to force you to stop celebrating this pagan ritual. All I am doing is exposing it for what it really is and giving you the evidence of what I have found. You must weigh that evidence for yourself to decide if this applies to you as well. This is a powerful worldly traditional celebration. But the truth is more powerful than vain tradition and I am confident that you too can see through its disguise for what it really is which is an attempt to deceive Christians into taking part in pagan idol worship rituals without them even realizing it. Please don't allow yourself to be deceived any longer by this trick. Free yourself from this charade and do what we just read in John 8:31-32. Let the truth make you free.

### THE END

CPSIA information can be obtained
at www.ICGtesting.com
Printed in the USA
LVHW101656021121
702256LV00011B/309